GREAT
TRAVEL
VALUES™

GERMANY

FODOR'S TRAVEL PUBLICATIONS

are compiled, researched, and edited by an international team of travel writers, field correspondents, and editors. The series, which now almost covers the globe, was founded by Eugene Fodor in 1936.

OFFICES
New York & London

Fodor's Great Travel Values: Germany

Contributing Editors: Laura lo Bianco, Andrea Dutton, Birgit Gericke, Jackie Krendel, Bob Tilley
Editor: Thomas Cussans
Maps and Plans: Swanston Graphics

FODOR'S

GREAT TRAVEL VALUES™

GERMANY

FODOR'S TRAVEL PUBLICATIONS, INC.
New York & London

ISBN 0-679-01480-2

MANUFACTURED IN THE UNITED STATES OF AMERICA
10 9 8 7 6 5 4 3 2 1

CONTENTS

FOREWORD

While every care has been taken to insure the accuracy of the information contained in this guide, the publishers cannot accept responsibility for any errors that may appear.

All prices quoted in this guide are based on those available to us at the time of writing. In a world of rapid change, however, the possibility of inaccurate or out-of-date information can never be totally eliminated. We trust, therefore, that you will take prices quoted as indicators only, and will double-check to be sure of the latest figure.

Similarly, be sure to check all opening times of museums and galleries. We have found that such times are liable to change without notice, and you could easily make a trip only to find a locked door.

When a hotel closes or a restaurant produces a disappointing meal, let us know, and we will investigate the establishment and the complaint. We are always ready to revise our entries for the following year's edition should the facts warrant it.

Send your letters to the editors of Fodor's Travel Publications, 201 E. 50th Street, New York, NY 10022. European readers may prefer to write to Fodor's Travel Guides, 9-10 Market Place, London W1N 7AG, England.

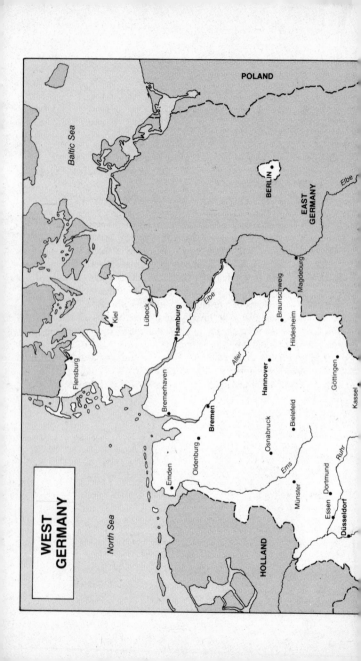

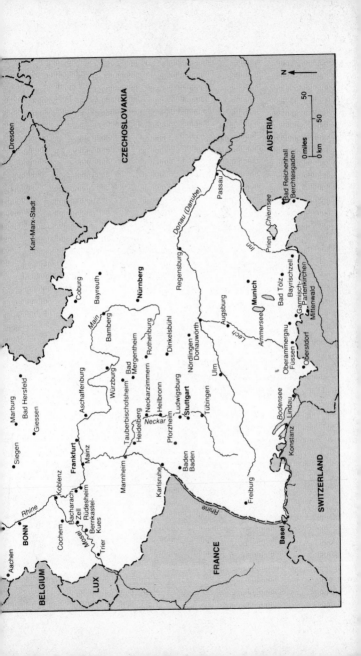

INTRODUCTION

West Germany is bordered by half a dozen countries with an enviably lower cost of living, and German airports are all within three hours' flying time of Mediterranean and Aegean resorts where a life of warm luxury can be bought for little more than the weekly housekeeping bills at home. Yet a third of the Germans who bolt their front door and take off on vacation each year stay within the borders of their own country.

These home-loving types are young and old, families and fun-seeking singles, package-tour tourists and trail-blazing adventurers. There's the expected proportion of people who shrink from the thought of stepping aboard a plane, let alone across a foreign frontier. But there's also more than a sprinkling of hardier individuals who have rounded the world and now feel it's time to take a square look at their own country. For them all, the expense of a German vacation holds no horrors—and for the simple reason that it need not be expensive to vacation in Germany. They have discovered the secret of enjoying a budget German vacation. Perhaps we can learn something from them.

Whomever they are and wherever in Germany they live, they virtually all begin their German vacation on the firm foundation of a planned program or itinerary. They would hardly be German if they didn't; the German is nothing if not methodical—particularly when it comes to financial matters. The German knows by intuition if not by experience that it's no good stepping off a plane or a train and heading into the blue yonder without a thought of where he (or she, or the whole family) is going to lay his weary head that night, or of how much the privilege is going to cost.

So it has to be said right at the start that the amount of time

1

spent planning a vacation in Germany is well invested, returning a dividend that can actually be measured in cash terms. It's not as if the hours of preparation and discussion are to be regarded as drudgery. Sifting leisurely through travel brochures and studying maps of yet-unknown territory are themselves a delightful introduction to a vacation. The travel agent that doesn't stock an evening's worth of reading on Germany isn't worth the name; but if a shortage is encountered, a letter to the German National Tourist Office will surely bring a heavy parcel of material by an early post. A package tour, offering pre-booked itinerary and hotel accommodations, is the most economical way of visiting Germany short of securing a charter flight and backpacking among the campsites and youth hostels with which the country is so well and efficiently served.

The first pleasant surprise for the hotel visitor in Germany is that although the country is generally expensive, good, comfortable accommodations can be reasonable in price—even (dare one say it?) cheap. The Germans run their hotels as they handle most other sectors of the economy: efficiently. The largest hotels hum along beautifully with squadrons of highly capable staff, while small family units run spotless and snug pensions in the most out-of-the-way places with no apparent problem at all.

It can safely be said that, with very few exceptions, value for money will be offered in whatever class of hotel or pension you stay in.

German hotels are waking up to the fact (perhaps later than hotels in many other Western countries) that rooms that remain empty on weekends, when business travelers are recovering at home from the labors of the week, can be profitably filled by offering them to tourists. Discounts of up to 50% are now quite common; they just have to be ferreted out by calls to the hotels themselves or to city tourist offices.

A logical course is for you to plan your itinerary so that you visit German cities on weekends (there are other advantages here, such as free entrance to museums, to be touched on later), leaving weekdays open to tour the countryside.

In Germany's lovely and varied countryside, accommodations are not only cheaper than in the cities—they can be unbelievably inexpensive. There are enchanting farmhouses in the depths of the Bavarian Forest or the far reaches of the Lüneberg Heath where a simple but spotless room, with a genuine featherbed and a morning call from the resident rooster can cost as little as $7. A farmhand's breakfast of cold meats and cheeses, fresh rolls, home-made butter and jam, and unlimited coffee *might* push the price into double figures.

Every small town and most villages have a central inn where a night need not cost much more than a farmhouse room, while everywhere there are small guest houses where a Frau Schmidt or a Frau Mayer has a welcoming sign outside (*Zimmer Frei* means "room to let") and a warm welcome inside.

Farmhouse, inn, or guest house—they might vary marginally in price and in comfort, but all share one quality: cleanliness. That guarantee is taken for granted in rural Germany, where no Hausfrau would risk the shame of having her hospitality faulted.

In the anonymity of the cities there is understandably no such guarantee, and one secure piece of advice for the visitor seeking reasonably-priced and clean accommodations is to avoid the seedy areas of town. The Reeperbahn of Hamburg, Frankfurt's Schillerstrasse, and some of the streets south of Munich's main train station are definitely *not* the places to find a quiet night's sleep. City tourist offices are able to blue-pencil the red-light districts on your visitor's street-map.

Transports of Delight

These three cities are among those that have highly-developed urban transport systems that give speedy and affordable access to and from the suburbs. Consequently, one possibility for the cost-conscious tourist who doesn't want to forego the city lights, is to take a hotel room on the outskirts of town and join the commuters. The cost of a daily ticket—no more than $5—and the inconvenience of a half-hour train ride can be more than compensated for by the lower cost and perhaps higher comfort of a suburban hotel.

On the subject of travel, advance planning is again the key to the potentially complicated business of getting around Germany as inexpensively as possible. One has to start out from the premise that—with the exception of two wheels, two legs or four—there is no really inexpensive form of transport in Germany. There are many ways of cutting the cost, but they have to be hunted out with the same nose for bargains that one needs in sniffing out the special hotel deals.

Starting at the top of the league—air travel—Germany has a wonderfully efficient national airline, Lufthansa, but flights are expensive by American standards. On the other hand, Lufthansa, in common with all other European airlines, offers a fly-and-save deal that gives considerable discounts on certain prepaid flights.

Rivaling Lufthansa for sheer efficiency is the German rail system, whose trains don't just arrive on time, but are frequently early. A fast Inter-City service links up with branch lines gathering up country towns and villages in a finely-spun web of a communications network. German railways offer a bewildering array of special fares, which require the assistance of a ticket clerk or a travel agent to sort out. For an enterprise so deeply in debt, German railways go to great lengths to explain to the puzzled traveler how to accomplish his journey most affordably.

The major cities, and some of the minor ones, have fast, efficient urban transportation systems, usually combinations of suburban trains, subways, buses—and the much slower but well-loved tram, still rattling its defiant way through many long-since modernized downtown areas. Special daily or weekly tickets cut the cost of city travel dramatically.

The days are long since gone when the country's *autobahns* (expressways) were a tourist attraction in themselves and visitors would rent or borrow a car for a spin on the smooth, straight tarmac. But there's still an indefinable sense of personal contact with European history to motor down roads laid out with military precision 50 years ago. Germany has Europe's most developed expressway network, free of the tolls demanded by several of its neighbors—and consequently more crowded. Car rental charges in Germany are higher than in the States, but savings can be made by careful planning and comparison shopping. Many smaller rental firms offer older cars at a fraction of the usual charge, and big discounts are available on weekends and public holidays.

Germany's biggest car-maker produces one of the world's most popular camping vehicles, which is to be found in the fleet of every major car-rental firm. Behind the wheel of one of these, you are released from hotel and transport cares and can enjoy the kind of independence that is attracting more and more Germans. German camp sites are reputedly the cleanest and best-run in Europe, and many of them—particularly those in the foothills of the Bavarian Alps—are set amid spectacular scenery. The charges for parking a camper or pitching a tent are minimal, but for individualists who want to cut costs still further the German motoring organization ADAC (an excellent source of information not only on motoring matters but for any tourist question) has won from local authorities a slightly grudging assurance that camping vehicles can legitimately stay on public parking lots for no longer than a night.

In the mountains above those idyllic camping sites are strategically positioned huts and lodges for upland walkers and mountaineers. Beds—usually simple bunks in dormitory-like conditions—can be booked by foreign visitors. Walking is a mass pursuit in Germany, to judge by the crowded mountain trails on fine summer and fall weekends, so it's advisable to work out a route carefully and make reservations as far ahead as possible.

Germans aren't only passionate walkers, they rival the Dutch as cyclists. Munich, for example, has more bicycles than cars, and most cities have central points where visitors can rent a sturdy machine for a few marks and explore the sights on two wheels. German railways have caught up with the trend and offer bicycles to rent at many country stations.

Of Beer and Shops

Beer—that's one thing the budget-conscious visitor to Germany can enjoy without consulting the vacation balance-sheet. German beer is good—and it's affordable. It's so nutritious and pure (still brewed strictly according to a 17th-century Bavarian recipe, despite conformist pressures by Common-Market bureaucrats) that nursing mothers are sometimes prescribed a daily bottle or two. German beer is the perfect complement to German food, which is best described as wholesome. The increasing German hunger for exotic holidays has brought a refreshing variety to the restaurant scene, and French bistros now compete with Italian pizzerias and trattoria, and they in turn compete with culinary delights from other corners of the globe. Exotic is synonymous with expensive, however, so with some exceptions (Italian pizzerias, Yugoslav grills) it's advisable to stay with the homespun cuisine of the German *Gaststätte*, where a plate of pork, Sauerkraut, and dumplings, with enough calories to provide the daily intake of a ditch-digger, can be had for $6 or so.

The visitor to Germany in late spring, summer, and fall can save money by avoiding restaurants, buying cheese, cold meats, and salads at the nearest shop, packing them in a picnic basket and taking them to the local beer-garden, where it's not only accepted but expected practice to bring along whatever goes well with the beer. A check of the packed tables, groaning under the weight of beer and good food, will confirm that Germans aren't shy about it.

Shopping may be an expensive pursuit in West Germany, but most municipalities have made it a delight by building leafy pedestrian malls in cities once choked with traffic. Restricting your tour to window shopping and perhaps a drink at one of the outdoor cafes that line every mall can be one of the most pleasant and economical ways of getting to know what makes the typical German city tick. There's even free entertainment; the malls have become the open-air stage of a growing company of itinerant Europeans, who sing and dance through all winds and weathers for the chance of gathering a few marks in an upturned hat.

Entertainment and Nightlife

In a country where a ticket to the opera can cost $50 or more, there is still a refreshing repertoire of free or extremely low-cost entertainment.

In the summer, most towns have a program of open-air theater and concerts, often free of charge. Wherever there is a castle—and that's just about every place on the map—there is usually a year-long series of performances within and without its ancient walls. A concert of early music experienced in the ivy-hung confines of a castle courtyard provides memories far exceeding in value the nominal price of a ticket.

In cities with a music academy there are always free concerts to be enjoyed, featuring advanced students who are likely to become the stars of tomorrow. Germany's ancient churches and cathedrals also provide rich hunting grounds for the music-lover, who is rarely asked to part with more than $5.

For the opera-lover with a fixed budget and sturdy legs, the so-called "Stehplätze" (standing places) in the country's opera-houses are also to be recommended. For those who love music, the pubs and clubs of Hamburg, Berlin, Munich, and many other cities charge a nominal entry fee.

The local press can be an invaluable key to opening the door to the bargain basement of Germany. Every newspaper has a "What's On" column listing entertainment and leisure activities.

PLANNING YOUR TRIP
Before You Go

NATIONAL TOURIST OFFICE. The best starting point for any trip to Germany is the German National Tourist Office (GNTO). It produces a wealth of tourist literature, most of it free and all of it useful. It is a strikingly efficient organization and the expert staff will be able to give you advice and information on every aspect of your vacation.

You will find offices at the following addresses:

In the U.S.: 747 Third Ave., New York, NY 10017 (212–308–3300); 444 South Flower St., Suite 2230, Los Angeles, CA 90017 (213–688–7332).

In Canada: PO Box 417, 2 Fundy, Place Bonaventure, Montreal H5A 1B8 (514–878–9885).

In the U.K.: 61 Conduit St., London W1R 0EN (01–734–2600).

ENTRY REQUIREMENTS. All visitors to Germany from the U.S., Canada, and Britain must have a valid passport. Visas are not required. However, if you plan to drive or go by train to West Berlin, you must have a transit visa from the East German authorities to cross East Germany. These are available at the border points and it is not necessary to arrange them in advance. A small fee is charged.

HEALTH AND INSURANCE. Travel insurance can cover everything from health and accident costs to lost luggage and trip cancellation.

Try to make your insurance arrangements *before* you leave, rather than at the last minute from, say, an airport vending machine or insurance company counter, so you can be sure you are getting the coverage you need. It is a good idea to take out separate health and accident insurance for your trip but make sure that you do not duplicate coverage you already have. Check whether emergency evacuation back home is covered by your insurance and bear in mind that most insurance issued specifically for travel does *not* cover pre-existing conditions, such as a heart problem.

Several organizations offer coverage designed to supplement existing health insurance and to help defray costs not covered by many standard policies, such as emergency transportation. Some of the more prominent are:

Carefree Travel Insurance, c/o ARM Coverage, Inc., 120 Mineola Blvd., Box 310, Mineola, NY 11510 (212–683–2622), offers medical evacuation arranged by Europ Assistance of Paris. Carefree coverage is available from many travel agents.

International SOS Assistance, Inc., PO Box 11568, Philadelphia, PA 19116 (800–523–8930), has fees from $15 a person for seven days, to $195 for a year.

IAMAT (International Association for Medical Assistance to Travelers), 417 Center St., Lewiston, NY 14092 (716–754–4883) in the U.S. or 188 Nicklin Rd., Guelph, Ontario N1H 7L5 (519–836–0102) in Canada.

Travel Assistance International, offers a comprehensive program providing medical and personal emergency services, and offering immediate medical, personal, and financial help. Trip protection ranges from $35 for an individual for up to eight days, to $220 for an entire family for a year. Full details are available from travel agents and insurance brokers, or from **Europ Assistance Worldwide Services, Inc.,** 1333 F. St. NW, Suite 300, Washington, DC 20004 (800–821–2828). **In the U.K.** contact **Europ Assistance Ltd.,** 252 High St., Croydon, Surrey CRO 1NF (01–680–1234).

The Association of British Insurers, Aldermary House, Queen St., London EC4N 1TT (01–248–4477) will give comprehensive advice on all aspects of vacation insurance.

Germany and Britain, as members of the **EEC,** have reciprocal medical arrangements. Get form CM1 from any DHSS office, complete it, and return it well in advance of your trip. You will then be sent form E111 which entitles you to the same emergency medical treatment as a national of the country in which you are staying. This does *not* cover transportation back home and you are strongly advised to take out personal accident insurance for that.

You have to pay for any medical treatment you receive in Germany but you should get most of your money back provided you follow the directions on the back of the E111 form exactly; if you don't you could lose a lot of money. Different instructions apply to each EEC country so make sure you follow the ones which apply to the country in which you are staying.

Loss of luggage is another frequent inconvenience to travelers, and although insurance companies are reluctant to arrange coverage solely for luggage, you may be able to include it in your health and accident policy. Remuneration is often determined by weight, regardless of the value of the contents of your luggage. Also, check your home-owner's policy before you buy luggage insurance, as you may find you are already covered for loss of luggage while traveling.

Finally, trip cancellation insurance is especially important for travelers on APEX or charter flights. Should you get sick abroad or for some other reason be unable to continue your trip you may have to buy a new one-way ticket home, and also pay for the ticket which you're unable to use. You can guard against this with trip cancellation insurance available from most travel agents.

BUDGET PACKAGE TOURS. There is no doubt about it: If your priority is to stick to a modest budget, then you cannot do better than to buy a package tour to Germany. Tours are numerous, however, so it is best to get expert advice from your travel agent or from the German National Tourist Office nearest to you.

Among tour operators in the U.S. are:

Bennett Tours, 270 Madison Ave., New York, NY 10016 (212–532–5060) offers a variety of tours through Germany, Switzerland, and Austria. Among its offerings are inexpensive city tours of Berlin, Frankfurt, and Munich. Cost of the tours range from $300 to $600.

Cosmos/Globus Gateway, 95–25 Queens Blvd., Rego Park, NY 11374 (718–268–1700).

Lufthansa, 680 Fifth Ave., New York, NY 10010 (718–895–1277).

Pan Am, Pan Am Bldg., New York, NY 10017 (212–687–2600).

TWA, 28 S. Sixth St., Philadelphia, PA 19106 (215–925–7885).

Many U.K. operators have German packages and most of them are in the budget range. Here is just a selection of the firms who deal with the German market:

Angel Travel Ltd., 34 High St., Borough Green, Sevenoaks, Kent TN15 8BJ (0732–883868), offers city vacations by rail or own car, and self-catering vacations.

Cosmos Tours Ltd., Cosmos House, 1 Bromley Common, Bromley, Kent BR2 9LX (01–464–3400).

DER Travel Service, 18 Conduit St., London W1R 9DT (01–408–0111). DER has an extensive range of ski, fly-drive, walking, and "Go-As-You-Please" vacations, and many other options.

German Tourist Facilities, 184–186 Kensington Church St., London W8 4DP (01–229–2474), offers a variety of winter and summer, multi-center, and city vacations.

KD German Rhine Line, G.A. Clubb Rhine Cruise Agency Ltd., 80–81 St. Martin's Lane, London WC2 4AA (01–836–1876), for a wide choice of cruises.

Thomson Holidays Ltd., Greater London House, Hampstead Rd., London NW1 7SD (01–387–9321).

WHEN TO GO. The main tourist season in Germany runs from May to late October, when the weather is at its best but when the crowds are at their thickest. This is also the season for the hundreds of folk festivals. The main winter sports season in the Bavarian Alps runs from Christmas to mid-March.

Prices everywhere are, as you would expect, generally higher during the summer, so you may find there are many advantages in visiting Germany off-season. Most large resorts offer special *Zwischensaison* (low season) or *Nebensaison* ("edge of season") rates. Tourist offices can provide lists of hotels offering *Pauschalangebote*—special low-price, inclusive weekly packages. Similarly, many winter resorts offer *Weisse Wochen*—winter off-season rates for the periods immediately before and after the high season. These rates normally include seven days' bed-and-breakfast and skiing lessons.

However, there are a few disadvantages. First, the weather, which during the summer is usually quite reliable, is pretty miserable for sightseeing in the winter. Second, many tourist attractions, particularly those in rural areas, close down, though, of course, the winter attractions will be in full swing. Carnival time—February or March—brings in the crowds and with them the higher prices to cities like Köln, Aachen, Düsseldorf, and Munich. You may find that many hotels close down completely or have reduced staff and service between the end of October and Christmas.

CLIMATE. Germany's generally mild climate makes it an ideal country for traveling. Average temperatures during January, the coldest month, are about 0°C (32°F) dropping to several degrees (though sometimes as much as −20°C) below freezing in the mountains. The winter season begins in December, and it is possible to ski in the Bavarian Alps into April. Spring comes early, except in the Alpine resorts, and in some areas such as the Bergstrasse (between Darmstadt and Heidelberg) orchards bloom as early as April.

The average temperature during the summer months is a pleasant 20°C–25°C) (68°F–77°F), but be prepared for a few cloudy and wet days from time to time. The south is usually warmer than the north, but as you get nearer the Alps the summers are much shorter. Swimming is at its best from June through August. The only real exception to the above is the strikingly variable weather in southern

Bavaria caused by the Föhn, a warm Alpine wind that gives rise to clear but rather oppressive conditions in summer and sudden thaws in mountainous regions in winter.

Average afternoon temperatures in degrees Fahrenheit and centigrade:

	Jan.	Feb.	Mar.	Apr.	May	June	July	Aug.	Sept.	Oct.	Nov.	Dec.
Berlin												
F°	35	38	46	55	65	70	74	72	66	55	43	37
C°	2	3	8	13	18	21	23	22	19	13	6	3
Munich												
F°	33	37	45	54	63	69	72	71	64	53	42	36
C°	1	3	7	12	17	21	22	22	18	12	6	2

SPECIAL EVENTS. The German National Tourist Board, Beethovenstrasse 69, 6000 Frankfurt am Main 1, publishes a calendar of folklore events and local festivals, musical and theatrical events, exhibits, conventions, congresses, and trade fairs (useful to know about as hotels in the cities where these are held are always booked far in advance). The calendar appears in April and October; write the address above for a free copy, or get one from your nearest GNTO (for addresses see National Tourist Offices above). Local and regional tourist offices also produce calendars of local events, usually monthly, which are available either from tourist offices or from newsstands.

January. International World Cup Ski Races (downhill and slalom) at Garmisch-Partenkirchen in the second weekend of the month. Berlin's *Grüne Woche* (Green Week) gets under way with a traditional agricultural and garden show.

February. This is the month for the Frankfurt International Trade Fair for consumer goods. Berlin holds its famous film festival later in the month. The *Fasching* (carnival) season peaks with Shrove Tuesday processions in the Rhineland, Munich, and Bavaria. In Nürnberg there's the Toy Fair for trade only but worth mentioning as all the hotels will be booked solid.

March. Munich's International Fashion Fair is held, which again means that hotels will be fully booked. If you like beer then you won't want to miss Munich's *Starkbierfest* (strong beer festival).

April. This month sees the start of the folk festivals with Mannheim's traditional May Market, and Spring Festivals in Stuttgart and Munich. *Walpurgis* festivals are held throughout the Harz Mountains on the last day of the month, while Frankfurt holds it Fur Trade Fair. The Hannover Industrial Fair begins at the end of April and continues into early May.

May. The festival season continues with Wiesbaden's three-week international May Festival of opera, drama, music, and ballet. Augsburg's German Mozart Festival is held at the end of the month. The theatrical theme carries on with the Theater Festival in Berlin, and Killisberg's open-air summer theater in Stuttgart begins. In Rothenburg-ob-der-Tauber the traditional *Meistertrunk* play is staged.

June. Yachtsmen make their way to Kiel for the regatta, while Augsburg's open-air opera season gets under way (continuing into September). There are Corpus Christi parades at Freiburg and Berchtesgaden. Mozart-lovers flock to Würzburg's festival. Nürnberg offers two attractions this month—the International Organ Week and the "200 Miles of Nürnberg" car race on the Noris Ring. In Heidelberg the first summer castle illuminations take place.

July. The historical *Kinderzeche* open-air play is performed in Dinkelsbühl, while Würzburg holds its Kiliani Folk Festival. If you're interested in music there's the choice of Munich's opera festival or the Wagner festival in Bayreuth. At St. Goarshausen on the Rhine there's the Lorelei Festival and Düsseldorf's *Kirmes am Rhein* folk festival. Between Bingen and Rüdesheim the "Rhine in Flames" celebrations are held.

August. There's open-air theater at Heidelberg's castle and a "Rhine in Flames" festival between Braubach and Koblenz. There are also festivals to celebrate the start of the grape harvest at Rüdesheim, Stuttgart, and other towns in the Rhineland, and a beer festival at Kulmbach. Motor racing enthusiasts won't want to miss the German Grand Prix at the Hockenheim Ring in southern Rhineland.

September. Celebrations continue all over the wine-producing areas of the country—particularly interesting is Bad Dürkheim's *Wurstmarkt,* or Sausage Fair, and Worm's *Backfischfest,* the largest in the Rhineland. In Stuttgart there's the Cannstatt Wasen folk festival, and at St. Goar and St. Goarshausen the most spectacular of the Rhine's summer Rhine-in-Flames illuminations are held. Munich's famous Oktoberfest begins at the end of the month.

October. The International Book Fair is held at Frankfurt—hotels are reserved months before. The oldest folk festival in Germany is held at Bremen, and if you're in Munich you might pick up a bargain at the autumn *Auer Dult,* the flea- and antique market.

November. There are St. Martin's Day parades all over the country, particularly in the Rhineland, Heidelberg, and Bavaria. Jazz lovers will be interested in Berlin's Jazz Festival. If you're in Hamburg don't miss the *Hamburger Dom* folk festival. In Munich there's the international six-day indoor cycle race—the *Sechs Tage Rennen*.

December. *Christkindl-markets*—Christmas open-air markets— are held in Nürnberg, Rothenburg-ob-der-Tauber, Munich, Stuttgart, and other cities.

WHAT TO PACK. The first principle is to travel light. The restrictions by size or weight that are imposed on air travelers are an added incentive to keep baggage within the bounds of commonsense. Transatlantic passengers may take two pieces of luggage; these are subject to a size allowance, not a weight one. The total sum of their height, length, and width must not exceed 270 cms. (106 inches), and neither of the two must exceed a total of 158 cms. (62 inches). Extra pieces of luggage are prohibitively expensive.

If you are traveling to Germany on a European flight, luggage is subject to a weight allowance and you will be charged extra if your luggage weighs more than 20 kg. (44 lbs.). All travelers are entitled to one piece of hand luggage only.

Clothing. The mild climate calls for lightweight clothing from June through September, with a sweater or light jacket for the evening. A light raincoat is essential at any time.

If you wear glasses or contact lenses, take an extra pair if possible. If you take prescription medicines regularly pack a good supply. Other medicines are not difficult to find.

If you intend to swim in either indoor or outdoor pools, take your swimcap; they're obligatory in Germany.

LANGUAGE. Most people will understand and be able to speak some English. The Germans are great linguists and you will find English spoken in all hotels, restaurants, airports, train stations, museums, and other places of interest. Similarly, tourist offices will have at least one staff member who can speak English. However, don't assume that everyone you deal with will automatically speak English; it is not always widely spoken in rural areas, and it is, in any case, only common courtesy to ask beforehand if the person you are addressing speaks English. Needless to say, the Germans respond warmly to anyone who makes the effort to master a few words or phrases of German (we give a basic vocabulary at the end of the book) but the chances are that the reply will be in perfect English!

TIME ZONES. During the summer (dates vary every year, but generally this means from the end of March to the end of September), Germany is six hours ahead of Eastern Standard Time, seven hours ahead of Central Time, eight hours ahead of Mountain Time, and nine hours ahead of Pacific Time. During the winter, Germany puts her clocks back one hour, but as all America does likewise, the time difference remains the same.

Similarly, Germany is one hour ahead of British Summer Time and, during the winter, one hour ahead of Greenwich Mean Time.

TRAVEL FOR THE DISABLED. Thousands of disabled people who are physically able to travel do so enthusiastically when they know they will be able to move about in safety and comfort. A growing number of travel agents specialize in this market, with tours that generally parallel those of the non-disabled traveler. The tours are taken at a more leisurely pace, with everything checked out in advance to eliminate inconvenience, whether the traveler is blind, deaf, or in a wheelchair.

The **Information Center for Individuals with Disabilities,** 20 Park Plaza, Rm. 330, Boston, MA 02116 (617–727–5540) is a helpful organization.

The **Society for the Advancement of Travel for the Handicapped,** 26 Court St., Brooklyn, NY 11242 (718–858–5483) can supply a complete list of travel agents who arrange such travel.

The **Travel Industry and Disabled Exchange,** 5435 Donna Ave., Tarzana, CA 91356 (818–343–6339) is another possibility.

The **Travel Information Center,** Moss Rehabilitation Hospital, 12th St., and Tabor Rd., Philadelphia, PA 19141 (215–329–5715), offers Travel Accessibility information packages detailing travel problems and possibilities to various destinations. The cost is $5, allow a month for delivery.

Several publications are available, including the excellent *Access to the World: A Travel Guide for the Handicapped,* by Louise Weiss. It's published by Henry Holt & Co., but must be ordered through your local bookstore. *The Itinerary,* a bimonthly magazine for travelers with disabilities, is published by Whole Person Tours, PO Box 1084, Bayonne, NJ 07002 (201–858–3400).

A number of car rental companies offer cars with hand controls, including Avis (800–331–1212), Hertz (800–654–3131), and National (800–328–4567). All have European divisions.

Britain's major center for help and advice for the disabled traveler is the **Royal Association for Disability and Rehabilitation,** 25 Mortimer St., London W1N 8AB (01–637–5400). It has a library of helpful pamphlets, including the Access guides.

The Airline Transport User's Committee, 129 Kingsway, London WC2B 6NH (01–242–3883), publishes a useful booklet, *Care In The Air,* free, which includes advice for disabled passengers.

STUDENT AND YOUTH TRAVEL. Germany is an excellent low-cost destination for the young. There are many well-organized hostels, campsites, travel discounts, and study possibilities available.

Student travelers should get an International Student Identity Card (ISIC), which is usually needed to get student discounts, rail and bus passes, and European student charter flights. In the U.S. apply to the Council on International Educational Exchange, in Canada apply to the Association of Student Councils; addresses of both are given below. Passes cost $10.

All the following organizations will be helpful in finding student flights, educational opportunities, and other information. Most deal with international student travel generally, but materials of those listed cover Germany.

Council on International Educational Exchange (CIEE), 203 East 42nd St., New York, NY 10017 (212–661–1414) and 312 Sutter St., San Francisco, CA 94108 (415–421–3473) provides information on summer study, work/travel programs, travel services for college and high school students, and their free *Charter Flights Guide.* Their *Whole World Handbook* ($7.95, plus $1 postage) is the best listing of both work and study possibilities.

Educational Travel Center, 438 North Frances, Madison, WI 53703, is also an organization worth contacting.

The Institute of International Education, 809 United Nations Plaza, New York, NY 10017 (212–883–8200) is primarily concerned with study opportunities and fellowships for international study and training. The New York office has a visitors' information center, and there are satellite offices in Chicago, Denver, San Francisco, and Washington.

In Canada, contact the **Association of Student Councils** (AOSC), 187 College St., Toronto, Ontario M5T 1P7 (416–979–2604). This is a non-profit student cooperative, owned and run by over 50 college and university student unions. Its travel bureau provides information on tours and work camps worldwide. Try also **Tourbec,** 535 Ontario East, Montreal, Quebec H2L 1N8 (514–288–4455).

In Britain, student travel arrangements can be made through a variety of organizations. Here are just a few useful addresses:

Centro Turistico Studentesco (CTS), 33 Windmill St., London W1P 1HH (01–580–4554).

London Student Travel (LST), 52 Grosvenor Gardens, London SW1W 0EB (01–730–8111): try also the **Union of Student International Travel** (USIT), at the same address.

Worldwide Student Travel, 39 Store St., London WC2E 7HY (01–580–77330).

See also Youth Hostels in "Where To Stay In Germany" for other useful addresses. Specific information on rail and other discounts is listed in the relevant sections.

Getting to Germany

From North America

BY AIR. Most of the major transatlantic airlines operate services to at least one of Germany's larger cities but the leading carriers are:

Lufthansa, 680 Fifth Ave., New York, NY 10010 (718–895–1277).

Pan Am., Pan Am. Bldg., New York, NY 10017 (212–687–2600).

TWA, 605 Third Ave., New York, NY 10016 (212–290–2141).

Fares. As is so often the case with budget travel your best hope of finding an inexpensive plane ticket is with the help of a travel agent. Bargain fares appear and disappear with such rapidity that often they're not announced publicly; these are the fares only a travel agent can find for you.

The best buy is not an APEX (advance purchase) ticket on one of the major airlines. APEX tickets carry certain restrictions: they must be bought in advance (usually 21 days), they restrict your travel, usually with a minimum stay of seven days and a maximum of 90, and they also penalize you for changes—voluntary or not—in your travel plans. But if you can work around these drawbacks (and most can), they are among the best-value fares available. Mid-1987, the New York–Frankfurt APEX ticket cost $756.

Charter flights offer the lowest fares but often depart only on certain days, and seldom on time. Though you may be able to arrive at one city and return from another, you may lose all or most of your money if you cancel your ticket. Travel agents can make bookings though they won't encourage you, since commissions are lower than on scheduled flights. Checks should as a rule be made out to the bank and specific escrow account for your flight. To make sure your payment stays in this account until your departure, don't use credit cards. Don't sign up for a charter flight unless you've checked with a travel agency about the reputation of the packager. It's particularly important to know the packager's policy concerning refunds should a flight be cancelled. One of the most popular charter operators is **Council Charters** (800–223–7402), a division of CIEE (Council on International Educational Exchange). Other companies advertise in Sunday travel sections of daily newspapers.

Somewhat more expensive—but up to 50% below the cost of APEX fares—are tickets purchased through companies known as consolidators that buy blocks of tickets on scheduled airlines and sell them at wholesale prices. Here again you may lose all or most of your money if you change plans, but at least you will be on a regularly scheduled flight with less risk of cancellation than a charter. Once you've made your reservations, call the airline to make sure you're confirmed. Among the best known consolidators are **UniTravel** (Tel. 800–325–2222) and **Access International** (250 West 57th St., Suite 511, New York, NY 10107. Tel. 212–333–7280). Others advertise in the Sunday travel section of the daily newspapers as well.

A third option is to join a travel club that offers special discounts to its members. Four such organizations are **Moments Notice** (40 E. 49th St., New York, NY 10017. Tel. 212–486–0503); **Stand-Buys Ltd.** (311 W. Superior, Suite 414, Chicago, IL 60610. Tel. 800–255–0020); **Discount Travel International** (114 Forrest Ave., Barberth, PA 19072. Tel. 215–668–2182) and **Worldwide Discount Travel Club** (1674 Meridian Ave., Miami Beach, FL 33139. Tel. 305–534–2082). These cut-rate tickets should be compared with APEX tickets on the major airlines.

From Great Britain

BY AIR. There are currently very few real budget flights to Germany from the U.K. Prices remain unjustifiably high.

The major airlines from the U.K. are:

British Airways, Speedbird House, PO Box 10, London-Heathrow Airport, Hounslow, TW6 2JA (01–897–4000).

Lufthansa, Lufthansa House, 10 Old Bond St., London W1X 4EN (01–408–0442).

Both these airlines operate a wide range of scheduled services from London to destinations including Berlin, Düsseldorf, Frankfurt, Hamburg, Hannover, Munich, and Stuttgart.

Fares. In early '88, the round-trip fare to Munich from London, flying Lufthansa, ranged from £248 on their Eurobudget ticket, where both your outward and inward journey must be booked at the same time, to £159 for their Fly-and-Save ticket where reservations and payment must be made at least 14 days in advance, with a minimum stay of one Saturday night. Best value of all was the Early Saver Return at £107; only available on certain flights and again reservations and payment must be made at least 14 days in advance, and the minimum stay is one Saturday night.

In competition with these fares are regular charter flights operated by **German Tourist Facilities,** 182–186 Kensington Church St., London W8 4DP (01–727–6676). However, these flights may not always work out as best value. Depending on season their London–Munich round-trip fare ranged from £79 to £119, plus £10 supplement if you booked less than 14 days before flying. Alternatively, for the Rhineland you could fly Virgin to Maastrict, southern Holland, for around £75 round-trip from Gatwick. From Maastrict there are good train services to Köln via Aachen. Contact **Virgin Atlantic Airways,** 7th Floor, Sussex House, High St., Crawley, West Sussex RH10 1BZ (0293–38222).

BY TRAIN. Train travel is an excellent budget option. There are three main routes from London. The quickest is via Dover and then across the Channel by Jetfoil to Oostende, in Belgium. From here, trains run through to Germany, many via Köln where they connect with the Inter-City network. Using the Jetfoil you can be in Köln by early evening, and Stuttgart and Würzburg by 10 P.M. You can use the conventional ferry on this route but it is a much slower way of making the Channel crossing.

There are overnight trains to all parts of Germany from Oostende. The "Tauern Express" heads south to Munich (day carriages and bunk beds/sleepers available) and numerous trains head north to Hannover, Bremen, and Hamburg (all of which can be reached by 10:30 P.M., if you use the Jetfoil).

The second route to Germany is from London (Liverpool St. Station) to Harwich and then to the Hook of Holland. It's a long sea crossing which means that the route is really only suitable for overnight travel. Rail connections from London to Harwich are good—use the comfortable connecting EuroCity services; seat reservations are recommended. The Hook is reached in the early morning from where there are excellent rail connections to all parts of Germany via Köln.

The third route again runs from London to Harwich and then by DFDS Prins Ferries to Hamburg. This service runs throughout the year on alternate days and takes longer than either of the other two routes.

Fares. It's worth buying tickets in advance to take advantage of the special all-inclusive rates offered on routes from London to Germany. Fares vary considerably depending on how and when you travel, so explore all the possibilities carefully to get the best deal.

In early '88 three different fares were offered for the London–Köln (via Dover/Oostende) route: A round-trip at £78; an economy day return at £75.60; and a five-day excursion return at £49. Remember, too, that you will have to pay a supplement if you travel by Jetfoil. The journey via Harwich is more expensive. The London to Hamburg trip with DFDS worked out at around £88 plus cabin accommodations, while via Harwich and the Hook of Holland the basic fare was £134.

Remember that British Rail, with their Mini Breaks, as well as DB/DER Travel and the ferry companies all operate a wide range of inclusive rail/ship holidays to Germany which can offer substantial savings, so if you are on a tight budget consult the brochures carefully.

Ticket Bargains. Discounts available include the **Inter Rail Card** for those under 26 years. It costs around £140 and is valid for one month. It allows half-price travel on British Rail services, reductions on cross-Channel services (these vary according to the route taken), and unlimited second-class rail travel in 26 European countries, including Germany. Inter Rail Cards are available from many train stations in Europe and the U.K.

If you're under 26 and just going to one place, then get a **Eurotrain** or **Transalpino** ticket; they offer reduced-rate rail travel. You can get more information from **Eurotrain,** 52 Grosvenor Gardens, London SW1W OEB (01–730–6525) and **Transalpino,** 71–75 Buckingham Palace Rd., London SW1W OQU (01–834–9656).

If you're traveling in a group of three or more you can save money by buying a **Rail Europe Family Card.** This gives discounts of up to 50%. The card is available to a family, or a group of people, living at the same address, up to a maximum of eight, all of whom must be named on the card. A minimum of three of the named fare-payers, at least one of whom must be an adult, must travel together throughout the journey to qualify for the reductions. The first adult pays the full ordinary fare and subsequent adults pay half fare, and children under 12 years pay half the child's reduced fare.

Senior citizens should buy a **Rail Europe Senior Card** (the price in early '88 was £5). This card is only issued in conjunction with a valid British Rail Senior Citizen Card. It entitles the holder to reduced-rate rail travel in 19 European countries. The reductions in Germany are about 30%.

If more than six people are traveling together they will be eligible for a group discount. Full details of all these offers and the Inter Rail Card are available from the **European Rail Travel Center,** Box 303, Victoria Station, London SW1V 1JY (01–834–2345).

Note: If you want to be really knowledgeable about train times in Europe, then buy the **Thomas Cook Continental Timetable.** It is packed with information and is issued monthly, so make sure you get the correct issue for when you'll be traveling. It's available in the U.S. from Travel Library, PO Box 2975, Shawnee Mission, Kansas 66201. In the U.S. call toll-free on 1–800–FORSYTH: in Canada call collect on 913–384–0496. In Britain it can be ordered from Thomas Cook Ltd., Timetable Publishing Office, PO Box 36, Peterborough, Cambridgeshire PE3 6SB (0733–502568), price £6.60.

BY BUS. Germany has relatively few scheduled bus services from the U.K. There are really only two main routes: one to Munich, and one to northern Germany.

The main operators have grouped together under the banner of **International Express,** and details of their services are available from International Express, 13 Regent St., London SW1Y 3LR (01–439–9368).

During the summer **Eurolines** runs a daily service to Munich. This leaves London Victoria Coach Station mid-evening and crosses the Channel at Dover in the middle of the night. En route the next day, the bus calls at Köln (8:30) and Frankfurt (1 P.M.) reaching Munich at 6:45. Three days a week the service goes from Frankfurt to Munich via Nürnburg, and on the remaining days via Mannheim and Stuttgart.

Transline serves the Rhineland and northern Germany and destinations include Düsseldorf, Munster, Osnabruck, Hannover, and Celle. However, many extra buses run just before national holidays and in summer, so check with International Express for the latest details.

Fares. Although the magnificent German *autobahn* (expressway) network makes journey times fast, the fares are not very competitive with air travel at around £100 round-trip from London to Munich.

BY CAR. There is only one direct car ferry service to Germany from Britain; this is the DFDS Prins Ferries service, which runs on alternate days from Harwich to Hamburg. The ships sail at mid-afternoon, arriving at Hamburg in the early afternoon the following day.

However, there are a number of other indirect car ferry routes good for Germany, though there is little to choose between them. On all routes it is possible to cut your costs by using off-peak sailings. For example, there are reduced rates on Sealink British Ferries' sailings from Harwich to the Hook of Holland. Similarly, Olau Line, sailing from Sheerness to Vlissingen, offers reduced rates for travel on their day-time sailing, though, of course, these have the disadvantage of your not reaching deep into Germany until nightfall.

For travelers from northern England, North Sea Ferries operates a service from Hull to Rotterdam (Europoort) and Zeebrugge. Fares include evening meal, breakfast, and a reclining seat with rug. Daily departure from Hull is at 6 P.M., arriving in Rotterdam at 8 A.M., and Zeebrugge at 9.

The Belgian ports of Oostende and Zeebrugge have excellent road links, via Brussels, to Aachen and Köln, where you can join the main expressway network. P & O European Ferries operates services from Dover to Oostende with up to four day-time sailings and to Zeebrugge with three. Again, substantial savings can be made on these routes by taking your vacation before the main summer season and by traveling off-peak in the early morning or afternoon. P & O European Ferries also operates a service to Zeebrugge from Felixstowe with three sailings a day. Sally Viking Line operates a service from Ramsgate to Dunkirk at competitive rates when several people travel together.

The "bus service" routes from Dover to Calais and Boulogne are the shortest with the cheapest fares, but they do not leave you very well placed for a speedy drive to Germany. The Hoverspeed service from Dover to Calais or Boulogne will zip you across the Channel in about 40 minutes, which gives you a flying start even if the drive from both French ports to Germany is long.

Fares. To give an idea of cost, the round-trip for a car and two passengers from Harwich to Hamburg, during the summer, is expensive, at about £340, though this does include a berth in a four-berth cabin.

For the shorter routes, say between Felixstowe and Zeebrugge or Ramsgate and Dunkirk, an off-peak round-trip for two people plus car works out at about £150.

All the large ferry companies operate inclusive car-based vacations at affordable rates, and often to less well-known destinations, too; ask for their brochures. DFDS, for example, offer a range of inclusive and attractively priced vacations throughout Germany. An eight-day vacation with six nights in a country guest house (half board) during July and August, only costs about £430 for two, including ferry charges.

DFDS Seaways, 199 Regent St., London W1R 7WA (01–488–2952).

Hoverspeed Ltd., Maybrook House, Queens Gardens, Dover, Kent CT17 9UQ (0304–216205).

North Sea Ferries, King George Dock, Hedon Rd., Hull HU9 5QA (0482–796145).

Olau Line Ltd., Ferry Terminal, Sheerness, Kent ME12 1SN (0795–666666).

P&O European Ferries, 7 Arundel St., London WC2R 3DA (01–240–9071).

Sally Lines Ltd., Argyle Center, York St., Ramsgate, Kent CT11 9DS (0843–595522).

Sealink British Ferries, 163 Eversholt St., London NW1 1BG (01–387–1234).

For details of car rental see "Getting Around Germany—By Car."

Getting Around Germany

BY TRAIN. German Federal Railways—or DB (Deutsche Bundesbahn) as it is usually called—is one of the most comprehensive rail systems in Europe. Services are reliable, fast, and comfortable.

The main-line passenger service consists of Inter-City (IC) expresses. There is an hourly service on IC routes and all trains have both first- and second-class cars. There is a supplement payable for travel in these trains; currently DM 6 for second class and DM 10 for first. Every IC train has a buffet car; prices are reasonable. Some even have train phones for urgent telephone calls. Seat reservation is recommended, the price of reservation being included in the IC supplement if you buy your ticket in advance.

The IC trains system is complemented by the *Fernexpress* (FD)—long-distance express trains—and *Schnellezüge*—ordinary fast trains. On both of these a small supplement, currently DM 3, is payable on trips of 50 km. (31 miles).

No supplements are payable on the semi-fast *Eilzüge* trains or very local services.

Fares. A new system of fares was introduced in 1987. The rate is calculated at DM 0.20 per kilometer (second class; first class at DM 0.30 per kilometer); a single trip of 105 km. thus costs DM 21. First-class fares are exactly 50% more than the second-class fares.

Ticket Bargains. There is a wide range of special discount tickets available, all of which provide substantial savings. About the best value is offered by the **DB Tourist Card.** It entitles the holder to unlimited travel on all scheduled trains (with the exception of some special trains and the motorail) and covers the complete German rail network, as well as the complimentary Bahnbus system (buses which replace trains at off-peak times and on branch lines); Deutsche Touring bus services, including those along the Romantik Road and the Rhine-Moselle line (Frankfurt–Trier); and scheduled ferry services of Köln-Düsseldorfer Rheinschiffart AG on the Rhine, Moselle, and Main (excluding their hotel cruises and hydrofoil services). In addition, the card entitles you to a reduced fare—only DM 48, available with nine and 16-day cards—to cross East Germany and visit West Berlin, with a free bus tour thrown in. The DB Tourist Card is available for four, nine, or 16 days and costs, for second-class travel, DM 160, DM 260, and DM 340, respectively. First-class tickets are available, as are DB Junior Cards for people under 26 years, second-class only. Price for nine days is DM 150, and for 16 days DM 200. You can get your DB Tourist Card either before you leave or from stations in Germany.

Another card worth considering is the **Vorzugskarte.** This gives reductions of about 20% on journeys of more than 201 km. (124 miles) in one direction. You can also use it for round-trips, and can make detours and stop-overs. Check the distances on a map: It may be worth making a detour, if you have the time, to qualify.

Complementing this card is the **Tourenkarte** (DB Regional Rail Rover). Having got to your vacation destination by using the Vorzugskarte, you can then buy the Tourenkarte to explore the area in which you are staying. The card entitles you to unlimited travel for a ten-day period. It costs around DM 45 for one person, DM 60 for two people, and DM 75 for families, including unmarried children under 18 years.

Among the variety of other bargain tickets is the **Bezirkswochenkarte,** though this isn't quite such good value as the others. It covers the same area as the Tourenkarte but costs around DM 85 and is only valid for seven days, plus each adult must buy his own card (children under 12 can share one card). **Tramper Tickets** are available to students under 27 and other people under 23. This card gives one month's unlimited travel, second-class, on DB lines (fast train supplements included) and bus services. The ticket costs around DM 238 and can be bought either before you leave for Germany or once you have arrived there. It's valid for 31 days and includes all supplements. Get the brochure *Make Tracks For Germany* from DER (see "Budget Package Tours" for address. This gives a brief rundown on the range of discount tickets available in Germany.

The **Eurailpass** and the **Eurail Youthpass** are unbeatable value if you are planning on traveling extensively by train through Europe, including Germany. They give unlimited mileage through western and central Europe (but *not* the U.K. or Ireland) by train, on railway-operated bus routes, many ferries, and certain river boat services and lake steamers—over 160,000 km. (100,000 miles) in all. The Eurailpass is available for 15 or 21 days, or one, two, or three months at $280, $350, $440, $620, and $760, respectively. The great advantage of the pass, apart from being amazing value for money, is that you travel in the spacious comfort of first-class compartments, so you can travel on a budget *and* in great style! Bunk beds are also available, so save money on hotel prices by traveling overnight and arriving early at your next destination.

If you can get a small group together (minimum of three people in summer, two in winter) you can get 15 days' first-class travel for a remarkable $210 each.

For the under 26s there's the Eurail Youthpass which gives unlimited second-class travel for one or two months for $310 or $400, respectively.

The Eurail company have introduced the **Eurail Flexipass** which gives you nine-days' rail travel in a 21-day period so you can break your journey without losing any time on your pass. The Eurail Flexipass costs $310.

These excellent money-saving passes are only available to citizens from the U.S., Canada, and South America. These passes *must* be bought *before* you leave for Europe.

In the U.S. contact: **French National Railways,** Eurail Division, 610 Fifth Ave., New York, NY 10020 (212–582–2110).

German Federal Railways, 747 Third Ave., New York, NY 10017 (212–308–3106).

Italian National Railways, 630 Fifth Ave., New York, NY 10103 (212–397–2666).

In Canada: **French National Railways,** 409 Granville St., Suite 452, Vancouver, BC V6C 1T2 (604–688–6707).

German Federal Railways, 1290 Bay St., Toronto, Ontario M5R 2C3 (416–968–1570).

Italian National Railways, 2055 Peet St., Montreal, Quebec H3A 1V4 (514–845–9101) or 13 Balmuto St., Toronto, Ontario M4Y 1W4 (416–927–7712).

What To Look For. Supplements must be paid on all IC trains; there are currently around DM 5 in second-class, irrespective of distance traveled or whether a change of train is involved. If you do have to change trains this couldn't be easier as you will only have to cross to the other side of the platform; if you have reserved your seat the carriage you will board will stop exactly opposite the one you got off (this is Germany, after all). Before boarding your train look at the notice board on the platform; it will show how the train is made up. For example, where the first- and second-class carriages and the restaurant car are. Then look for the carriage identification letters (A–E) which hang from the station roof. These show where each pair of carriages will come to a halt, and will also correspond with the carriage letters on your reservation.

Seat reservation, which costs an extra DM 3–4, is strongly recommended for high-season and weekend travel. If you buy your ticket in advance the cost of reservation is included in the IC supplement.

If you're visiting Germany by rail, consider the DB tours/DER Travel Service brochure, *Summer Holidays in Germany*. It contains some fantastic bargains, including city vacations and combined road-and-rail vacations on the Romantik Road. AMEROPA, the official tour operator of German Railways, offers special rail packages throughout Europe, with new, great-value deals within Germany.

BY BUS. Germany is well-endowed with bus services, most of them using vehicles of the latest design. You can buy a timetable of all the buses operated by the Federal Railways (including Bahn- and Postbuses) from DB ticket offices and at main bus stations. These buses are closely integrated with train services, and usually take over where the rail lines come to an end, penetrating some of the remote regions.

German Railways also operate the German services of the Europabus network, the **Deutsche Touring** company. Two of the best services is provided by the Romantik Road Bus (EB190) between Würzburg (with connections to Frankfurt and Wiesbaden) and Füssen (connections to and from Munich, Augsburg, Nürnberg, and Garmisch-Partenkirchen); and the Burgenstrasse (Castle Road) Bus (EB 189) from Mannheim to Nürnberg. Both are daily services in each direction in reserved-seat buses with stewardesses.

Numerous other buses (T–lines) run across the Federal Republic. For full details and routes, timetables, and prices write: **Deutsche Touring,** Am Römerhof 17, Postfach 900244, 6000 Frankfurt/Main 90. Or inquire at DER travel agencies or one of the Deutsche Touring branch offices in Hannover, Köln, Dortmund, Munich, or Nürnberg.

BY CAR. Germany encourages tourists to take advantage of her *autobahns* (expressways) and excellent roads by making entrance formalities as simple as possible and by imposing hardly any tolls. You will need an international car registration and international drivers' license but *not* if your car or your license is from an EEC country or from Austria, Norway, Switzerland, Sweden, or Portugal. Then, only your domestic license, plus proof of insurance, are required. All foreign cars must have a country sticker and have liability insurance. Although green-card insurance is not compulsory, it is advisable.

All three German automobile clubs are ready to help foreign motorists. Their addresses are:

ADAC (Allgemeiner Deutscher Automobile Club), Baumgarstr. 53, D–8000 Munich 70 (089–76761).

AvD (Automobilclub von Deutschland), Lyonerstr. 16, D–6000 Frankfurt-Niederrad (069–66061).

DTC (Deutscher Touring Automobile Club) Amalienburgstr. 23, D–8000 Munich 60 (089–8111048/9).

ADAC and AvD operate breakdown services on the whole German expressway network, which is constantly patroled by their cars. There are emergency phones located along the expressways: Ask for Road Service Assistance if you run into trouble. This breakdown service is free except for replacement parts. The ADAC (southern Germany) also has a telephone service for emergency medical help: call 089–222222. If you need police or an ambulance call 110.

The GNTO booklet *Happy Days In Germany* gives excellent information on motoring in Germany, as well as being a colorful guide to the country.

Rules Of The Road. The speed limit in built-up areas is 50 kph (31 mph). On all other roads speeds are limited to 100 kph (62 mph) *except* on expressways, where there is presently no limit though there is a "recommended" 130-kph (about 80-mph) limit; this effectively means only that if you are involved in an accident at a higher speed, this fact will weigh against you.

Seat belts *must* be worn—you'll be fined if you're caught not wearing one—and children under 12 years must not sit in the front seat.

All expressways in the Federal Republic are distinguished from the highways by the preceding letter followed by the route number. Other main roads, *Bundersstrassen,* are designated by the letter "B". There is also a network of major European highways crisscrossing West Germany, incorporating the expressways, but lettered "E" for Europaroute. Don't get confused if a particular stretch of expressway appears with an "E" number.

Gas Prices. Gas prices are not fixed so they may vary considerably but one liter of regular should cost around DM 0.98; super DM 0.96; diesel DM 1.03; and oil DM 8–DM 10.

Car Rental. This is an option worth considering even if you are on a fairly tight budget; there are some good-value schemes on offer. There are branches of Avis, Hertz, National, and Europcar in most large cities and you can make arrangements to rent a car either before you leave or when you get to your German destination.

In the U.S. **Hertz,** PO Box 2692, Smithtown, New York, NY 11787 (800–654–3001), in conjunction with British Airways, operates the Affordable Europe Scheme, with prices ranging from $78 for three-days' hire to $136 for seven.

In the U.K.: **Avis,** Hayes Gate House, Uxbridge Rd., Hayes, Middlesex UB4 0JN (01–848–8733) runs a number of excellent schemes, including their Super-Value Scheme. Prices range from £20 per day for six-days' rental, to £18 per day for 13. Don't forget to add on 14% local tax to your final bill and to budget for the price of gasoline.

BY BIKE. Bicycles can be hired in many vacation areas; the tourist offices will usually be able to provide you with addresses of rental firms. Hotels sometimes have bikes for hire by guests, too. Bicycles can also be hired at more than 280 German railroad stations. The cost per day, including insurance, is about DM 10. If you arrive by rail it is only DM 5. You can often return your bicycle to another station, thus saving money on train fares, but check first.

Staying In Germany

CUSTOMS ON ARRIVAL. There are three levels of duty-free allowance depending on which is your country of origin. For those entering Germany from a country outside Europe the allowances are: 1) 400 cigarettes or 100 cigars or 500 gr. of tobacco; 2) one liter of spirits over 22 proof or two liters of spirits less than 22 proof or two liters of sparkling wine or liqueur wine and two liters of wine; 3) 50 gr. of perfume; 4) other goods to the value of DM 115.

For travelers originating from a country belonging to the EEC (except Denmark) and providing goods have not been bought in a duty-free shop, the allowances are: 1) 300 cigarettes or 75 cigars or 400 gr. of tobacco; 2) three liters of wine or one-and-a-half liters of spirits over 22 proof or three liters of liqueur wine or sparkling wine up to 22 proof and five liters of other wine; 3) 75 gr. of perfume and 0.375 liters of toilet water; 4) goods up to the value of DM 780.

For those entering Germany from a European country outside the EEC, the allowances are: 1) 200 cigarettes or 50 cigars or 250 gr. tobacco; 2) liter of spirits over 22 proof or two liters of spirits up to 22 proof or two liters of sparkling wine or liqueur wine and two liters of wine; 3) 50 gr. perfume; 4) other goods to the value of DM 115.

CUSTOMS ON RETURNING HOME. U.S. Residents.

U.S. residents may take home $400 worth of foreign merchandise as gifts or for personal use duty-free, provided they have been out of the country for at least 48 hours, and that they have not claimed a similar exemption within the previous 30 days. Every member of a family is entitled to the same exemption, regardless of age, and the exemptions may be pooled. For the next $1,000 worth of goods a flat 10% duty, based on the price usually paid, will be charged, so keep all receipts.

Included in the $400 allowance, for travelers over the age of 21, are: 200 cigarettes, 100 non-Cuban cigars, and one liter of alcohol. Only one bottle of perfume trademarked in the U.S. may be brought in. You may not import meats, fruit, plants, soil, or other agricultural products. Gifts valued at under $50 may be mailed to friends or relatives back home, but not more than one gift per day of receipt to any one addressee. These gifts must not include perfume costing more than $5, tobacco, or liquor. If you are traveling with foreign-made articles such as cameras, watches, or binoculars bought on a previous trip or at home, either carry the receipt, or register them with the U.S. Customs before departure.

Canadian Residents. In addition to personal effects, and over and above the regular exemption of $300 per year, Canadian residents may import the following into Canada duty-free: 200 cigarettes, 50 cigars, two pounds of tobacco, and 40 ounces of liquor, provided these are declared in writing to Customs on arrival. Canadian Customs' regulations are strictly enforced, so you are recommended to check what your allowances are and to make sure that you have kept receipts for whatever you have bought abroad. Small gifts can be mailed home and should be marked "Unsolicited gift (nature of gift), value under $40 in Canadian funds". For other details get the Canadian Customs leaflet *I Declare*.

British Residents. There are two levels of duty-free allowance when returning to the U.K.: one, for goods bought outside the EEC, or for goods bought in a duty-free shop within the EEC; two for goods bought in an EEC country, but not in a duty-free shop.

In the first category you may import duty-free: 1) 200 cigarettes or 100 cigarillos or 50 cigars or 250 gr. of tobacco; 2) two liters of still table wine plus one liter of alcohol over 22 proof or two liters of alcohol under 22 proof or a farther two liters of still table wine; 3) 50 gr. of perfume and 1/4 liter of toilet water; 4) other goods up to a value of £32 but not more than 50 liters of beer.

In the second category, you may import 1) 300 cigarettes or 150 cigarillos or 75 cigars or 400 gr. of tobacco; 2) five liters of still table wine plus one-and-a-half liters of alcohol over 22 proof or three liters of alcohol under 22 proof or a further three liters of still table wine; 3) 75 gr. of perfume and 3/8 liter of toilet water; 4) other goods to the value of £250 but not more than 50 liters of beer.

CURRENCY. The German monetary units are the Deutsch Mark (DM) and the Pfennig (Pf): there are 100 Pf. to 1 DM. There are 1, 2, 5, 10, and 50 pfennig and 1, 2, and 5 DM coins in circulation, as well as 10, 20, 50, 100, 500, and 1,000 DM bills. As we went to press in early '88 the Deutsch Mark stood around 1.67 to the dollar and at 2.9 to the pound. It is essential to keep a sharp eye on the exchange rates during your trip.

CHANGING MONEY. The best place to change your money is in banks, where you will have to pay a small fee but you will get the best exchange rate. You can also change money at the Wechelstuben (official exchange offices) which you will find in most major towns, train stations, and airports.

Travelers' Checks. Travelers' checks are still the best way to safeguard your money while you're traveling, as most companies will replace them quickly and efficiently should they be lost or stolen. Always keep a separate note of the numbers of your checks to help in the recovery process, if this should be necessary. You will also usually get a better exchange rate for travelers' checks than you will for cash in Germany.

In the U.S. many of the larger banks issue their own travelers' checks which are almost as well recognized as those of the established firms, such as American Express, Cooks, and Barclays. Most banks will carry one or other of these brands of checks as well as their own.

Britons holding a Uniform Eurocheck card and check book can cash checks for up to £100 a day at banks, and write checks in some hotels and restaurants, etc.

It is always wise to have some small change when you arrive in Germany to pay for phone calls and buses, etc.

Credit Cards. As a budget traveler, you may decide to use your credit card to spread the cost of your trip—vacation now, pay later! Although credit cards are now an integral part of the Western Way of

Financial Life, there is still a certain amount of resistance on the part of some hotels, restaurants, and shops. Be sure to check before reserving your room or ordering a meal that your particular piece of plastic is accepted. Generally, Visa is probably the most widely accepted credit card, while practically all larger and more expensive establishments will accept American Express. If you lose your card, immediately notify the relevant office: **American Express** tel. 069–720016; **Diners Club** tel. 069–26030; **Master Card/Access** tel. 069–79330; **Visa** tel. 069–7562537.

TOURIST OFFICES. Almost every town of every significance has its own local *Verkehrsamt* (tourist office) and there are also a series of larger, regional tourist offices located throughout the country. Generally located at the *Rathaus* (city hall) or main train station, these offices produce an abundance of material on their regions—what to see, how to get around, special discount travel, where to eat, hotel reservations, etc. Be warned, though, that in some smaller offices this information may only be available in German, but as there is always someone who can speak English you should not encounter too many problems. These offices will also be able to book accommodations for you—look for the sign *Zimmernachweis*.

TIPPING. The service charges on hotel bills suffice, except for bell hops and porters (DM 2 per bag or service). Whether you tip the hotel concierge depends on whether he or she has given you any special service.

Service charges are included in restaurant bills (listed as *Bedienung*), as well as tax (listed as *MWST*), but it is customary to round up the bill to the nearest mark or give about 5% to the waiter or waitress at the same time as paying the bill. You don't leave it on or under the plate as is customary in the U.S.

If you do indulge in a taxi, round the fare up to the nearest full mark as a tip. More is not expected, except of course for special favours or if you have particularly cumbersome or heavy luggage.

ELECTRICITY. In nearly all areas, the voltage is 220, AC current, 50 cycles. Better check before plugging in, however. Transformers to step down too-high voltages can be bought in special shops everywhere, along with adaptors for German sockets and plugs, which differ from the American and British varieties.

BATHROOMS. Public conveniences are to be found in most towns, especially at train stations. A charge of around DM 0.30 is usually made.

CONVERSION CHARTS. One of the most confusing experiences for many motorists is their first encounter with the metric system. The following quick conversion tables may help to speed you on your way.

Motor Fuel. An Imperial gallon is approximately 4½ liters; a US gallon about 3¾ liters.

Liters	Imp. gals.	US gals.
1	0.22	0.26
5	1.10	1.32
1 0	2.20	2.64
2 0	4.40	5.28
4 0	8.80	10.56
1 00	22.01	26.42

Tire Pressure measured in kilograms per square centimeter instead of pounds per square inch; the ratio is approximately 14.2 pounds to 1 kilogram.

Lb per sq. in.	Kg per sq. cm.	Lb per sq. in.	Kg per sq. cm.
2 0	1.406	26	1.828
2 2	1.547	28	1.969
2 4	1.687	30	2.109

Kilometers into miles. This simple chart will help you to convert to both miles and kilometers. If you want to convert from miles into kilometers read from the center column to the right, if from kilometers into miles, from the center column to the left. Example: 5 miles = 8.046 kilometers, 5 kilometers = 3.106 miles.

Miles		Kilometers	Miles		Kilometers
0 .621	1	1.609	37.282	60	96.560
1 .242	2	3.218	43.496	70	112.265
1 .864	3	4.828	49.710	80	128.747
2 .485	4	6.347	55.924	90	144.840
3 .106	5	8.046	62.138	100	160.934
3 .728	6	9.656	124.276	200	321.868
4 .349	7	11.265	186.414	300	482.803
4 .971	8	12.874	248.552	400	643.737
5 .592	9	14.484	310.690	500	804.672
6 .213	10	16.093	372.828	600	965.606
12.427	20	32.186	434.967	700	1,126.540
18.641	30	48.280	497.106	800	1,287.475
24.855	40	64.373	559.243	900	1,448.409
31.069	50	80.467	621.381	1,000	1,609.344

WHERE TO STAY. Accommodations in Germany are plentiful and varied to suit all tastes and pocketbooks; moreover, they are generally of a high standard. There are luxurious hotels (though definitely *not* for the budget conscious), inns, Romantik hotels, youth hostels, plenty of self-catering options, or, if the rural life appeals, you can even stay on a farm.

HOTELS. In addition to hotels proper (which can be expensive), Germany also has many *Gasthof* or *Gasthaus,* attractive, and often small, country inns. There's usually plenty of local atmosphere and wholesome, homey cooking. *Fremdenheim* (boarding house) and pensions are next down the scale and usually offer bed-and-breakfast only. At the lowest end of the scale are rooms in private houses which can be identified by the sign *Zimmer* displayed outside. If you see the word *Frei* there are vacancies; the word *Besetzt* means there is none. If a hotel describes itself as *Garni* it means it has no restaurant, though breakfast will be provided. Sometimes these hotels provide light snacks for residents only.

As a general rule, you are more likely to get better value for money in hotels and pensions in the suburbs of larger towns and cities rather than in the center. However, the additional cost of getting into the city should be taken into consideration before deciding to go for accommodations out of town. Another point to note is that the more idyllic the location and atmospheric the *Gasthof,* the higher the price, particularly in popular tourist areas.

Many larger hotels in the upper price categories vary their prices according to the demand. If you happen to be in a particular city in the *Nebensaison* (off-season) and at a time when there are no trade fairs or special events taking place, it can often be worth inquiring at hotels such as Sheraton, Intercontinental, and Ramada, etc., to see if they are offering reduced rates. Don't be offended if you receive a short, sharp *"Nein"* to your question; if you get a *"Ja",* you could be lucky to get first-class accommodations at moderate rates.

Prices. There is no official hotel grading system in Germany and we have accordingly divided accommodations in our listings into two categories, determined solely by price. In our Moderate (M) price category, two people sharing a double room (nearly always with a bath or shower) can expect to pay DM 75–DM 150. Two people sharing a double room in our Inexpensive (I) category, without bathroom (though some rooms may have a shower en suite) can expect to pay DM 35–DM 70. Obviously, the more popular the resort, the higher the prices and the smaller choice of affordable accommodations. In some lesser-known or outlying areas it may be possible to get bed-and-breakfast for as little as DM 15 per person.

Prices always include service and taxes, continental breakfast may also be included but check first; larger breakfasts will certainly cost extra, so check before you book in.

The symbol ● in our listings means highly recommended.

Making Reservations. The earlier you book your hotel room the greater will be your choice of budget accommodations. As you'd expect, hotels in popular resorts and major cities will be full during the high season, and during trade fairs and carnival times.

Within Germany reservations can be made either through the computer reservations system operated by **ADZ** (German Hotel Reservation Service), Beethovenstr. 61, Frankfurt/Main 1 (069–740767), which also request written confirmation of the booking or by simply calling the hotel in advance. Again, you will probably be asked to confirm the booking in writing or to give a telephone number in Germany where you can be contacted.

You can also try the local accommodations service; there's a *Zimmernachweis* office in all cities, towns, and many smaller villages, usually at the tourist office. Sometimes a small charge is made for this service. These offices are generally open during business hours, though in some cities they stay open late. However, don't leave it too late in the day to look for somewhere to stay—about 4 P.M. in the high season—and don't forget that weekends can be busy.

The German Hotel and Restaurant Association publishes *The German Hotel Guide* which lists all hotels, pensions, guest houses; get a copy free from the GTNO.

RENTALS. The Germans go in for rentals in a big way. You can rent fully-furnished *Ferienwohnungen* (apartments or bungalows) in all parts of Germany. Rates are relatively inexpensive, about DM 30–DM 100 a day depending on size, and are particularly good value for families. Sometimes utilities, such as heating, electricity, water, or bed linen, are charged extra. There is also a charge for cleaning at the end of the period of lease, between DM 25–DM 40.

Accommodations range from the simplest mountain chalet to apartments or bungalows with all modern conveniences. Details are available from tourist offices, which also issue lists of vacation apartments available in their areas. Or get the brochure *Self-Catering in Germany,* published by the GNTO; lists accommodations in chalets, villas, apartments, and holiday villages, all of which may be reserved centrally through the GNTO's reservation service (ADZ).

YOUTH HOSTELS. There are over 600 youth hostels available to members of the International Youth Hostel Federation Organization. Membership cards must be produced when you check in. German hostels are efficient, comfortable, and often located in historic buildings. Although primarily for those under 20, families are welcome in many hostels, as well as those over 20 years who belong to any of the Youth Hostel organizations. The exception is Bavaria, where the age limit is 27.

You can buy a family pass for about DM 20 and an International membership card for a nominal fee from the **Deutsche Jugendherbergswerk,** Hauptverband, Bülowstr. 26, D–4930 Detmold. They also publish a list of German youth hostels at DM 6, plus postage.

You'll find ample information about these accommodations from, in the U.S.: **American Youth Hostels,** Inc., PO Box 37613, Washington, DC 20013 (202–783–6161).

In Canada from the **Canadian Hosteling Association National Office,** Tower A, 333 River Rd., 3rd Floor, Ottawa K1L 8H9 (613–748–5638).

In Britain from the **Camping and Caravan Club Ltd.,** 11 Lower Grosvenor Place, London SW1W 0EY (01–828–1012).

The Cyclists Touring Club, 69 Meadrow, Godalming, Surrey GU7 3HS (04868–2717).

The Youth Hostels Association, 14 Southampton St., London WC2E 7HY (01–836–8541), which publishes an International Youth Hostel Handbook, also listing German hostels, price £1.50.

FARM VACATIONS. Another excellent budget option, again particularly for families, is to vacation on a farm. There is a wide range of accommodations—self-catering or bed and breakfast—available in most rural areas. The German Agricultural Society (DLG) publishes a brochure listing 1,500 farms throughout the country, all of which have been quality controlled by the DLG and bear their blue seal of approval. The brochure costs about DM 5 and is available from **DLG-Reisendienst,** Rüsterstr. 13, D–6000 Frankfurt/Main. This brochure also includes a section on vacations in *Winzer Urlaub* (vineyards) covering over 60 approved vintner's estates along the Moselle, in Rhineland-Hesse, Rhineland-Palatinate, in Baden-Württemberg, and on Lake Konstanz.

In Bavaria a list of *Urlaub auf dem Bauernhof in Bayern* (vacation apartments on farms) is published by **Bayerische Bauernverband,** Max Josef Str. 9, D–8000 Munich 2.

CAMPING. This is probably the least expensive way of staying in Germany, and there are over 2,000 sites to choose from. Campsites are often located in the most beautiful and popular areas. Most will have good facilities, so you don't necessarily have to sacrifice all comforts for budget prices. Look for signs with the international camping sign—a black tent on a white background.

The GNTO can give you a free list of some of the best sites (about 40) graded from "good" to "excellent". A fuller list is available from the **German Camping Club (DCC),** Mandlstr. 28, D-8000, Munich 70. This costs about DM 18.80. The German Automobile Association (ADAC) also publishes a map of all campsites located within six miles of expressways; it's available free from the ADAC (see "Getting Around Germany—By Car").

Campsites are open to all, and the average cost for a car and trailer/tent is about DM 10–DM 15 per night. Note, however, that you are not allowed to camp outside the recognized sites without the permission of the landowner or police. You may not sleep in a trailer parked in the street though you may sleep in it when parked in a parking lot, so long as it's for no more than one night.

WHERE TO EAT. The selection of eating places in Germany is extremely varied, both in style and in price. Naturally for the budget-conscious visitor, culinary flirtations with the gastronomic high life—of which there is an endless choice—will not figure as high on a list of priorities as good-value, wholesome food. Fortunately, Germans have a marked preference for *Gut bürgerliche Küche* (home-cooking), backed up by a considerable variety of regional specialties. The ideal place for this type of fare is at one of the many *Gasthofs* (inns or beer restaurants) found throughout the country, or the *Gaststätte,* "local," around the corner. They usually serve hot meals from 11:30 A.M. to 8:30 or 9 P.M.

It's wise to select the *Tageskarte* (fixed-price menu of the day) rather than eating *à la carte*. To help you budget, the menu is posted outside every *Gasthof* or *Gaststätte* so you can decide how much you want to spend before you enter. Drinks are normally ordered by the glass; beer either by the half-liter *(ein grosses Bier);* or a quarter-liter *(ein kleines Bier)*. Wine is served in quarter-liter glasses *(ein viertel)*. If you want coffee after your meal it's better value (and often nicer) to go to a café; cheapest of all is to drink it standing up in one of the numerous coffee houses, such as *Tschibo* or *Eduscho,* where it will cost about DM 2.50. If you order water to drink with your meal, you will automatically be served a small bottle of mineral water, and this is often more expensive than beer. To keep the cost down ask for *Leitungswasser*—tap water—which should be served free.

Prices. We have graded the restaurants in our listing in two categories, both determined by price. A set meal for one person in a Moderate (M) restaurant will cost about DM 18–DM 25; the same type of meal for one in an Inexpensive (I) restaurant would cost about DM 12–DM 20, both excluding drinks.

The symbol ⬤ in our listings means highly recommended.

BUDGET EATING TIPS. Stand-up Snack Bars *(Imbiss)*. Often on wheels or in pedestrian zones, these can be found in almost every busy shopping street, at parking lots, rail stations, near markets or outdoor activities, and often just on the street corner. They serve *Würst* (sausages) grilled, roasted, or boiled, of every shape and size, and rolls filled with cheese, cold meat, or fish, usually accompanied by French fries. Prices range from DM 3 to DM 6 per portion.

Department stores *(Kaufhäuser)*. For lunch the restaurants in local department stores are especially recommended. Their meals are wholesome, appetizing, and inexpensive. **Kaufhof, Karstadt, Horton** and **Hertie** are some names to note, as well as the enormous **Ka-De-We** in Berlin, particularly famous for its food, and the new **Kaufmarkt** in Munich's suburb of Oberföhring.

Butcher's shops *(Metzgerei)*. These often have a corner serving warm snacks. The **Vincenz-Murr** chain in Munich and Bavaria have particularly good-value food. Try *Warmer Leberkäs mit Kartoffelsalat,* a typical Bavarian specialty, which is a sort of baked meat loaf served with sweet mustard and potato salad; or, in northern Germany, try *Bouletten,* small hamburgers, or *Currywurst* (sausages in piquant curry sauce).

Fast Food. A number of good fast-food chains exist all over the country. The best are **Wienerwald, McDonald's** (there's even a drive-in branch in Garmisch-Partenkirchen), **Burger King,** and **Wendy's.** Also good value are the **Nordsee** fish bars, serving hot and cold fish dishes for lunch.

Foreign Food. Another good budget bet is the vast selection of moderately-priced pizzerias, Greek, Chinese, Italian, and—largely as a result of the numbers of Yugoslav and Turkish "guest-workers" in Germany—Balkan restaurants. All are good value; the choice depends on your taste. Italian restaurants are about the most popular of all the specialty restaurants (some can also be exclusive, so stick to the simple pizzerias), and the pizza to-go is as much a part of the German's diet as *Bratwürst.*

Picnics. Buy some wine or beer and some cold cuts and rolls

(Brötchen) from a department store, supermarket, or delicatessen and turn lunchtimes into picnics. You'll not only save money, but you'll also be able to enjoy Germany's beautiful scenery. Or leave out the beer and take your picnic to a beer garden, sit down at one of the long wooden tables and order a *mass* (liter) of beer. You'll quickly strike up conversation with your neighbors.

SHOPPING. It is worthwhile keeping receipts for more expensive items and then getting them stamped by customs on leaving the country. If you send them back to the shop, your VAT will be refunded. VAT in German is called *Mehrwertsteuer* and at present is 14% of the net value.

OPENING AND CLOSING TIMES. Shops. Shops are generally open from 9 A.M. to 6 or 6:30 P.M. Monday to Friday, and closed on Saturday afternoons (larger department stores often stay open until 2 P.M.), and on Sundays. On the first Saturday of every month shops in large towns stay open all day. Longer hours may apply at larger resorts. All shops and banks close on public holidays.

Banks and Post Offices. Banks are open 8:30 A.M. to 1 P.M. and 2:30 to 4, Monday to Friday, and until 5:30 on Thursday. In Bavaria, they are open 8:45 to 12:30 and 1:45 to 3:30, Monday to Friday, and until 5:30 on Thursday.

Post offices are generally open from 8 A.M. to 6 P.M. Monday to Friday and 8 to 12 on Saturday. Post offices in stations are open until late evening on all weekdays.

Places of Interest. Museum opening times vary, but most museums are closed Mondays and open late (usually until about 9 P.M.) one evening a week. Opening times are normally listed in the monthly calendar of events issued by the tourist offices in most large towns.

National Holidays. January 1 (New Year's Day); Good Friday, Easter Sunday, and Easter Monday; May 1 (Labor Day); May 12 (Ascension); May 23 (Whit Monday); June 17 (German Unity Day); November 16 (Day of Prayer and Repentance); December 24 to 26 (Christmas).

MAIL AND TELEPHONES. *Postamt* (post offices) are identified by a yellow sign bearing a post-horn; mail-boxes are also yellow, with the same symbol. Postage stamps can be purchased from vending machines (make sure you have some small change handy) bearing the words *Postwertzeichen* or *Briefmarken* or at the appropriate counter at the post office. At the time of writing (early '88) mail costs are as follows: postcards within the EEC 60 pfennigs; other countries 70 pfennigs; U.S.A. 90 pfennigs. Letters up to 20 grams, within the EEC 80 pfennigs (except Britain—DM 1.00); other countries DM 1.20. Air mail letters are DM 1.40 to the U.S.A. and Canada for 5 grams.

Telephones. Local calls from pay stations (yellow booths) cost 30 pfennigs. Cheap rates on long-distance calls within the Federal Republic operate between 6 P.M. and 8 A.M. and at weekends. There are no cheap rates for calls to the U.S., the unit price remaining DM 4.66 per minute. Calls to the U.K. cost DM 1.15 per minute from 8 A.M. to 6 P.M. and 86 pfennigs thereafter and at weekends. Foreign calls can be made from call-boxes bearing the sign *Inlands und Auslandsges- präche.* But as you will probably need such a large amount of small change, it is more convenient to inquire at a post office. Phone calls from hotels are considerably more expensive (often as much as four times the normal price) and not in the budget realm.

To call the operator, dial 1188 for local directory information and 00118 for international directory inquiries.

◆

MUNICH

Though Berliners will deny it vehemently, if there really is a spiritual capital of Germany, it's Munich, München to the Germans, capital of the free state of Bavaria (Bayern) and the third largest city in the Federal Republic. Dating from around 1100, beer capital of the world—Munich University even has a Beer Faculty—and cultural epicenter of Germany, it is an intellectual, entertaining, and earthy meeting place which attracts the young much as does the West Coast or the French Riviera. The city has about it an air of permissiveness that contrasts sharply with the puritanical uprightness of the Prussians in the north. The people of Munich are good- natured and easy-going, possessing an almost infinite capacity for fun and laughter. This bonhomie reaches its peak during Fasching, the carnival that runs from Epiphany on January 6 through Mardi Gras, and which encompasses almost 2,000 masked balls. Real Fasching enthusiasts end these wild nights only the next morning with a breakfast of *Weisswürst*—a traditional Munich white sausage—and a glass of beer before heading straight to work. Munich's other great festival, one that says just as much about the soul of the city, is Oktoberfest, the mammoth beer-drinking celebration held at the end of September. This is stein-swinging time with a vengeance; if you plan to visit, reserve several months in advance and expect higher room rates.

Don't think that Munich means only highlife and hangovers, though. Few German cities are as rich in art, and no other German city of comparable size has anything like the same elegance or architectural style. Much of this is the heritage of Bavaria's 19th-century rulers, in particular Ludwig I (not to be confused with "mad" Ludwig II, builder of Neuschwanstein) and his son, Prince Luitpold. Between them, they laid out spacious boulevards, put up imposing churches, and founded great museums. The Alte Pinakothek, the Ludwigstrasse, the Residenz, the Prinzregentenstrasse, the Deutsches Museum, and the Neues Rathaus were all built by this imaginative pair of city planners.

The drawback to Munich is that though good value may not be hard to find the same can't be said of low prices. So stay in a hotel or pension in the suburbs rather than in the center; the comprehensive network of trams and subways makes getting around easy, and there are some excellent-value tourist tickets for all city transportation that help keep costs low (see below). If you want to take in some of the city's immense variety of nightlife, check out one of the tours offered by the city tourist office; there are considerable reductions for groups. Best of all, buy yourself picnic-makings *(Brotzeit)* from the open-air food stalls in the Viktualienmarkt, the food market, and carry it off to a beer garden in the Englischer Garten. After buying your liter mug of beer—they sell nothing smaller—from the *Ausschank,* take a seat at one of the long wooden tables. It won't be long before you are swept into conversation with your neighbors who will be just as keen on trying out their English on you as introducing you to the Bavarian dialect. On the warm velvety nights of late summer, it can be a magical experience. This is the real Munich. And it's affordable.

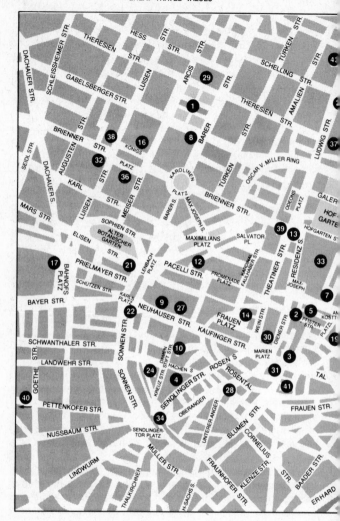

MUNICH

0 Miles   ¼
0 Kilometers ¼

ENGLISCHER
GARTEN

Points of Interest

1 Alte Pinakothek
2 Alter Hof
3 Altes Rathaus
4 Asamkirche
5 Bayerisches Hauptmünzamt
   (State Mint)
6 Bayerisches Nationalmuseum
7 Bayerisches Nationaltheater
8 Bayerisches Staatsarchiv
9 Bügersaal Kirche
10 Damenstiftskirche
11 Deutsches Museum
12 Dreifaltgkeitskirche
13 Feldherrnhalle and Preysing
   Palais
14 Frauenkirche
15 Gasteig Kulturzentrum
16 Glyptothek
17 Hauptbahnhof
18 Haus der Kunst
19 Hofbräuhaus
20 Isartor
21 Justizpalast
22 Karlstor
23 Kleine Komödie am Max II
   Denkmal
24 Kreuzkirche
25 Ludwigskirche
26 Maximilianeum
27 Michaelskirche
28 Münchner Stadtmuseum
29 Neue Pinakothek
30 Neues Rathaus
31 Peterskirche
32 Propyläen
33 Residenz
34 Sendlinger Tor
35 Siegestor
36 Staatliche Antikensammlungen
37 Staatsbibliothek
38 Stadtische Galerie
39 Theatinerkirche
40 Theresienwiese
41 Viktualienmarkt
42 Universität

PRACTICAL INFORMATION

GETTING IN FROM THE AIRPORT. Munich's Reim airport is located about 10 km. (six miles) from the city center. A bus leaves from outside the Arrivals (Ankunft) building for the train station, the Hauptbahnhof, in Munich every 20 minutes between 6:40 A.M. and 9 P.M. (Buses to the airport leave the train station every 20 minutes between 5:40 A.M. and 8:40 P.M.) You can also take the S-Bahn train from the airport; line 6 takes you to the Hauptbahnhof. Bus 37 makes the short ride from the Arrivals building to the S-Bahn station at Reim.

Taxis take about 20 minutes from Reim to central Munich; fare is around DM 22.

Facts and Figures

USEFUL ADDRESSES. Tourist Offices. The main tourist office is at Rindermarkt. 5 (tel. 089–239171), near Marienplatz. Note that the building is not easy to find, and that the third-floor office is only open during working hours. The office can help with room reservations; if you arrive out of hours, call for the recorded message detailing hotel vacancies.

There are also tourist offices at Reim airport (open Mon. to Sat. 9 A.M.–10 P.M., Sun. 11–7); in the town hall on Marienplatz; and at the Bayerstr. exit of the Hauptbahnhof.

For information on regions outside Munich, contact the Fremdenverkehrsverband München-Oberbayern (Upper Bavarian Regional Tourist Office). Sonnenstr. 10 (tel. 089–597347).

The tourist office produces an official listing of upcoming events every month, the *Monatsprogram*. It's available at most hotels and newsstands, and all tourist offices. Cost is DM 1.30.

Consulates. American Consulate General, Königinstr. 5–7 (tel. 089–23011). Canadian Consulate, Maximiliansplatz. 9 (tel. 089–558531). British Consulate General, Amalienstr. 62 (tel. 089–394015).

Lost and Found. Municipal office: Ruppertstr. 19 (tel. 089–2311), open Mon. to Fri. 8:30–12 and 2–5:30. At main train station: Bahnhofsplatz 2 (tel. 089–128 6664), opposite track 26. At the post office: Arnulfstr. 195 (tel. 089–126 2552).

Emergencies. Police: call 110. Ambulance: call 222666.

Pharmacies: International Ludwigs Apotheke, Neuhauser Str. 8 (tel. 089–260 3021).

Main Post Office. Bahnhofsplatz 1 (tel. 089–5388 2732). Open 24 hours. There are also post offices in the train station itself and at Reim airport. Both will change money.

Getting Around

Munich has an immensely efficient and well-integrated network of subway trains (U-Bahn), suburban trains (S-Bahn), buses, and trams (streetcars). The heart of the system is Marienplatz. Pick up a free copy of *Rendezvous mit München* at any tourist office for a clear explanation in English of how the system works and how to get the most from it.

Fares are uniform for the entire network, and, so long as you are traveling in the same direction, you can transfer from one system to another on the same ticket. A basic one-way ticket *(Einzelfahrkarte)* for a ride in the inner zone costs DM 2.30 (or DM 1.86 for a ride of just a few stops). You'll save money by buying a *Mehrfahrtenkarten*, or strip ticket. A strip of seven red tickets, valid for rides in the inner zone and for both zones for children under 15, costs DM 5. A strip of eight or 12 blue tickets, valid for rides in the outer zone, cost DM 6.50 and DM 12 respectively.

Note that you must cancel your ticket in one of the blue machines at station entrances and on all buses and trams *before* starting your journey; spot checks, which carry an automatic DM 40 fine if you're caught, are common.

Best value of all is the **24-Stunden-Ticket,** the 24-hour tourist ticket. This gives unlimited travel on all public transportation in any 24-hour period. Costs are DM 6.50 (children under 15 DM 2) for an inner-zone card and DM 12 (children under 15 DM 4) for the entire network.

You can buy all these tickets from the blue dispensers at U-and S-Bahn stations and at some bus and tram stops, from bus and tram drivers as you board, all tourist offices, and booths displaying a white "K" on a green background and the word *Mehrfahrtenkarten*.

Holders of a Eurail Pass, a Youth Pass, Inter-Rail Card, or a DB Tourist Card can travel free on all S-Bahn trains.

BY TAXI. Munich's cream-colored taxis are numerous. Hail them in the street or call 086–21611 (there's an extra charge for the drive to the pick-up point). Charges are high, however. Rates start at DM 3 and rise by around DM 1.50 per kilometer. There are additional charges for luggage and waiting.

ON FOOT. The whole of downtown Munich is compact and easily explored on foot. Almost all the major sights in the city center stand on

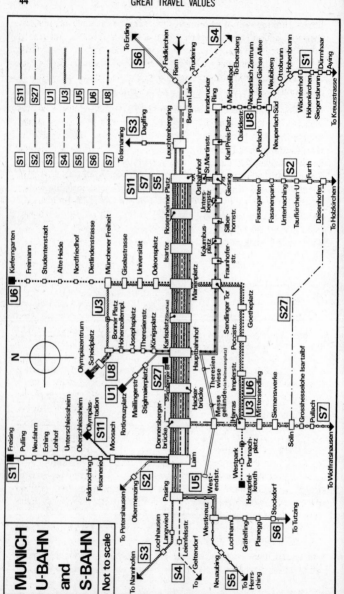

MUNICH U-BAHN and S-BAHN

Not to scale

the interlinking web of pedestrian streets that runs from Karlsplatz by the train station to Marienplatz and the Viktualienmarkt and extend north around the Frauenkirche and up to Odeonsplatz. The tourist office issues a free map with suggested walking tours. Sights and attractions away from the city center are too scattered to reach easily on foot. Make use of the excellent U- and S-Bahn.

BY BIKE. Munich and environs can be delightfully explored on two wheels. The city is threaded with a network of specially designated bicycle tracks. A free map showing all bike trails and suggested biking tours is available at branches of the Bayerische Vereinsbank. You can rent bikes at any S-Bahn station; costs are DM 5 per day if you take the S-Bahn to the station where you rent your bike; otherwise DM 10. You can also rent bikes in the Englisher Garten at the corner of Königinstr. and Veterinärstr. Costs are DM 5 for one hour, DM 6 for two hours, and DM15 for a whole day. Call 089–397016 at weekends; during bookings are available for groups only. Call 089–529943. Otherwise, try Lothar Borucki, Hans-Sachs-Str. 7 (near Sendlinger Tor Platz) tel. 089–266506.

Where to Stay

Make reservations well in advance, and be prepared for higher-than-average rates. Though Munich has a vast number of hotels in all price ranges, most are fully-booked year-round; this is a major convention city as well as a prime tourist destination. If you plan to visit during the "fashion weeks" (Mode Wochen) in March and September or during the Oktoberfest at the end of September, make your reservations at least two months in advance. The tourist office at Rindermarkt 5 has a reservations service, though note that they will not accept telephone reservations. There's also a reservations office at the airport. Best bet for finding a room if you haven't reserved in advance is the tourist office at Bayerstr. by the train station. They charge a small fee, but are supremely well organised.

The closer the city center you stay, the higher the price. Consider staying in a suburban hotel and taking the U- or S-Bahn into town. Rates are much more affordable, and a 15-minute train ride is no obstacle to serious sightseeing. There are three youth hostels, all in the suburbs. Advance reservations are essential.

Check out the city tourist office "Key to Munich" packages. These include reduced-rate hotel reservations, sightseeing tours, theater visits, and low-cost travel on the U- and S-Bahn. Write the tourist office at Rindermarkt 5.

In our listings, the symbol ⊖ means we highly recommend this selection.

Moderate

Am Markt, Heiliggeiststr. 6 (tel. 089–225014). 30 rooms, none with bath. Head here for a terrific central location and a relaxed, almost gracious, town-house atmosphere. The hotel is a favorite with singers and musicians performing at the State Opera. Rooms are on the small side. Make reservations well in advance.

Ariston, Unsöldstr. 10 (tel. 089–222691). 59 rooms, all with bath. The building and decor have a functional austerity, but the location at the southern end of the Englischer Garten by the Bayerisches Nationalmuseum is excellent. It's a 20-minute walk from center city.

Arnulf, Arnulfstr. 12 (tel. 089–598641). 136 rooms, all with bath. A city-center location and functional atmosphere make this a reasonable spot for overnighting. It's located a couple of minutes' walk from the train station. No restaurant.

Biederstein, Keferstr. 18 (tel. 089–395071). 28 rooms, all with bath, and 3 apartments. Small, almost rustic, hotel in Schwabing close to the Englischer Garten. The service is efficient and friendly. No restaurant.

⊖ **Bräupfanne,** Oberföhringerstr. 107 (tel. 089–951095). 25 rooms, with bath. The rough concrete exterior of the Bräufpanne belies the considerable comforts within. Rooms are sparsely furnished but well designed, with writing desks and sofas. The restaurant offers excellent local specialties at affordable prices. It's located a 25-minute tram ride from center city in the northeast suburbs.

Consul, Viktoriastr. 10 (tel. 089–334035). 27 rooms, all with bath. The Schwabing location and professional staff make this an excellent choice. Rooms are plain but with appealing touches, and service is excellent. Bar, but no restaurant.

Uhland, Uhlandstr. 1 (tel. 089–539277). 25 rooms, most with bath. This is one of the few town-house hotels in Munich; it's located a five-minute walk south of the train station near the Theresien Wiese, the site of the Oktoberfest. Rooms are comfortable and well furnished. No restaurant.

Inexpensive

Ariane, Pettenkoferstr. 44 (tel. 089–535529). 12 rooms, most with bath. Make reservations well in advance for this small pension. It's located a five-minute walk due south of the train station.

Augsburg, Schillerstr. 18 (tel. 089–597673). 30 rooms, some with bath. Gasthof atmosphere and central location south of the train station make the Augsburg an evergreen among Munich pensions.

Kriemhild, Guntherstr. 16 (tel. 089–170077). 18 rooms, some with bath. Small and efficiently run pension in the peaceful area around Nymphenburg, a 30-minute tram ride from the city center. No restaurant.

●**Monopteros,** Oettingenstr. 35 (tel. 089–292348). For charm and excellent service, you'll be hard put to find a better deal than the little Monopteros. It's located just south of the Englischer Garten, with a tram stop for the 10-minute ride to the city center right by the door. No restaurant.

Youth Hostels

You'll need an international Youth Hostel card to stay in any of Munich's three youth hostels. Note that the age limit for staying in a youth hostel is 27. Contact Jugend Informationszentrum, Paul-Heyse-Str. 22 (tel. 089–531655) for further details.

DJH Jugendherberge, Wendl-Dietrich-Str. 20 (tel. 089–131156). Nearest tram stop is Rotkreuzplatz.

DJH Jugendgästehaus Thalkirchen, Miesingstr. 4 (tel. 089–723 6550). Nearest tram stop is Boschetriederstr.

DJH Jugendherberge Burg Schwaneck, Burgweg 4–6 (tel. 089–793 2381). This is Munich's 5-star youth hostel. It's in a 19th-century castle in Pullach, 12 km. (eight miles) south of the city.

Camping

For full details on Munich campsites, write Deutsche Campingclub, Mandlstr. 28, 8000 Munich 40 (tel. 089–334021). All sites can take trailers.

Campingplatz am Lanwieder See, tel. 089–814 1566. North of the city; take Langwieder See exit from the Stuttgart autobahn. Open Apr. through mid-Oct.

Camping Nordwest in Ludwigsfeld, tel. 089–150 6936. North of city center off Dachaustr. Open May through mid-Oct.

Camping Thalkirchen, tel. 089–723 1707. In Isar Valley nature park near Hellabrunn Zoo on the Isar Canal. Open Mar. through Oct.

Internationaler Wald-Campingplatz Obermenzing, tel. 089–811 2235. Near the start of the Stuttgart autobahn. Open year-round.

Where to Eat

Munich boasts as wide and as fine a range of places to eat as any city in Germany. Great for a splurge, perhaps, but what about low-cost eating? In fact, the picture is pretty good. For hearty and wholesome fare, with the accent firmly on good value, try one of the numerous beer restaurants. The food naturally takes second place to the drinking, but this is about the best and most atmospheric way to fill up at minimal cost. Alternatively, investigate the restaurants in department stores: All offer solid value. Another low-cost option, especially at lunch, is the snack bars (Imbiss-Buden) at the Viktualienmarkt; eat at one of the round stands there. The Vinzenz-Murr chain of butchers' shops also have good-value food to take out or to eat on the spot, as do the Nordsee fish shops. Munich's large Turkish and Yugoslavian population have given rise to a number of excellent-value restaurants, especially in Schwabing. Check out Türkenstr., Amalienstr., Barerstr., and Adalbertstr. There's no shortage of fast-food outlets around town—all the familiar names are here—and they at least offer good value if not much in the way of local color.

Every visitor to Munich should try *Weisswürst,* a delicate white sausage traditionally eaten only between midnight and noon. Wash it down with a large glass of cold beer.

In our listings, the ☻ symbol means we highly recommend this selection.

Moderate

Augustiner Grossgaststätte, Neuhauserstr. 16 (tel. 089–26041). A traditional rendezvous for late-nighters, especially during Fasching. Zither music, lots of beer, even more sausages, and enormous helpings make sure you know you're in Bavaria. It's open from 8 A.M. to 3 A.M.

Feldherrnkeller, under the Feldherrnkeller, entrance from Residenzstr. and Theatinerstr. (tel. 089–229 537). Somewhat up-market rustic-style haunt offering traditional fare in the heart of the city. Cozy wood paneling and good-value wines guarantee an authentically German experience.

Gasthof Seerose, Feilitzstr. 32 (tel. 089–331116). Longtime Schwabing favorite where Bavarian specialties are offered at strikingly low prices. Try *Schweinebraten mit Knödel,* roast pork with dumplings.

Mykonos, Georgenstr. 105 (tel. 089–271 6742). This is about the pick of Schwabing's Greek restaurants. The food is reliable, if not outstanding, and the decor convincingly Mediterranean.

●**Nürnberger Bratwurstglöckl am Dom,** Frauenplatz 9 (tel. 089–294469). Make reservations as far in advance as you can: This is about the most authentic old-time Bavarian sausage restaurant in Munich, and always crowded. Wobbly chairs, pitch-black wooden paneling, tin plates, and lace curtains set the mood. Unless you're in a group, expect to share a table. The menu is limited, with *Nürnberger stadtwurst mit kraut* taking pride of place. The beer, never in short supply, is served straight from wooden barrels. The restaurant is right by the Frauenkirche—the entrance is set back from the street and hard to spot—and makes an ideal lunchtime halt.

Ratskeller, Marienplatz (tel. 089–220313). Dine beneath the painted vaults of Munich's late 19th-century town hall. The menu offers a wide range of Bavarian specialties as well as some international dishes. Reservations are recommended.

Inexpensive

Berni's Nudelbrett, Petersplatz (tel. 089–264469). Pasta and pizza at low prices; choose from one of the fixed-price menus for best value. It's located near the Rindermarkt, in the center of the city.

Handskugel, Hotterstr. 18 (tel. 089–264272). Head here for wholesome and good-value home cooking in the oldest restaurant in the city. It dates from 1640.

●**Max-Emanuel-Brauerei,** Adalbertstr. 33 (tel. 089–271 5158). Music, floor-shows, beer, and immense quantities of hearty German food make this a standout among the city's eating places. It's also one of the oldest genuine Bavarian taverns in Munich.

●**Mövenpick,** im Künstlerhaus, Lenbachplatz 8 (tel. 089–557865). Five restaurants in one, ranging from expensive to low budget; make sure you pick the right one (menus are displayed outside). There are few better-value places in town, and quality is always tops. Choose from a wide range of salads and hot dishes, partly Bavarian, partly international. The mood is discreetly modern. It's located just northwest of the historic center, a five-minute walk from the train station.

Wienerwald. This is Germany's premier fast-food outlet, offering excellent all-round value if not much atmosphere. The three most centrally located are at: Ungererstr. 56; Fraunhoferstr. 39; and Odeonsplatz 6.

Beer Restaurants

Donisl, Weinstr. 1. Donisl is located just off Marienplatz, and in summer tables spill out onto the sidewalks. But the real action is inside. The large central hall, with painted and carved booths ranged round the sides and garlands of dried flowers, is animated night and day with locals and visitors alike. The atmosphere, like the food, is rough and ready. The beer flows freely.

●**Franziskaner and Fuchsenstuben,** Peruastr. 5. Vaulted archways, cavernous rooms, long wooden tables, and a sort of spick-and-span medieval atmosphere—the look without the dirt—set the mood. This is the place for an early-morning *Weisswürst* and a beer; the Bavarians swear it will banish all trace of that morning-after feeling. It's right by the State Opera.

Haxnbauer, Münzstr. 2. This is about the most sophisticated of the beer restaurants. There is the usual series of interlinking rooms—some small, some large—and the usual sturdy/pretty Bavarian decoration. But there is much greater emphasis on the food here than elsewhere. Try *Leberkäs,* meat loaf made from pork and beef, or *Schweinshaxe,* pork shank.

Spartenhaus, Residenzstr. 12. More Bavarian atmosphere, food, and beer. You can eat in one of the little booths or take your chance at one of the long wooden tables in the central hall.

Beer Halls and Gardens

Am Chinesischen Turm, Englischer Garten. This is about the most famous of the city's beer gardens. Certainly it's the most popular. It's not unusual to find up to 6,000 people squeezed along the wooden tables under spreading chestnut trees. Food is available, but it's cheaper to bring your own picnic. The garden is located by the Chinese pagoda in the Englischer Garten.

Hofbräubaus, Platz. If the Chinesischer Turm is the most famous beer garden, the Hofbräuhaus is unquestionably the most famous of the beer halls. It's a series of massive stone-vaulted, interlinking rooms, each filled with crowds of singing, shouting, and swaying beer drinkers. Picking their way past the tables are hefty waitresses in traditional garb bearing frothing steins. Some people love it. Others deplore the rampant commercialism and the fact that the whole place is now so obviously aimed at the tourist trade. See it for yourself and make up your own mind. It's just north of Marienplatz.

Salvatorkeller, Hochstr. 77. The time to visit is March, when the strong Salvator beer is on tap. The attractive garden comes into its own in the summer.

Zum Aumeister, Sondermeierstr. This is the other great Englischer Garten beer-drinking haunt. It can be delightful in the summer, though there are times when the lines can seem endless.

Wine Taverns

⊖ Pfälzer Weinprobierstube, Residenzstr. 1. A warren of stone-vaulted rooms of various sizes, wooden tables, candles, dirndl-clad waitresses, and a vast range of wines add up to an atmosphere as close to timeless, tourist Germany as you're ever likely to get.

St. Georg's Stuben, Prinzregentenplatz. 13. Late-nighters and wine lovers will appreciate the splendors of this ancient farmhouse. The food is excellent—this is really somewhere for serious eating than for casual wine sipping—and the mood intimate.

Weinhaus Neuner, Herzogspitalsstr. 8. Again, this is a place for eating rather than drinking *per se*. The atmosphere is darkly discreet, and the food hearty.

⊖ Weinstadl, Burgstr. 5. The oldest and most picturesque house in Munich—it was built in the 15th century—provides the setting for a memorable meal. If you only have one night in town, spend it here.

Cafes

Eduscho and **Tschibo** are two chains offering good-value coffee and pastries. Their stand-up coffee shops are cheaper than those with waitress service. There are branches on Rosental, right by the Viktualienmarkt, and in Leopoldstr., where you'll also find one cafe and ice-cream shop after another.

Alte Börse, Maffeistr. 3. You'll find this cosy coffee house in the passage between Maffeistr. and Schäfflerstr. in the city center. There's an attractive covered courtyard. Breakfast is served from 7 A.M.

Café Extrablatt, Leopoldstr. If you have a yen to mingle with Munich high society, make for this vaguely Manhatten-style cafe in the throbbing heart of Schwabing. There's a wide range of food—including breakfasts, which you can order up at midnight—and an even wider range of drinks. Stick to beer to keep costs within range.

Café Glockenspiel, Marienplatz 28. The entrance to this third-floor cafe is not easy to find, but make the effort: There's no better place to see the glockenspiel in the Rathaus opposite or to watch the endless comings and goings of the crowds in Marienplatz.

Café Luitpold, Briennerstr. 11. This pre-war haunt is probably the best known and most elegant of Munich's cafes. Prices for the glorious cakes and pastries can be high.

Café Reitschule, Königinstr. 34. The draw here is the riding school next door; the cafe overlooks the arena. Sip a coffee and watch the horses. It's in Schwabing, by the Englischer Garten, and is popular with students and other young people.

Note that nearly all museums and other places of interest are closed on Mondays; the Deutsches Museum is a rare exception. All museums, except Nymphenburg, the Residenz Museum, and the Deutsches Museum are free on Sundays. If you have a student card, most museums have free entry, while others give reductions.

What to See and Do

MAJOR ATTRACTIONS. Alte Pinakothek, *Barerstr. 27. Open year-round Tues. to Sun. 9–4:30 (Tues. and Thurs. also open 7 P.M.–9 P.M.). Buy a money-saving double ticket good for both the Alte and Neue Pinakotheks.* This is one of Europe's great picture galleries; if you're interested in northern European painting of the 15th to the 19th centuries, it will be one of the highlights of your visit to Munich. The collection was begun by Duke Wilhelm IV in the 16th century and added to by succeeding generations of Wittelsbachs, rulers of Bavaria. Standouts include luminous and delicate works by Jan van Eyck, a series of tortured figures by Cranach, some sturdy Dürers, and a number of massive history paintings by Rubens.

Asamkirche (Church of St. John Nepomuk, or Church of the Asam Brothers), *Sendlingerstr.* Some think the little Asamkirche no more than a preposterously over-decorated jewelbox; others consider it one of Europe's finest late-Baroque buildings. One thing is certain: If you have any interest in church architecture, this is a place you shouldn't miss. It was built around 1730 by the Asam brothers—Cosmos Damian and Egid Quiran—next door to their home, the **Asamhaus.** They dedicated it to St. John Nepomuk, a 14th-century Bohemian monk who was drowned in the Danube. Pause before you go in to see the charming statue of him; angels are carrying him to heaven from the rocky river bank. Inside, there is a riot of decoration: frescoes, statuary, rich rosy marbles, billowing clouds of stucco, and gilding everywhere. The different decorative elements merge into each other to create a seamless sense of movement and color. Note the hidden light source over the altar, a typically theatrical Baroque device and one which, in this case, shows how cleverly the Asam brothers exploited the limitations of the cramped site to their advantage.

Bayerisches Nationalmuseum, *Prinzregentenstr. 3 Open year-round, Tues. to Fri. 9:30–4:30.* This is about the finest and most spectacular applied-arts museum in Germany, a rich store of sculpture, stained glass, jewelry, furniture, arms and armor, and ecclesiastical objects from the Middle Ages through the 19th century. As at the Alte Pinakothek, the nucleus of the collection came from the Wittelsbachs. It was Maximilian II who donated them to the State, and who, in

1855, began the immense and striking Renaissance "castle"—in itself a compelling reason to visit—in which they are housed.

Deutsches Museum, *Museuminsel 1. Open year-round, daily 9–5. Guided tours Sun. at 11.* The massive Deutsches Museum, located on an island in the river Isar, has long been touted as one of the most impressive and stimulating science museums in the world, only apt, really, given Germany's justly-famed technological achievements. It's very much a "hands-on" sort of place, with numerous working models and easy-to-follow demonstrations. Nonetheless, what was new in the '50s and '60s, when the museum was lavishly overhauled (it was actually built before World War I), seems rather dated in the age of the micro-processor. Still, even if the museum is showing its age a little it's still a great place for a half-day visit, especially if you have children in tow. There's a good-value restaurant for a lunchtime break.

Englischer Garten. The Englischer Garten, or English Garden (it takes its name from the man who laid it out back in 1790, Sir Benjamin Thompson), is the largest city park in Europe. It makes a great place to wander around, or maybe to have a picnic. There are a number of beer gardens for those in need of liquid refreshment—the most famous is the Chinescher Turm; see "Beer Gardens" above— plus a lake where you can rent row boats, and a network of bicycle paths. Don't be disconcerted to find nude sunbathers; the Germans are partial to taking their clothes off in public.

Frauenkirche (Cathedral of Our Lady). This lofty, red-brick medieval structure is Munich's cathedral, its twin onion-dome towers very much a symbol of the city. The most striking aspect of the church today is the obvious evidence of war-time damage. The exterior is pitted with shrapnel scars, while the interior, which had to be completely rebuilt after the war, is plain to the point of austerity. A series of photographs by the main entrance show the building as it was just after the war, a gaunt roofless skeleton filled with rubble. The effect of the church today is curiously moving. Though terribly scarred, the building has a strange, stiff dignity. Rebuilding it represented an enormous labor of love for the people of Munich, and their earnest efforts somehow permeate the echoing interior. Look for the splendid Baroque tomb of **Ludwig II** by the west door, put up in 1622. In the crypt you'll find an assortment of other Wittelsbach tombs. Beneath the organ loft is the so-called **"Devil's Footprint,"** a shallow indentation in one of the paving stones. Legend has it that it was made by Lucifer as he stamped his foot in fury after a pact he made with the original architect, Jörg Ganghofer, misfired.

Marienplatz. This is the heart of Munich, a substantial pedestrians-only square surrounded by shops, restaurants, and cafes, and permanently bustling with crowds and tourists. Dominating the north side of the square is the **Neues Rathaus,** Prince Ludwig's late 19th-century stage set of a town hall. It's built in a variety of medieval styles with, as with all Wittelsbach buildings, expense no object. The central tower contains a superb **musical clock.** Every day in summer, at 11 and 5, two tiers of figures—knights on horseback and folk dancers—revolve to the tunes of this giant musical box 90 meters (280 ft.) above the square. Take the elevator to the summit of the **tower** for the stunning view over the city to the Alps (weather permitting) and of the Frauenkirche, otherwise obscured by the cluster of buildings surrounding it. A brief but telling inscription on the facade of the Rathaus states simply that the building was "Built in 1867–1874, Enlarged 1888–1908, Destroyed 1944–1945, Rebuilt 1952–1956."

In the center of Marienplatz is a marble column, the **Mariensaüule,** topped by a statue of the Madonna—hence the name of the square. It was put up by the elector of Bavaria in 1638 to commemorate the sparing of the city by the occupying Swedish army in the Thirty Years' War.

Across from the town hall is the Gothic **Peterskirche,** another landmark of the old city and dating originally from the 11th century. Its tower, over 90 meters (280 ft.) high and offering terrific views, is fondly called **Der Alte Peter,** Old Peter. Climb the tower if a white disc is posted on the north side of the platform; it means the view is clear all the way to the Alps. A red disc means visibility is limited to Munich.

Michaelskirche, *Neuhauserstr. 52.* This is one of the most magnificent Renaissance churches in Germany, a spacious and handsome structure decorated throughout in plain white stucco. It was built for the Jesuits in the late 16th century, and the floor plan is closely modeled on the Jesuit church of the Gesú in Rome. Their intention was to provide a large preaching space, hence the somewhat barn-like atmosphere. Among much else of interest it contains the tomb of Napoleon's stepson, Eugene de Beauharnais; he lies in a suitably austere neo-Classical monument in the north transept. Ludwig II, doomed Dream King of Bavaria, is buried in the crypt.

Neue Pinakothek, *corner of Barerstr. and Theresienstr. Open year-round, Tues. to Sun. 9–4:30 (Tues. and Thurs. also open 7 P.M.–9 P.M.) Buy a money-saving double ticket good for both the Alte and Neue Pinakotheks.* The Neue Pinakothek—it means New Gallery—was founded shortly after the completion of the Alte

Pinakothek (see above), in 1846 to be exact, its purpose being to house modern—that is, 19th-century—works, carrying on where the Alte Pinakothek stops. Though the collection contains a small number of 18th-century English paintings, it is accordingly rich in Impressionists and works of the Munich school. However, the original 19th-century building that housed the collection was so severely damaged in the war that it eventually had to be demolished and a new and lavish building constructed.

Residenz, *Max-Joseph-Platz 3. Open year-round, Tues. to Sat. 10–4:30, Sun. 10–1; closed Mon. Guided tours twice daily (except Mon.): shorter tour from 10; longer tour from 12:30.* The great complex that is the Residenz has been the home of the dukes, princes, and kings of the Wittelsbachs for over 650 years. It has been rebuilt, enlarged, and restored for almost the whole of its life. It sustained severe bomb damage during the war, though has since been splendidly reconstructed. It is divided into four sections: the **Alte Residenz,** which includes the **Cuvilliés Theater,** the one-time court theater and a glittering specimen of Rococo architecture; the **Königsbau,** which houses the **Schatzkammer,** or treasury, containing, among its many treasures, a small Renaissance statue of St. George studded with 2,291 diamonds, 209 pearls, and 406 rubies; the **Residenz-museum** itself, a series of heroic interiors brimming with paintings and tapestries; and the **Festsaalbau,** which includes the **Hercules Saal** concert hall and, behind the palace, the **Hofgarten,** a trim, formal garden framed by arches and filled with flowers.

Schloss Nymphenburg. *Located about eight km. (five miles) northwest of the city center. Open year-round, Tues. to Sun. 9–12:30 and 1:30–5; closed Mon.* This is the most famous and most beautiful of the palaces surrounding Munich. It was built as a summer residence by the Wittelsbachs. The oldest parts of the building date from 1664, but construction continued over the next 100 years, the bulk of the work being undertaken in the reign of Max-Emmanueal between 1680 and 1730. The gardens, a mixture of formal French "parterres" (trim, ankle-high hedges and gravel walks) and English parkland, were landscaped over a similar period. The interiors are exceptional, especially the **Banqueting Hall,** a Rococo masterpiece in green and gold. Make a point of seeing the **Schönheits Galerie,** the Gallery of Beauties. It contains upwards of 100 portraits of women who had caught the eye of Ludwig I; duchesses rub shoulders with butchers' daughters. Among them is Lola Montez. This is kitsch of a very high order. About the greatest delight is the **Amalienburg,** or Hunting Lodge, in the grounds. It was built by Cuvilliés, architect of the

Residenztheater in Munich. That the hunting the lodge and it's design were not necessarily always outdoor pursuits can easily be guessed at by the sumptuous silver and blue stucco and the atmosphere of courtly high life. The palace also contains the **Marstallmuseum** (the Museum of Royal Carriages), containing a sleigh that belonged to Ludwig II among the opulently decorated vehicles, and, on the floor above, the **Nymphenburger Porzellan,** where examples of the gorgeous porcelain produced here between 1747 and the 1920s, when the factory closed, can be seen.

Theatinerkirche, *Odeonsplatz*. The Theatinerkirche, or Church of the Theatines (a monastic order), dominates Odeonsplatz, site of Hitler's doomed putsch, or uprising, of 1923. The church is about the best Italian-style building in Bavaria. It was built in the mid-17th century, though the handsome facade, with its twin eye-catching towers, was added in the following century. Despite its Italian influences, the interior, rather like that of the Michealskirche, is austerely white, though there's some good stucco work.

Theresienwiese. This large open space, originally a horse-racing track, located just southwest of the city center, is the site of the annual **Oktoberfest,** the great beer-drinking festival held every September. It's overlooked by a monumental statue of **Bavaria,** a sort of mini Statue of Liberty, about 35 meters (100 feet) high. Like her cousin in New York, the bronze statue has a hollow head which you can climb up to, if you can manage the 130 steps. But don't go in the afternoon: The interior becomes positively furnace-like as the day heats up.

Viktualienmarkt. This is the city food market. Stock up here on picnic-makings before heading to one of the beer gardens for an inexpensive meal. The market itself is filled with stalls selling fresh and inviting produce. It's a great meeting place for the locals, who come here to grumble and gossip about prices and politics. The market women are as strong-armed and direct as ever, and their regular customers much the same: self-confident, straightforward, distrustful, good-humored, sly, and always ready to lend a hand. The famous Munich comedian, **Karl Valentin,** has a statue and memorial here. A bouquet of flowers is thrust into his hand every day, an anonymous tribute of love.

OTHER ATTRACTIONS. Altes Rathaus (Old Town Hall), *Burgstr. Open year-round, Mon. to Fri. 10–5. Sometimes closed if official functions are being held.* Jörg Ganghofer, who also built the Frauenkirche, was the architect of this splendid medieval building. It was all but destroyed in the war, but, though the interior was lost for all time—the ballroom was considered one of the most beautiful Gothic halls in Germany—the exterior was carefully rebuilt.

Bayerisches Staatsbibliothek (Bavarian State Library), *Ludwigstr. 23. Opening times under review; check with the tourist office.* The library houses over three million volumes, among them around 16,000 medieval texts and illuminated manuscripts (the bible of Otto III, its ivory binding inset with gems, is a standout).

Deutsches Jagd and Fischerei Museum (German Hunting and Fishing Museum), *Neuhauserstr. 53. Open year-round, daily 9:30–5 (Tues. and Sun. closes at 4).* Anyone with a taste for hunting knives, deer heads mounted on wooden shields, and shotguns will feel at home.

Heiliggeistkirche (Church of the Holy Ghost), *Tal. 77.* Behind the Baroque facade of this little church lurks a 13th-century interior. It contains some excellent stucco work by the Asam brothers, and a ceiling fresco by Cosmos Damian Asam.

Isator. This is one of the original city gates. It's located at the lower end of Tal, just where it joins Zweibrücken Strasse. The exterior of the gate has a stirring 19th-century fresco illustrating the triumphal return to Munich of Ludwig of Bavaria after the battle of Ampfing in 1322. Inside, you'll find a small and curious museum dedicated to comedian **Karl Valentin,** and a coffee bar on the top floor.

KZ-Gedenkstätte Dachau mit Museum. *Located 18 km. (11 miles) north of the city and reached by S-Bahn or on a tour (see below). Open year-round, Tues. to Sun. 9–5; closed Mon.* 206,000 prisoners were systematically exterminated in this concentration camp by the Nazis. Those who wish to understand fully the horrors of the Hitler regime should visit. It is, to put it mildly, a sobering experience.

Ludwigskirche, *Ludwigstr. 22.* The largest church fresco in the world—it was painted between 1836 and 1840 by Peter Cornelius—and some rather improbable Byzantine touches make this unusual church worth visiting if only to see what can happen when a lot of money and rather less taste collide.

Münchner Stadtmuseum (City Historical Museum), *St-Jakobs-Platz 1. Open year-round, Tues. to Sun. 9–4:30; closed Mon.* Huge collections document Munich through the ages. There are sections on brewing, puppets, movies, and musical instruments, and an excellent wooden model showing the city in around 1570.

Tierpark Hellabrunn. South of the city center in Isar valley and reached by bus from Marienplatz. Open year-round daily 8–6. This is the only zoo in the world that arranges the animals according to their geographical origins. 4,000 animals are kept here in 170 beautifully landscaped acres.

Tours

A variety of bus tours are operated by Munich Sightseeing Tours, Arnulfstr. 8 (tel. 089–120 4248). Tours leave from the bus station at the corner of Prielmayerstr., opposite the Hauptbahnhof. The one-hour tour leaves daily at 10, 11:30, and 2:30; cost is DM 13. The two-hour tour leaves daily (except Mon.) at 10 and 2:30; cost is DM 23.

Shopping

Practically the whole of downtown Munich is one big pedestrian mall: **Karlsplatz, Neuhauserstr., Weinstr., Theatinerstr., Sendlingerstr., Dienerstr.,** and **Residenzstr.** are all lined with shops large and small. If prices in some are high, this is at least unsurpassed window-shopping territory. But there are always bargains during the sales *(Schlussverkauf)* in January *(Winterschlussverkauf)* and July *(Sommerschlussverkauf)*. Keep an eye open any time of year for *Sonderangebote* (special offers) and *reizierte Ware* (reduced goods). For consistently low prices and a wide selection, try the **Olympia-Einkaufszentrum** at Olympia Park (take the U-Bahn from Marienplatz); it's the largest purpose-built shopping mall in the city. You can nearly always find bargains and good value in the department stores *(Kaufhäuser);* the best are **Kaufhof, Karstadt, Beck,** and **Hertie.**

For typical souvenirs, especially dirndls and lederhosen, try **Loden Fry,** Maffeistr. 7–9, or **Dirndlkönigin,** Residenzstr. 19. Prices at both can be high, however, anything from DM 150 to DM 1,200. A wide variety of Bavarian handicrafts are available at **Wallach,** Residenzstr. 3 and Wurzerstr. 11. You may find better value at the **Viktualienmarkt,** especially for little bunches of dried flowers and bouquets of dried herbs. For beer steins and pewter mugs, try **Ludwig Mory** at the Rathaus in Marienplatz; for hand-painted glass mugs, try **Franz Mayer'sche Hofkunstanstalt,** Seidelstr. 20. Candles, wood carvings, and wax figures are available from **Pfarrhaus St. Peter** in the Rindermarkt.

The city has a number of flea markets, of which the best is the **Auer Dult,** held three times a year (end April, end July, and end October) on Mariahilfplatz in front of the church of the same name. Other regular markets are held in the courtyard of **Reitmoorstr.** 15 in Lehel every Saturday and at **Dachauerstr.** 128, near Olympia Park, every

Saturday and Sunday. There are also occasional flea markets at **Münchener Freiheit** in Leopoldstr. and at the **Theresienwiese.**

There are some good buys, especially for fashion, at **Etienne Aigner Secondhand Shop,** Türkenstr. in Schwabing, and at **Trödelkeller,** Agnesstr. 6. For secondhand Bavarian folk costumes, try **Traudl,** Marktstr. 15.

Entertainment and Nightlife

For many, there's no better way to spend an evening in Munich than in one of the traditional beer halls or wine taverns. This is the way to combine value for money with the authentic atmosphere of the Bavarian capital. See above for listings. But this is not to say that there's any shortage of culture in Munich; far from it. Equally, however, many of Munich's premier cultural attractions are both expensive and hard to get into; tickets are not usually easy to find. This is especially true of the state opera, though productions are often superb and opera-lovers may find the temptation irresistable. Theater tickets are not much easier to get, added to which only those with fluent German are likely to find a performance of interest. Performances of classical music are a different matter, and, though standards may not always scale the same heights as in Vienna, say, or in Berlin, concert-goers will find a rich selection from which to choose, though again tickets may be hard to obtain. Try Bavarian Official Travel Agency, Theater und Konzerthaus, Karlsplatz-Stachus (tel. 089–590 4419). Details of all performances are published in *Monatsprogram,* available monthly from tourist offices and newsstands at DM 1.30.

For superb **church music,** try Sunday mass at the Frauenkirche (9:30), Michaelskirche (9:00), or the Theatinerkirche (10:30). Many concerts of the **Musikhochscule** (Music Academy), Arcisstr. 12, are free of charge. For the price of no more than a beer you can enjoy live performances of **classical music** at Mariandl, Goethestr. 51. There are concerts of **Christmas music** during the December Christkindl Markt in Marienplatz at 5 P.M. every day.

Our listings here contain only the largest and/or most famous venues.

THEATERS. Bayerische Staatsoper im National Theater (Bavarian State Opera), Max-Joseph-Platz (tel. 089–221316). Box office open Mon. to Fri. 10–1:30 and 3:30–5:30, Sat. 10–12:30; also opens one hour before performances.
 Bayerische Staatsschauspiel/Neues Residenztheater (Bavari-

an State Theater/New Residence Theater), Max-Joseph-Platz (tel. 089–593427). Box office open Mon. to Fri. 10–1:30 and 3:30–5:30, Sat. 10–12:30; also opens one hour before performances.

Deutsches Theater, Schwanthalerstr. 13 (tel. 089–593427). Box office open Mon. to Fri. 12–6, Sat. 10–6.

CONCERTS. Gasteig Kulturzentrum, Rosenheimer Str. and Am Gasteig (tel. 089–41810). Built 1985, and the most prestigious concert hall in the city. Make reservations well in advance.

Herkules Saal der Residenz, Residenzstr. 1 (tel. 089–224641). Box office opens one hour before performances.

Kongress Saal Deutsches Museum, on island in Isar by the Deutsches Museum (tel. 089–298430). Box office open Mon. to Fri. 1:30–6:30, Sat. 11–2.

NIGHTLIFE. Steer clear of Goethestr., Schwanthalerstr., Schillerstr., and Josephsspitalstr. There's no shortage of low-life clubs among them, with high prices and tawdry shows. Tours of night-time Munich lasting around five hours and taking in three night spots and including dinner leave daily at 7:30. Contact Munich by Night, a division of Munich Sightseeing Tours, Arnulfstr. 8 (tel. 089–590 4248). Cost is around DM 120 per person.

◆

S P L U R G E S

Dinner at the Preysing-Keller, Innere-Wiener-Str. 6 (tel. 089–481015). Head here for a meal you won't forget in a hurry. Among the fancy restaurants of Munich, many charging astronomic prices for minute portions of nouvelle-inspired Bavarian cusine, the Preysing-Keller—it's in the basement of the hotel of the same name—is a breath of fresh air. That's not to say there's any lack of sublety about the food or that the service is in any way slapdash. But it *is* to say that the restaurant believes that haute cuisine and good value are compatible, and that good service doesn't have to mean obsequious deference. This is not the sort of place where you feel you can't raise your voice above a self-conscious whisper. The wine list, like the food, is terrific. Expect to pay from DM 180 for two people.

Raft Rides on the Isar. This is guaranteed to be a riotous day out, though make sure the weather's good before setting out. The large wooden rafts leave from Wolfratshausen and float down to Thalkirchen, near the Hellabrunn zoo, shooting the rapids on the way.

That it's not exactly the same as a trip down the Grand Canyon is made clear by the fact that there's a Dixieland jazz band on board and that liberal quantities of beer are available. Make reservations in advance from Bavarian Official Travel Agency, Theater and Konzerthaus, Karlsplatz-Stachus (tel. 089–590 4419). Cost is around DM 50.

◆

ALONG THE ALPS

The German Alps extend a full 240 kilometers (150 miles) from Lake Constance (Bodensee) in the west to Berchtesgaden in the east. They comprise in all nine different regions: The Allgäu (Westallgäu, Oberallgäu, and Ostallgäu); the Ammergau Alps; Werdenfelser Land; Isarwinkel; and Isar and Inn Valleys; the Chiemgau Alps; and Berchtesgadener Land. It is an area that corresponds more nearly than any other in Germany's largest state to most people's idea of Bavaria. Its multitude of little villages nestling among the rolling Alpine foothills, a welcoming *gasthof* on every street corner, zither music and brass bands abounding, and low-roofed houses bedecked with flowers exert a potent and irresistable appeal.

Between these picturesque small towns and villages are a number of sophisticated winter and summer vacation resorts, such as Garmisch-Partenkirchen, Bad Wiessee, Bad Reichenhall, and Berchtesgaden. And there are also such stalwart tourist favorites as Ludwig II's breathtaking castles and palaces, and a clutch of exquisite Roccoco churches.

No one could really be said to have visited Germany without having spent at least a day or two in the Alps. But, whatever is said in its favor, there's no getting away from the fact that this is not an area that offers terrific value. The major resorts, especially the winter resorts, *are* expensive, while even those places off the beaten tourist track are still not exactly low cost—even the Allgäu, where prices are generally 10 to 15% lower than elsewhere. But there's a lot you can do to keep costs within reasonable bounds. The one golden rule is that the farther from the Alps proper you are, the lower prices will be. Second, most of the resorts here have two peak seasons: summer, mid-June through early September; and winter, Christmas through late March. Visit away from these times and prices drop significantly. October can be a particularly good month; the weather is still usually reliable—it can even be hot—and the hillsides are ablaze with the fall foliage. Third, take advantage of the many excellent great-value deals available on accommodations. Staying in a farmhouse, for example, is both inexpensive, *and* an excellent way to get the real feel of the country. Tourist offices have full lists of properties, where you can always be sure of good value, plus high standards of comfort and, this being Germany, cleanliness. Fourth, explore the savings you can make by using local transport. Getting around in the Alps can sometimes be slow—on most trips you will have to return to your starting point before heading on to your next port of call—but there's a fully integrated network of buses and trains. Buses, especially, are inexpensive, and run like clockwork. Timetables and ticket prices are available from tourist offices, train stations, and post offices. This is also a terrific area for bicycling, something that's not as grueling as it sounds, so long as you stick to the Alpine lowlands, that is. You can hire bikes from almost every train station, and tourist offices issue cycling maps of their respective areas.

This symbol ☙ represents our highly recommended selection.

Ammersee

The Ammersee is one of the most important of the five lakes which comprise Fünf-Seen-Land (literally, Five Lakes Land) southwest of Munich. (The others are Pilsensee, Starnbergersee, Wesslingersee, and Wörthsee.) It's one of the most popular excursions from Munich, and offers excellent swimming, sailing, walking, and eating opportunities. This is also ideal bicycling country, a fact recognized by the local tourist office in Landsberg am Lech who recommend no less than 11 different bike routes around the lake and into the neighboring valley of the river Lech. They all start from a train station and take in at least one bathing beach and a *gasthof* en route.

For a combination of sparkling Alpine waters, rolling wooded hills, and typical villages and towns, all within easy reach of Munich, Ammersee is hard to beat.

GETTING THERE. Ammersee is easily reached by car from the Munich—Lindau A8. expressway. It's also accessible from Munich on the S-Bahn. In summer there are regular boat services around the lake with departures timed to coincide with S-Bahn arrivals.

TOURIST OFFICE. Fremdenverkehrsverband Ammersee-Lech, Von Kuhlmann Str. 15, 8910 Landsberg am Lech (tel. 08191–47177).

WHERE TO STAY. *Strandhotel Griesshuber* (M), Jahnstr. 10, Diessen (tel. 08807–5038). Located on own beach overlooking the lake, with waterside terrace and café, and good-value restaurant.

WHERE TO EAT. ● *Klosteregasthof Andechs* (M), am Heiligen Berg, Erling-Andechs (tel. 08152–3760). Closed Tues. Beer hall open daily. Fine traditional *gasthof* offering delicious spit-roasted pork (*Schweinshax'n*), grilled chicken, and various cold snacks, the whole accompanied by a full range of local beers.

ATTRACTIONS. Kloster Andechs. This lovely Benedictine priory sits perched on the Heiligen Berg (Holy Mountain), overlooking the southeast corner of the lake at Erling-Andechs. Founded toward the end of the 14th century, the monastery rapidly became a place of pilgrimage, and the church itself has been rebuilt several times. Its greatest glory is the superb Roccoco decoration, the work of 18th-century architect and monk Johan Baptist Zimmermann. Visit the **Schatzkammer,** the abbey treasury, which contains numerous precious and bejeweled religious objects. Opening times are erratic; if the complex is closed, inquire at the caretaker's house.

The monastery has its own brewery, and the shaded **beer garden** by the church is a great place to sample its wares.

Klosterkirche Diessen. This is one of the finest Baroque churches in Germany. It's in the attractive summer resort and market town of Diessen, at the southern end of the Ammersee. The church was part of the original Augustine monastery and was completed in 1739 by Johann Michael Fischer. You should also pay a visit to Diessen's **craftsmen's quarter** in Herrenstrasse. You probably won't find many bargains, but its a charming place to browse around.

Bad Reichenhall

Bad Reichenhall, a few miles north of Berchtesgaden at the eastern tip of the German Alps, is home to the most powerful saline springs in Europe. The fashionable 18th-century enthusiasm for health cures drew a wealthy clientele to the town, who established a smart and correspondingly expensive spa and resort. If you fancy a spot of old-fashioned Alpine glamor, or a flutter in the casino, this is the place to be. Likewise, most hotels specialize in expensive health treatments. Best bet for keeping costs low is to stay in one of the outlying suburbs—try Marzoll, Karlstein, Nonn, or Thumsee. Or get the tourist office list of farmhouses offering affordable and atmospheric rooms.

GETTING THERE. Bad Reichenhall can be reached from either the Munich–Salzburg highway or the scenic Deutsche Alpenstrasse. From Munich both rail and bus services stop at the town en route to Berchtesgaden.

TOURIST OFFICE. Verkehrsamt, am Bannhof, 8230 Bad Reichenhall (tel. 08651–1467).

WHERE TO STAY. Bergfried (M), Adolf-Schmidstr. 8 (tel. 08651–4398). Good town-center location. Most rooms have own facilities. Breakfast only, but cold evening meals can be provided for residents.

Berghotel Predigtstuhl (M) (tel. 08651–2227). Located at the top of the cablecar run, the hotel rejoices in panoramic views, absolute peace and quiet, and a good restaurant. Transportation via the cablecar is included in the room rate.

● Schlossberghof (M), Schlossberg 5 (tel. 08651–3002). Four km. (three miles) east of the town center, in the suburb of Marzoll, the 100-bed Schlossberghof harbors a good restaurant, cosy bar, and comfortable rooms with own facilities. Other bonuses include a beer garden, sunbathing, and pony riding.

WHERE TO EAT. Kammererbräu (M), Poststr. 23 (tel. 08651–2444). Local specialties prepared with the finest local produce and meat from the family-owned butcher.

ATTRACTIONS. Alte Saline (Old Salt Works), Alte Saline 9. Open Apr. through Oct., daily 10–11:30 and 2–4. Lavish medieval-style edifice built by Ludwig I in 1834 on 16th-century origins. You'll be able to see examples of early machinery, visit subterranean passageways, and ogle the massive 19th-century pumping station.

Munsterkirche St. Zeno. Founded by Augustine monks in the

12th century, the huge Romanesque basilica of St. Zeno was partially destroyed by fire and rebuilt in late-Gothic style during the 16th and 17th centuries.

Predigtstuhl. Winter and summer a cablecar runs up to the viewing point on Predigtstuhl offering a spectatular view of the rocky giants of Berchtesgaden Land.

Bad Tölz

The dandies of the 18th century were not, of course, the first to appreciate a good spa when they saw one. Many European spas have revealed traces of Roman occupation, and Bad Tölz, on the river Isar south of Munich, is one. Today, the popular iodine-rich spa is famed for its long traditions and active conservation of local crafts and folklore, particularly the lovely hand-carved and painted peasant furniture known as **Bauernmöbel.** The Marktstrasse at the center of town is also a reminder of those ancient skills, with its fine patrician houses behind splendid painted facades. For outdoor types the surrounding woodlands offer a maze of hiking trails, or there's summer tobogganing on Blomberg mountain!

GETTING THERE. Take the Penzberg exit off the Munich–Garmisch highway or journey direct by bus or rail from Munich.

TOURIST OFFICE. Kurverwaltung, Ludwigstr. 11, 8170 Bad Tölz (tel. 08041-70071).

WHERE TO STAY. Alexandra (M), Kyreinstr. 13 (tel. 08041-9112). On the left bank of the river Isar, a short distance from the town center. Well-equipped rooms (many with balcony); facilities include sauna, solarium, sunbathing, and a restaurant (for residents only).

Kolberbräu (M), Marktstr. 29 (tel. 08041-9158). Family-run hotel dating back to 1600, with a variety of period styles in the rooms (most with bath or shower). Located in Old Town with good-value restaurant and children's playground.

Gästehaus Bergblick (I), Benedikt-Erhard-Str. 6 (tel. 08041-3622). Quiet hotel with 16 rooms (half with own facilities); no restaurant.

Gasthof am Wald (I), Austr. 39 (tel. 08041-2788). Good-value pension on right bank of Isar. 35 rooms with own bath; indoor pool and sauna. Medium-priced restaurant with garden.

WHERE TO EAT. Altes Fahrhaus (M), an der Isarlust 1 (tel. 08041-2873). Situated in a former ferryboat station on the banks of the Isar, this restaurant serves typical Upper Bavarian specialties with flair.

Schwaighofer (M), Marktstr. 17 (tel. 08041–2762). Closed Wed. and Whitsun. Located in center of Old Town.

ATTRACTION. Heimatmuseum (Local Museum), *Old Rathaus, Marktplatz*. Open year-round, daily 8 A.M.–9 P.M., Fri. and Sat. until 10 P.M. Underlining the town's long-standing interest in preserving rural crafts, the museum (founded in 1866) contains many fascinating exhibits, from furniture and historic firearms to period costume.

Bayrischzell

This tiny village at the foot of the Schliersee Mountains, southeast of Munich, owes its origins to an 11th-century monastic settlement. The town has a long association with Bavarian folklore traditions today; the Bayrischzell *Trachtenbewegung* (folklore movement) has branches in countries the world over, including the US. The picturesque village offers cure pools, idyllic scenery, and a chairlift to Sudelfeld Peak. Twelve km. (eight miles) down the Deutsche Alpenstrasse, you'll find Tatzelwurm. This dramatic, rugged gorge thunders with the sound of waterfalls, and was once, so rumour would have it, inhabited by a fire-eating dragon!

GETTING THERE. Drivers can take the Deutsche Alpenstrasse, or the Miesbach exit off the Munich–Salzburg highway and continue on B307 via Schliersee. Trains run direct from Munich, and buses via Tegernsee.

TOURIST OFFICE. Kuramt, Kirchplatz 7, 8163 Bayrischzell (tel. 08023–648).

WHERE TO STAY. Alpenrose (M), Schlierseestr. 6 (tel. 08023–620). All rooms have bath or shower. Popular restaurant serving Bavarian specialties, as well as international menu. Garden-terrace.

Berghotel Sudelfeld (I), Unteres Sudelfeld (tel. 08023–607). 71 rooms right up by the ski slopes; accessible by car or bus along the mountain road out of the village.

Gästehaus Effland (I), Tannermühlstr. 139 (tel. 08023–263). Comfortable hotel with 14 rooms (all with bath or shower). No restaurant, but generous breakfasts and evening snacks for residents.

Berchtesgaden

At the heart of Berchtesgadener Land, surrounded by rugged mountains and exquisite mountain lakes, lies the ancient market town of Berchtesgaden. Climatic health spa and winter sports center, Berchtesgaden is also an excellent base from which to explore the riches of the eastern alps. The main sight in the town is the Royal

Castle: Originally an Augustine abbey, it was requisitioned by the Wittelsbachs, rulers of Bavaria, in 1810. The other major attraction is the Salzbergwerk (Salt Mines), source of the town's prosperity since the 16th century.

The town and surroundings offer all kinds of activities from concerts and theater to tennis, golf, and horse-back riding. There are plenty of opportunities for mountaineering, hiking, and skiing, and many out-of-town excursions. The most popular are to Königsee (King's Lake) in the Berchtesgaden National Park, a nature and wildlife reserve; and to Kehlstein, once the site of the Eagle's Nest, Hitler's Alpine retreat.

GETTING THERE. Take the Bad Reichenhall exit off the Munich–Salzburg highway. The town is also accessible by train direct from Hamburg/Dortmund as well as Munich/Salzburg. Buses run from Munich, and there is an excellent local network throughout the region. Check out the RVO pass system if you plan on staying a while.

TOURIST OFFICE. Kurdirektion, Königseer Str. 2, 8240 Berchtesgaden (tel. 08652–5011).

WHERE TO STAY. Hotels tend to be expensive in the center of town, but there are plenty of *gasthof* and farmhouse accommodations in the surrounding area. Full lists from the tourist office.

●**Gasthof Theresienklause** (M), Gerner Str. 18 (tel. 08652–3445). Friendly, family-run establishment in Maria Gern on the outskirts of town. Quiet, comfortable rooms with shower; garden terrace; restaurant, and cafe. Vegetarian meals on request.

Pension Gröll (M), Alte Königseer Str. 51 (tel. 08652–4161). Quiet family boarding house on the outskirts of town. All rooms have bath or shower, and balcony or terrace. Breakfast room.

Café Waldluft (I), Bergwerkstr. 37 (tel. 08652–2328). 10-minutes' walk from center, on the edge of the forest. 55 beds (most with shower); restaurant and quiet, sunny terrace cafe.

●**Haus Schneiderlehen** (I), Hinterschönauerweg 19 (tel. 08652–3256). Beautifully situated farmhouse-pension at the foot of Watzmann peak. Eight rooms; traditional Berchtesgaden breakfast made with produce from the farm.

WHERE TO EAT. Le Gourmet (M), Demming Hotel, Sunkerleg 2 (tel. 08652–5021). Hotel restaurant offering substantial and wholesome local specialties; try one of the fixed-price menus to keep costs low.

MAJOR ATTRACTIONS. Kehlstein *Open mid-May to mid-Oct. Bus* *information, call 08652–5473*. Hitler's notorious mountain retreat lies some three miles out of town via Obersalzburg. During 1937–39 a private road was built to give access to the Eagle's Nest, and there's a special bus service to the lift which carries you the last few meters. Now the building is an Alpine inn and restaurant; the view is breathtaking.

Königliches Schloss (Royal Palace), *Schlosspslatz. Open Easter through Sept., Sun. to Fri. 10–1 and 2–5; Closed Sat.* The 13th-century cloisters and Gothic dormitory of the Augustine monks date from the earliest period of the castle, though building and expansion continued through to this century. The **museum,** founded by Prince Rupert of Bavaria, who died here in 1955, contains many treasures; of particular interest are the fine 15th- and 16th-century German wood carvings.

Salzburgwerk (Salt Mines). *Open May through mid-Oct., daily 8–5.* This will rate as one of the most surprising and exciting visits of your trip. Fitted out in protective clothing you slide down a 500-meter (1,640 ft.) chute into a labyrinth of subterranean galleries shimmering with mountain crystal. The guided tour includes a boat trip on an underground lake and a film presentation.

OTHER ATTRACTIONS. Almbachklamm. A ten-minute ride from the center of town brings you to this striking gorge and rapids which, improbably, power Germany's only existing glass-marble factory. Daily tours.

Deutsches Wappenmuseum (Germany Museum of Heraldry), *Haus Fröhliche Wiederkehr, Jennerbahnstr. 30. (tel. 08652–61910).* If geneology is your hobby, don't miss this fascinating museum, which contains around 4,000 examples of family crests. It is also possible to research family trees and apply for your own coat-of-arms. Visits by appointment only.

Enzianbrennerei, *Salzburger Str. 105, Unterau. Open year-round, Mon. to Fri. 8–12 and 1–5.* Visit Germany's oldest Gentian schnaps distillery; after your tour you'll be offered free samples.

EXCURSIONS. Jennerbahn, *Königsee. Open Summer 8–5:30, winter 9-4:30.* The cablecar climbs 1,874 meters (6,150 ft.) above Königsee to the panoramic terrace and restaurant at the peak of Jenner mountain. There are hiking and mountaineering trails in summer; skiing in winter.

Königsee. Enclosed like a jewel in the heart of the Berchtesgaden Nature Park, Königsee is one of the biggest attractions in the region. From the village of Schönau, you can walk along the banks of the

Königseer Ache river to picturesque Malerwinkel; or take a boat trip across the lake to the pretty 18th-century chapel of St. Bartholoma. In summer boats depart every 10–20 mins. between 7:15 and 6:30.

Rossfeld–Höhenringstrasse. This 16 km. (10 mile) scenic road climbs 1,600 meters (5,250 ft.) between Rossfeld and Obersalzburg, and affords a memorable view of the countryside. There is a toll for private cars, so you may prefer to take a bus from the town. There's plenty of opportunity for hikers to stretch their legs along the marked trails from Hennenköüfl.

Füssen

The story of Füssen stretches back over 1,000 years. Once the site of a fortress guarding the pass through the Alps, the town now marks the southern end of the famous Romantischestrasse, the Romantic Road. Füssen is also a popular spa town, surrounded by majestic mountains and cooled by the rushing waters of the river Lech. The medieval center offers an abundance of architectural treasures, and the busy cultural life of the city is well worth investigating. If you enjoy playing around on the water there are six lakes to choose from, and a variety of water sports. Füssen is also on the King Ludwig Hiking Trail, which links the fabulous and fantastic royal palaces of Ludwig II and his father, including Hohenschwangau and Neuschwanstein. For most people, the visit to Neuschwanstein is the highlight of their trip to Germany. Make sure you don't miss it.

There's so much to see and do that you'll probably want to stay a few days; the good news is that Füssen offers a wide variety of accommodations at prices often 10 to 20% lower than elsewhere in the Alps.

GETTING THERE. Take the Ulm–Kempten highway, and then B309/310. Trains run from Munich on the Kaufbeuren line, with carriages from Hamburg/Dortmund. Buses leave from Munich and Frankfurt. You can also take the EB 190A service, which runs the length of the Romantischestrasse.

TOURIST OFFICE. Kurverwaltung Füssen, Augsburger Torplatz 1, 9858 Füssen (tel. 08362–7077).

WHERE TO STAY. Alpenblick (M), Uferstr. 10, Hopfen am See (tel. 08362–7018). Comfortable, lakeside hotel. 60 beds with bath/shower, rustic-style; terrace-cafe, attractive bar, and first-class restaurant.

⊖**Geiger** (M), Uferstr. 18, Hopfen am See (tel. 08362–7074). Traditional, family-run hotel in good position overlooking the lake. Most rooms have own facilities; breakfast buffet and restaurant.

Kurhotel Filser (M), Saulingstr. 3 (tel. 08362–2068). Quiet, central, and good-value hotel with full cure facilities, own garden, and views across to Neuschwanstein. 45 beds with shower/bath; good restaurant.

Sonne (M), Reichenstr. 37 (tel. 08362–6061). Pleasant 64-bed hotel near center. All rooms have bath. Beer garden and Café Sonnenstube which serves snacks; no restaurant.

WHERE TO EAT. ◒ **Zum Schwanen** (M), Brotmarkt. 4 (tel. 08362–6174). Try the fixed-price menus in this sturdily old-fashioned haunt. Food is always fresh, and service is excellent.

ATTRACTIONS. Hohes Schloss, Magnusplatz. Once the medieval summer residence of the prince-bishops of Augsberg, the Hohes Schloss now houses the law courts and **Staatsgalerie** (Municipal Art Gallery). The collection focuses on Swabian-Bavarian art from the 16th century onwards, and includes late-Gothic Allgäu sculpture. The splendid Gothic-style ceiling of the **Rittersaal** (knights' hall) dates from 1500.

St. Mangkirche, *Schlossberg.* With the exception of a 10th-century tower, this fine Baroque church dates from 1707, and possesses a 1,000-year-old fresco of the patron saint, St. Magnus. You can also visit the ancient monastery buildings which shelter the **local history museum** *(Open Mon. to Sat., guided tours 10 A.M.).*

THE ROYAL PALACES. Schloss Hohenschwangau. *Open Apr. through Sept., daily 9–5:30; Oct. through Mar., daily 10–4. Two miles east of Füssen.* This was Ludwig II's childhood home, and the decisive influence on the strange young man who was to build ever more lavish fantasy palaces of his own. The castle was originally built in the 12th century, and was remodeled by Maximilian II, Ludwig's father, between 1832–36. It was here that Ludwig met Wagner, the German composer and the man who was to confirm Ludwig's obsessive interest in German mythology—the story of Lohengrin in particular—and love of the theater (a love that extended to employing a set designer rather than an architect to build his most celebrated castle, Neuschwanstein). There's a bus to Hohenschwangau from Füssen, or you can take the marked path for the 15-minute walk.

Schloss Neuschwanstein. *Open Apr. through Sept., daily 9–5:30; Oct. through Mar., daily 10–4.* Neuschwanstein rises dream-like from a pinnacle of rock above the Pöllat Gorge a mile or two south of Füssen. Building began in 1869, but despite the immense sums lavished on it Neuschwanstein was never entirely completed before, in

1886, the Bavarian government had Ludwig declared insane. He drowned, in mysterious circumstances, shortly afterwards. The building exudes a theatrical quality—it's no surprise Walt Disney used it as the model for his castle in *Sleeping Beauty*—and in fact it's hard to imagine any building less like a real castle than this wonderful stage-set of a building. This is a castle for dreaming of gallant deeds, not for performing them. Inside, walls are covered with immense frescoes depicting German mythological figures—the swan themes of Lohengrin predominate. Perhaps the two standout rooms are the extraordinary **grotto**—again a motif borrowed from Wagner; it recalls his opera *Tannhäuser*—and the **bedroom,** with a quite astounding Gothic-style bed like a huge choir-stall; pinnacles rise in majestic profusion from it. The irony is that poor Ludwig hardly slept in it before his demise. In similar vein, the sumptuous Oriental-style **throne room** doesn't even have a throne. Ludwig was dead before it could be installed.

After seeing the castle, walk along the gorge to **Marienbrücke** bridge. It provides a magnificent vantage point from which to see the building.

Garmisch-Partenkirchen

Among the world's top winter sports centers and site of the 1936 Winter Olympics, the twin towns of Garmisch and Partenkirchen lie in the valley formed by the Loisach and Partnach rivers beneath the unique backcloth of the Wendelsteingebirge range. Most famous of the startling silhouettes is the Zugspitz, at 2,964 meters (9,710 ft.) Germany's highest mountain. Take the cogwheel railway to the summit.

Garmisch-Partenkirchen makes an ideal base for excursions and sporting holidays, but it can be expensive, especially at the height of the winter season. Take advantage of the low-season rates and special offers in spring and fall; seek accommodation in the neighboring villages of Grainau, Farchant, Oberau, or Eschenlohe. Another money-saving idea is the *Kurkarte,* or visitors' card, available from your hotel or the tourist office. It entitles you to a wealth of reductions on mountain railways, local buses, and places of interest, as well as providing accident insurance for the length of your stay!

GETTING THERE. The tour is easily accessible from anywhere in Germany. Drivers will find a highway link with Munich and the Deutsche Alpenstrasse. Direct Inter-City trains from Hamburg, Düsseldorf, Bonn, Munich, and many other points; numerous long-distance buses including the EB165 route from Oostende.

TOURIST OFFICE. Vekehrsamt der Kurverwaltung, Bahnhofstr. 34, 8100 Garmisch-Partenkirchen, (tel. 08821–1800).

WHERE TO STAY. **Aschenbrenner** (M), Loisachstr. 46 (tel. 08821–58029). Attractive hotel in a house once owned by the Princes of Reuss. 25 rooms with bath or shower; terrace cafe; great views; cosy tavern serving light evening meals for residents.

Buchenhof (M), Braunhausstr. 3 (tel. 08821–52121). Traditional Bavarian hotel across the river Loisach from the town center. Large breakfasts served in Wintergarden; no restaurant.

Garmischer Hof (M), Bahnhofstr. 53 (tel. 08821–51091). Good-value hotel in the town center. Alpine-style decor; pleasant atmosphere; no restaurant, but hearty breakfast buffet.

⊖ Gästehaus Barbara (I), Am Krepbach 12, Grainau (tel. 08821–8924). 13 rooms, most with bath, and two apartments in quiet village close to town. Breakfast only, but excellent value.

Gästehaus Bernrieder (I), St. Martin Str. 39 (tel. 08821–57581). Centrally located pension belonging to luxury Kur-Hotel Bernrieder Hof. 15 rooms; no restaurant.

WHERE TO EAT. The sprawling layout of Garmisch-Partenkirchen makes it difficult for the visitor to seek out good-value eating places, and you are often restricted by the whereabouts of your hotel or *gasthof*. The majority of the better restaurants are found in the large hotels, but the **Dorint** at Mittenwalderstr. 59, offers a good-value Sunday brunch (12–2) for all the family.

Café Bauer (M), Griesstr. 1 (tel. 08821–2109). Centrally located near the Marienplatz; plenty of atmosphere, and music in the evenings.

⊖ Gasthof Fraundorfer (M), Ludwigstr. 24 (tel. 08821–2176). Typical Bavarian tavern in Partenkirchen, with loud music and *Schuhplattler* dancing. Very popular, so reservations are essential; some rooms available.

Reindl's Drei Mohren (M), Ludwigstr. 65 (tel. 08821–2075). Hearty home-cooking and local specialties grace the menu of this old-fashioned gasthof dating from 1870. Good value; also some simple rooms available.

⊖ Zum Rassen (M), Ludwigstr. 45 (tel. 08821–2089). Amazingly good value in the heart of Partenkirchen. The beautifully painted facade of this historic house contains Bavaria's oldest folk theater, and a restaurant serving excellent local food and beer.

EXCURSIONS. **Alpspitz** At 2,219 meters (7,280 ft.), this is the second largest peak after Zugspitz, and a popular skiing area. There are a variety of different cablecar rides which complete a round tour of the mountain, and special deals available to rail travelers—check with German Railways or the tourist office in Garmisch.

Hausberg. Another of the peaks around town—1,330 meters (4,362 ft.)—and famous for the challenging run which forms part of the German Alpine World Championships. Cablecar departures from 8:30–5 from the parking lot near the Ice Stadium.

Jagdschloss Schachen. This is Ludwig II's hunting lodge perched 1,850 meters (6,070 ft.) up to the Schachen peak, and accessible only on foot. It's a three-to four-hour hike along the lovely Königsweg trail, and there's an Alpine Botanical Garden with 1,500 different species of mountain plants.

Partnachklamm. This is one of the loveliest hiking trails in the area. It leads through a romantic gorge, tunnels through the rock, and leads past mountain lakes and galleries, before finally reaching Zugpitz. The trail leaves from the Ice Stadium and takes 10 hours. However, for those in search of beauty without blisters, the Graseckbahn cablecar is at hand, or take a horsedrawn carriage or sleigh for the first section of the journey. Enquire at the tourist office for further details.

Postkutsche. Stagecoach rides to Badersee lake and back. Open from July through Sept. Tickets and reservations from the Main Post Office (Hauptpostamt).

Wank. The third highest peak in the district at 1,780 meters (5,840 ft.), and assailable by cablecar from the station near the Schützenhaus (shooting range) from 8:30–5:30.

Zugspitz. Right on the German-Austrian border, the mighty Zugspitz boasts a massive skiing area between 2,000 and 2,830 meters (6,560 ft. and 9,280 ft.). To see for yourself you can either take the cogwheel railway from the Bayerische Zugspitzbahn (tel. 08821–58058), which takes about an hour; or the cablecar, which leaves from the shores of the beautiful Eibsee lake, and reaches the Schneefernerhaus hotel and restaurant on the summit in just ten minutes.

Mittenwald

Mittenwald, located about 15 km. (eight miles) southeast of Garmisch, is a favourite center for climbers and mountaineers, both summer and winter, and renowned for the precipitous slopes of the Dammkar, considered the longest and one of the most difficult Alpine ski runs in Bavaria. Less experienced winter sportsmen should stick to skiing on the Kranzberg, tobogganing, or perhaps a sleigh ride! In addition to its sporting pedigree, the town has been famous since the 17th century for the manufacture of stringed instruments, particularly violins and for its beautiful Alpine houses. For the best examples, make your way to Obermarktstrasse (south of the town center) and inspect the fabulous painted facades of Neuner Haus and Goethehaus amongst others.

Accommodations can be expensive, particularly during the winter high season, so investigate the good value self-catering and farmhouse accommodations lists at the tourist office. Another money saver is the visitor's pass, which entitles you to reductions on recreation facilities and public transport.

GETTING THERE. Drivers should leave the main highway at Garmisch-Partenkirchen and take the Karwendel Panoramic route (B2) or B11 via Kochel am See. Inter-City and express trains run via Munich on the Innsbruck line; and local buses run throughout the Werdenfelser Land district.

TOURIST OFFICE. Kurverwaltung, Dammkarstr. 3, 8102 Mitterwald (tel. 08823–1051).

WHERE TO STAY AND EAT. ◒ **Alpenrose** (M), Obermarkt 1 (tel. 08823–5055). A converted 13th-century house with a Baroque painted facade; 49 rooms, two apartments and two holiday apartments in the main building; annex five-minutes walk away. The rooms are all decorated in local style, and there's a restaurant serving game dishes, plus a cellar tavern. Check out the special winter inclusive packages.

Post (M), Obermarkt 9 (tel. 08823–1094). Another historic building, dating back to 1632, with a modern annex. 92 rooms, most with bath; sauna and solarium; restaurant and cafe.

◒ **Isarlust** (I), Albert Schott Str. 27 (tel. 08823–1274). Quiet, centrally located *gasthof* with 18 simple but spotless rooms. Full board is available.

ATTRACTIONS. Geigenbau and Heimatmuseum (Museum of Violin-Making and Regional Life), Ballenhausgasse. *Open year-round, Mon. to Fri. 10–11:45 and 2–4:45, Sat. and Sun. 10–11:45 only.* Interesting display of local crafts and history, with particular emphasis on the development of the violin-making industry started by Mathias Klotz in the 17th century.

Glenleiten. *Open Apr. through Oct., daily 9–6.* Bavaria's largest open-air museum lies on the road from Mittenwald to Kochel (there are trains and buses from Mittenwald). Overlooking the Kochelsee lake, the museum presents 20 different types of traditional Alpine buildings from the various Upper Bavarian districts. The interiors have been carefully recreated and contain period furniture, machinery, and farming implements.

Pfarrkirche St. Peter & St. Paul. Originally a Gothic structure, this delightful church was transformed into a Baroque extravaganza by the architect Josef Schmuzer. The tower and ceiling frescoes deserve special attention.

EXCURSION. Karwendelbahn.
A cablecar runs up the Karwendelspitze, 2,385 meters (7,805 ft.) to a mountain station and restaurant just short of the summit. This is the start of the Dammkar ski-run, and there's a panoramic view from the terrace.

Oberammergau

Oberammergau is internationally renowned for its famous Passion Play, an event which traces its origins back to 1634. In the midst of a dreadful epidemic the village was miraculously saved, and the inhabitants made an oath to present a Passion Play every decade. The play requires over 1,000 performers, all of whom must be natives of the village (population 5,000). It takes place throughout the summer every ten years in years ending with a zero.

The town is also a spa and year-round resort with skiing on the Laberberg in winter and along the gruelling international crosscountry King Ludwig Round Course. In summer, King Ludwig is celebrated again on *Gebirgswandertag* (Mountain Hiking Day). This takes place on August 24, and is open to all, culminating at dusk in a spectacular blaze of bonfires on the mountainside.

GETTING THERE. From the Munich–Garmisch highway, take Ohlstadt exit for Oberammergau. Fast rail services run to Murnau, from where there are connecting local buses and trains; also, regional bus services run from Garmisch.

TOURIST OFFICE. Verkehrsbüro, Eugen-Papst-Str. 9a, 8103 Oberammergau (tel. 08822–4921).

WHERE TO STAY AND EAT. Reservations are made as much as one year in advance for Passion Play years, so be warned: Next performance is in 1990.

●Alte Post (M), Dorfstr. 19 (tel. 08822–6691). Centrally located in an historic building with a magnificent facade and lots of atmosphere. 27 rooms, six apartments, and a rustic restaurant serving Bavarian specialties; also, a cafe and beer tavern.

Wittelsbach (M), Dorfstr. 21 (tel. 08822–4545). A member of the Inter-Europe group (U.S. reservation service), the hotel has 40 rooms plus two apartments with all facilities. The restaurant serves both Bavarian and international cuisine.

Ambronia (I), Ettaler Str. 5 (tel. 08822–532). Typical, good-value local *gasthof* with 42 beds, some with bath or shower. Friendly cafe-restaurant with hearty home-cooking, and large beer garden.

Reiser (I), In der Breitenau 6 (tel. 08822–4747). 29 rooms with bath/shower in quiet, central location and own garden. Breakfast and small evening menu for residents.

ATTRACTIONS. Festspielhaus an der Passionswiese. The Passion Play Theater has a covered auditorium seating 4,700, and an open-air stage served by the splendid natural backcloth of the Ammergauer mountains. Daily guided tours are arranged from the tourist office and take in the wardrobe and backstage area, as well as the permanent wood-carving exhibition in the foyer.

Heimatmuseum (Local History Museum), *Dorfstr. 8*. Opening times available at the tourist office. The Passion Play is not all there is to know about Oberammergau——the little also boasts a famous wood-carving school. You'll find many superb examples, including a delightful **Christmas Crib** exhibit.

EXCURSION. Schloss Linderhof. *Eight miles west of Oberammergau. Open Apr. through May and Sept., daily 9–12:15 and 12:45–5; June through Aug., daily 9–12:15 and 12:45–5:30; Oct. through Mar., daily 9–12:15 and 12:45–4.* It took nine years (1870–79) for architect Georg Dollman to complete Linderhof, one of Ludwig II's more fanciful creations. The magnificent rooms include the **King's Bedroom,** with intricate painted ceiling and a Venetian chandelier lit by 108 candles. The **dining room** contains the famous "Tischleindecktisch" disappearing table, which descends through the floor to the kitchens below. Outside, the French Baroque-style **gardens** dance with fountains and conceal numerous grottoes.

Oberstdorf

The most popular spa resort and winter sports center in the Allgäu, Oberstdorf is also Bavaria's most southerly mountain village. The mountains are the main attraction, and there are cablecar rides up the three major peaks: Nebelhorn, Fellhorn, and Söllereck. Other diversions include golf, riding, and water sports on Freiberg Lake in summer; and all forms of winter sport. Oberstdorf is also a good starting point for excursions into the Kleinwalsertal valley, and there are miles of well-tended hiking trails to seven traffic-free valleys and beyond.

Hotel prices tend to reflect the popularity of the resort, but there are many summer spa packages and winter ski deals available. Also, look to the outlying areas to Kornau, Tiefenbach, Rübi, Reichenbach, and Schellang for good-value *gasthof* and farmhouse accommodations——lists kept at the tourist office.

GETTING THERE. Drivers should take the Kempten exit off the Stuttgart–Munich highway; rail travelers will find trains run from all over the country to Immenstadt, from where there is a connecting bus service. Oberstdorf is also on the Deutsches Alpenpost bus route.

TOURIST OFFICE. Verkehrsamt, am Marktplatz 7, 8980 Obersdorf (tel. 08322–7000). Room reservation service at train station.

WHERE TO STAY. Bergruh (M), Im Ebnat 2, Titefenbach (tel. 08322–4011). Friendly, rustic-style hotel in a sunny and quiet location near the woods. 13 comfortable rooms, plus sauna and solarium, and good restaurant with varied menu.

Hofatsblick (M), at the upper station of the Nebelhornbahn (tel. 08322–3086). A unique location high above the town, reached by cablecar, the hotel is ideal for winter sports or hiking. 99 beds with bath; a good restaurant and panoramic sun terrace.

Kappelerhaus (M), Am Seeler 2 (tel. 08322–1007). Quiet, but centrally located with a fine view and outdoor pool. 43 rooms with bath/shower; pleasant, modern interiors and friendly service. No restaurant, but evening snacks for residents on request, and club room bar.

●**Weller** (M), Fellhornstr. 22 (tel. 08322–3008). Quiet *gasthof* with a superb view of the mountains and hiking trails or ski paths on the doorstep. Well-furnished rooms with bath/shower and balconies; also, holiday apartments decorated in rustic-style. Breakfast only; indoor pool and sauna; good value.

WHERE TO EAT. Bacchus Stuben (M), Freibergstr. 4 (tel. 08322–4787). Good-value restaurant and wine bar (good local wines) with a pretty garden terrace.

Sieben Schwaben Restaurant (M), Pfarrstr. 9 (tel. 08322–3870). Pleasant restaurant with both international and regional cuisine, good value house wines, and a series of good-value fixed-price menus.

ATTRACTIONS. Breitachklamm. Open summer, daily 8–4; winter, daily 8–3 (according to weather conditions). Local bus services run from Oberstdorf, or you can make your way on foot (approx. one hour south of town). There are guided tours available through the dramatic one-mile long gorge, where the river Breitach flows through a massive

limestone rockface. Over thousands of years the fast flowing river has
carved a series of breathtaking rock formations and cascading waterfalls, over 100 meters (300 ft.) deep in parts. The trip can also be made
in winter, when ice festoons the galleries in glittering, magical
stalactites.

Heimatmuseum (Local History Museum), *Oststrasse 13. Open
summer, Tues. and Thurs. 2–5 (hours extended in bad weather).*
Housed in a 17th-century building, the museum contains a wide-
ranging collection of exhibits depicting the everyday life and culture of
the region. You can trace the history and development of skiing,
watchmaking, and even distilling!

Prien

Prien is the main resort on the Chiemsee, the largest lake in Bavaria,
also known as the "Bavarian Sea." A spa town, with a wide variety of
recreational facilities, particularly water sports and lakeside beaches,
Prien is one mile from Stock, the ferry point for excursions to the
islands of Herreninsel—site of Herrenchiemsee, another of Ludwig's
fantasy palaces—and Fraueninsel. The ten-minute journey can be
made by steam train—the oldest local steam railway in existence,
dating from 1887!

GETTING THERE. Prien is reached by road from the Bernau exit off
the Munich–Salzburg highway. Inter-City trains run the length and
breadth of the country via Munich; and buses link Munich and most
other Upper-Bavarian towns.

TOURIST OFFICE. Verkehrsamt, Haus des Gastes, Rathausstr. 11,
8210 Chiemsee, (tel. 08051–3031). The tourist office has a room
reservation service, and issues visitors' cards *(kurkarte)* which give
reductions on local facilities and transport.

WHERE TO STAY AND EAT. The nearer the lake, the higher the prices.
However, there are plenty of pretty local-style inns and *gasthofs* farther
inland, and a wide choice of private accommodations in farmhouses or
apartments. The tourist office has full lists.

●**Bayerischer Hof** (M), Bernauerstr. 3 (tel. 08051–1095).
Good, reliable hotel in the town center. 44 rooms furnished in
comfortable local style, and a good-value restaurant serving generous
Bavarian cuisine.

Reinhart (M), Seestr. 17 (tel. 08051–1045). 28 rooms right on the
lakeshore, and pleasantly decorated. There is a cafe in the summer
months, and a terrace-restaurant noted for its fish dishes.

Lindenhof (I), Rathausstr. 24 (tel. 08051–1525). Typical *gasthof* in a very central position. Ten simple rooms, and restaurant serving local cuisine, plus beer garden.

Mojerhof (I), Trautersdorf 4 (tel. 08051–1557). Quiet, but centrally located farmhouse with 6 rooms in the Trautersdorf section.

ATTRACTIONS. Heimatmuseum (Local History Museum), *Friedhofweg 1. Open year-round, Tues. to Fri. 10–12 and 3–5, Sat. 10–12 only.* Many exhibits depicting the traditional peasant lifestyle of the region, plus a unique **Bauerngarten,** a typical farm garden.

Herrenchiemsee. *Open summer, daily 10–5; winter, daily 10–4. Take the ferry from Stock, one mile from Prien.* The full range of Ludwig II's strange taste is demonstrated by this massive, stately palace. Where Neuschwanstein is romantically Gothic, Herrenchiemsee is formally classical, modeled in part on Louis XIV's palace at Versailles. There's no trace of the wildness or the fantasy of Neuschwanstein here. What the two buildings have in common, however, is extravagance. If anything, Herrenchiemsee is an even more lavish piece of work, even though, as at Neuschwanstein, Ludwig's untimely death in 1886 halted work on the building before it was anything like finished. Not that there's any shortage of things to see or glorious interiors to ogle. The **Hall of Mirrors** is about the most famous; it's a faithful copy of that at Versailles. The **bedroom** is a symphony in gilt and rich silks. The **dining room** has a table that sinks into the floor so that servants below could clear the dishes away. See the **Ludwig II museum,** too; it contains a fascinating range of exhibits charting the unhappy life of the haunted Ludwig.

Starnbergersee

The Starnberger Lake, in the alpine foothills southwest of Munich, is the largest of the group of lakes collectively known as Fünf-Seen-Land (see *Ammersee* above). The main town is Starnberg, which rises from the lakeside terraces in an elegant profusion of private villas, exclusive hotels, and expensive boutiques. There are several other resorts dotted around the lake and, although much of the shoreline is privately owned, a number of public beaches with watersports facilities.

After he was deposed in June 1886, Ludwig II was briefly interned in the Berg castle (three miles south of Starnberg), before drowning in the lake. The castle is not open to the public, but today a wooden cross marks the spot where his body was brought ashore.

GETTING THERE. Main roads link Starnberg with the Munich–Garmisch highway (E6); and there are buses and an S-Bahn connection from Munich, as well as regular train services on the Munich–Kochel line. Ferries run between the various east and west bank resorts.

TOURIST OFFICE. Fremdenverkehrsverband, Kirchplatz 3, 8130 Starnberg (tel. 08151–13274). Room reservation service available.

WHERE TO STAY. Rates can be high within the town, but smaller establishments in the surrounding area offer more affordable alternatives.

➡ **Hotel-Restaurant Café am See** (M), Marienstr. 16, Tutzing (tel. 08158–490). Rooms, apartments, and vacation flats in a perfect location on the lake, not far from the town center. Private beach; terrace-café and good restaurant with fish specialties.

Gasthaus zur Sonne (I), Hanfelderstr. 7 (tel. 08151–14571). Pleasant *gasthof* five minutes' walk from the S-Bahn station. All rooms have shower or bath; a particularly good-value restaurant serving local cuisine.

Seehof (I), Schlossstr. 3, Tutzing (tel. 08158–6314). Comfortable hotel set in own large park. Simple accommodations, plus attractive outdoor restaurant and café on the lakeside.

WHERE TO EAT. Forsthaus am See (M), Am See, Possenhofen (tel. 08157–1245). In a lovely lakeside location with its own little marina, the large country-style restaurant serves fresh locally-caught fish and home-made apple strudel, as well as international cuisine.

➡ **Hotel am See** (M), by the steamer landing stage at Münsing, (tel. 08177–212). Reached by ferry from Starnberg or Tutzing, the hotel has an attractive, shaded beer garden and good-value restaurant offering Bavarian specialties and afternoon coffee. Some rooms available.

Wieskirche

Normal opening hours year-round, daily 7:30–7. Guided tours. The culminating point of the Rococo period in German ecclesiastical architecture, the Wieskirche is as much a monument to its famed architect, Dominikus Zimmermann, as a pilgrim church. Commissioned to build a church dedicated to Christ Scourged, Zimmermann chose the lush meadowlands ("wiese") at the foot of the Ammergau Alps, and set to work redesigning the basic plans of his church at Steinhausen. The result is a simple exterior concealing a rich, harmonious tapestry of carved wood, stucco, and gilt beneath a glorious frescoed ceiling. At the time of writing urgent restoration work is underway and parts of the interior are not on view, but don't be dissuaded—this is a true highlight.

GETTING THERE. Wies lies close to the Deutsche Alpenstrasse north of Füssen (see separate entry), and three miles from Steingaden. Buses run from Schongau.

◆

S P L U R G E S

Evening Cruises on Chiemsee. From June through mid-September, there are cruises every night on Bavaria's largest lake. The boat leaves from the landing stage at Prien at 7:30, returning about 10. A brass band is on board and there is a selection of food and drink. On some Tuesday evenings there are also sailings from Chieming and Seebrück. Price, excluding food and drink, is an affordable DM 12 per person. Enquire at tourist offices for full details, or write **Chiemsee Schiffahrt Ludwig Fessler,** Seestr. 108, Prien (tel. 08051–6090).

A Night at Clausing's Posthotel, Marienplatz 12, 8100 Garmisch-Partenkirchen (tel. 08821–58071). Anyone who has dreamed of spending a night in a typical Bavarian chalet-style hotel, with sloping roofs, intricate balconies, scarlet geraniums in pots, and carved headboards over the beds, will feel very much at home here. There's an excellent restaurant, too; try suckling pig with dumplings. The hotel's right in the center of Garmisch–Partenkirchen, Bavaria's leading alpine resort, and located only 88 km. (55 miles) from Munich. Rates are around DM 200 for a double room with breakfast.

◆

AROUND THE
BLACK FOREST

The Black Forest lies within the state of Baden Württemberg—it's the third largest in Germany—and covers an area which extends from Heidelberg in the north right down to Bodensee (Lake Constance) in the south. West to east, it stretches from the border with France across the Rhine Plain to Ulm in the Schwäbische, or Swabian hills. The Schwarzwald (Black Forest) proper follows the east bank of the Rhine from Karlsruhe in the north to the city of Basel in Switzerland. It is an area which evokes a fairytale vision of dark romantic forests interspersed by broad meadows, and of picturesque thatched farmhouses and jolly farmers in traditional dress wolfing down rich chocolate cake surrounded by cuckoo clocks!

The major towns of the Black Forest are Freiburg-im-Breisgau, the ancient regional capital, backed by the southern mountains of the Black Forest range, and elegant Baden-Baden in the north. Baden in fact marks the start of the scenic Schwarzwald-Hochstrasse (the Black Forest High Road), and the Badische-Weinstrasse (the Baden Wine Road), which wends its way through the wine-growing villages of the Kinzig valley. This is wonderful walking country, too, with the best trails converging on Pforzheim. Hiking maps are available at every tourist office, and there's a great idea organized by a group of Black-Forest hoteliers, the "Wandern Ohne Gëpack" system (literally, "hiking without luggage"), with prices ranging from DM 430 to DM 640 per week depending on accommodations. A comprehensive brochure, *Discovering and*

Exploring Baden Württemberg's Towns covers 24 of the most beautiful and interesting towns, and details special deals and weekend packages. It's available from *Landesfremdenverkehrsverband Baden Württemberg,* Prospektservice, Postfach 420, 7290 Freudenstadt.

There is a huge variety of accommodations throughout the region, with numerous good-value *gasthof* and farmhouse rooms for as little as DM 15–20, with hotels weighing in from around DM 25. For specific information about farmhouse vacations *(Ferien auf dem Bauernhof)* write Ferienring Schwäbische Alb, Kreuzäckerstr. 11, 7414 Lichtenstein-Holzelfingen for the Swabian hills region; or to Urlaub auf dem Bauernhof, Postfach 5443, 7800 Freiburg for the Black Forest. Campsites are numerous; get a copy of *Camping in Baden Württemberg,* issued by the State Tourist Association Baden Württemberg, Postfach 304, 7000 Stuttgart 1.

This symbol ⬤ represents our highly recommended selection.

Baden-Baden

A noted spa since Roman times, Baden-Baden has got it all—from radioactive springs to mud baths. However, the cures were largely incidental to the fashionable pleasure-seekers of the 19th century who, attracted by the pleasant summer climate, transformed the town into a luxurious Belle-Epoque rendezvous. A token glass of spring water merely whetted the appetite for champagne, and a quick dip in the hot spring banished the worst excesses of the previous day in preparation for another long evening at the gaming tables.

Their spirit lives on, and the sheltered climate of the Oos valley remains a powerful attraction today. Still, times have changed in some ways, and modern facilities abound; accommodations have diversified, spreading out from the prohibitively expensive center to include good-value *gasthofs* in the suburbs of Ebersteinburg, Haueneberstein, and Sandweier, or farmhouses in the vineyard villages of the Badener. In town you'll find walking tours around the sights, and great shopping; window-shopping only in the exclusive Kastanienalle near the casino, but there are many less expensive stores providing for the souvenir hunter. Around town there are miles of hiking trails, or take a day trip to the Kinzig valley and the Badener vineyards.

GETTING THERE. Baden-Baden is reached via the Frankfurt–Basel highway (A5), or from Stuttgart on A8. The town is also on the

Heidelberg–Basel train line, with connections from all over the country. There's a good local bus service, and German Railways buses link the other Black Forest resorts.

TOURIST OFFICE. Bäder und Kurverwaltung, Haus des Gastes, Augustaplatz 8, 7570 Baden-Baden, (tel. 07221–275200).

WHERE TO STAY. A spa tax of between DM 1 and DM 2.50 per person per night is payable on all accommodations in town; it varies according to your location. However, it entitles you to a guest card for daily concerts and to visit the pump rooms, and gives reduced admission to some special events.

Panorama (M), Balger Hauptstr. 101a, (tel. 07221–62051). Modern hotel located on the forest edge in the quiet suburb of Balg. 23 rooms with bath, plus 2 apartments. Great views; riding and tennis; indoor pool and gym. No restaurant.

Suss (M), Friesenbergstr. 2, (tel. 07221–22365). 40 comfortable rooms near the cure park. Peaceful location and pleasant restaurant with varied menu; dine on the terrace in fine weather.

Zum Lamm (M), Mauerbergstr. 34, Neuweier, (tel. 07223–57212). A little off the beaten track, in the suburb of Neuweier, but a good-value rustic inn with a friendly atmosphere. 12 rooms with bath/shower and two apartments. The restaurant offers local and international cuisine.

Am Markt (I), Marktplatz 18, (tel. 0722–22747). Centrally located hotel; 27 rooms, all with bath; pleasant terrace. No restaurant.

Rebenhof (I), Rheinebene, Neuweier, (tel. 07223–5406). Small, friendly *gasthof* set among the vineyards in the suburb of Neuweier. All rooms have bath or shower, and there's a varied menu in the terrace restaurant.

WHERE TO EAT. The major hotels all offer haute cuisine of the highest order, *and* price bracket. However, there's a plentiful supply of inns and taverns where hearty local dishes are served up in generous portions. Particularly good value is the Badener vineyard area, where the delicious light wines are a big enough draw in their own right.

Cafe-König (M), Lichtentaler Str. 12, (tel. 07221–23573). For delicious pastries, and good-value food served on an attractive terrace, head for the König.

Ristorante-Pizzeria La Carrozza (M), Merkurstr. 3, (tel. 07221–26200). Right in the center of town, off the Augustaplatz, La Carrozza offers a warm Italian atmosphere and varied menu.

Zum Nest (M), Rettigsstr. 1, (tel. 23076). Popular restaurant renowned for local specialties; try the freshly-caught trout, and wash it down with Badener wines.

Zur Traube (M), Mauerbergsstr. 107, (tel. 07223–57216). Homey restaurant in the suburb of Neuweier. Good-value hearty meals, including a variety of steaks.

ATTRACTIONS. Altes Schloss (Old Castle), *Altes Schlossweg 10. Open year-round, Tues. to Sun. 10–8; closed Mon.* Also known as Hohenbaden Castle, the Altes Schloss was built by the Margraves of Baden between the 11th and 15th centuries, and largely destroyed by fire in the 16th century. From the ruins there is a fine view over the town. Just beyond Hohenbaden is **Ebersteinburg,** a 13th-century castle with more superb views over the Murg valley. Rebuilt during the 19th century, Ebersteinburg is now a wine-growing estate with a restaurant.

Brahmshaus, *Maximilianstr. 85. Open year-round Mon., Wed., and Fri. 3–5, and Sun. 10–1.* Romantic composer Johannes Brahms lived in Baden-Baden for over ten years; first at the Hotel Bären, and then from 1865–74 in this house on Maximilianstrasse. Today it is his sole remaining residence in the country, and has been turned into a memorial and small museum.

Kloster Lichtental, *Hauptstr. 40. Open year-round, Mon. to Fri., 9–12, 2–5; Closed Sat. and Sun.* A Cistercian abbey founded in 1245 by the Margravin Irmengard, today housing an interesting museum and the Gothic-style **Princes' Chapel,** which contains the graves of the Margraves of Baden.

Kurhaus, *Kaiserallee 1.* Set in the attractive cure park, the Kurhaus, built in 1821, was long the focal point of the social whirl. Alongside the gracious ballrooms and concert hall, you'll find the **casino**—it's the oldest and the largest in Germany, and said to be one of the most beautiful in the world. *(Guided tours 9:30–12 daily throughout the summer; tables open at 2 P.M.)* You can also take the waters in the 19th-century **Trinkhalle** (pump rooms) decorated with paintings depicting local scenes and folklore.

Lichtentaler Allee, Leading south from the Kurhaus along the banks of the river Oos, this world-famous promenade has attracted such diverse figures as Queen Victoria and Emperor Napoleon III. The rambling English-style garden was laid out in 1850, and boasts over 300 different varieties of shrubs and trees. There's a spectacular display of rhododendrons in early summer.

Neues Schloss, *Schlossstr. For guided tours check with the tourist office.* Originally a 14th-century fortress, the castle was rebuilt by the

Margraves of Baden in the Renaissance period, and acted as their summer residence until 1918. It now houses the **Zähringer Museum** of local art and history.

Römische Badruinen, Römerplatz. *Open year-round daily 10–12 and 1:30–4.* Between Friedrichsbad and the Caracalla Therme are the ruins of the ancient Roman baths. 2,000 years ago the Roman Emperor Caracalla visited Baden-Baden in the hope of curing his rheumatism, and following his example these baths were built for Roman soldiers. They were rediscovered and excavated in 1847.

Bad Mergentheim

From 1525 to 1809, Mergentheim was the center of the ancient Order of Teutonic Knights, a religious and military brotherhood with its origins in the great crusades of the Middle Ages. After the fall of Jerusalem, the Order redirected their attentions to Europe. They relinquished their religious precepts in the 16th century, and settled in Mergentheim to rule over an independent principality. When the Order was dissolved by Napoleon in 1809, Mergentheim threatened to disappear altogether, but the discovery of mineral springs in 1826 revived its fortunes, the town adopted the prefix "Bad" (meaning "spa"), and evolved into a popular resort in the shadow of its ancient castle.

Apart from the inevitable cure treatments, the town has much to offer outdoor-types, with riding and hiking, and boating on the river Tauber. There's also the huge Wildpark nature reserve, and a vintage car museum in the center of town. There are a variety of accommodations available with plenty of good-value inns and farmhouses, as well as a youth hostel and campsite; hotels tend to cater for longer-stay guests.

GETTING THERE. A good start point for excursions to Heidelberg, Würzburg, Nürnberg and Stuttgart, Bad Mergentheim is on the Romantischestrasse tourist route. There are good train links, and the town is served by the long-distance EB 190 Europabus between Wiesbaden and Füssen.

TOURIST OFFICE. Kultur- und Verkehrsamt, Marktplatz 3 (tel. 07668–57232).

WHERE TO STAY AND EAT. Bundschu (M), Cronbergstr. 15 (tel. 07668–3043). A modern cure hotel in the suburb of Weberdorf, with comfortable rooms and a good restaurant.

Weinstube Lochner (M), Hauptstr. 39, in Markelsheim district (tel. 07668–2081). 48 modern rooms with bath or shower; indoor pool; sauna and solarium. Pleasant restaurant with seasonal specialties, and a wine tavern.

Zum Wilden Mann (M), Reichengasse 6 (tel. 07668–7638). Good value *gasthof* in the center of town with 27 rooms; cure facilities and restaurant.

⬤ **Deutschmeister** (I), Ochsengasse 7 (tel. 07668–7285). 48 rooms with bath or shower. Centrally located in a quiet street, with comfortable furnishings, rustic restaurant serving local cuisine, and a cosy wine tavern.

ATTRACTIONS. Deutschordensschloss, *Open Mar. through Oct., Tues. to Fri. 2:30–5:30, Sat. and Sun. 10–12 and 2:30–5:30; closed Mon. Regular guided tours, concerts, and son-et-lumiere.* Built by the Grand Master of the Order of Teutonic Knights, one of the Hohenzollen family, the castle dates from 1526. It now houses a museum tracing the history of the Order from the 12th century, with displays of military objects from firearms to dioramas of famous battles. Also has a collection of historic dolls' houses.

Stuppacher Madonna, Stuppacher Parish Church. *Four km. west of town. Guided tours Apr. through Sept., daily 8–6; Oct. through Mar., 8–12 and 1:30–5:30.* Painted in 1519, by the German Master Matthias Grünewald, the single altar panel [from a composition entitled "St. Mary of the Snows"] was brought to Mergentheim by the Teutonic Knights in 1532. Transferred to the parish church in 1812, the Stuppach Madonna has enchanted thousands of visitors every year.

Freiburg-im-Breisgau

Generally known simply as Freiburg, the city is the largest and, arguably, the most attractive in southern Germany, an ancient university and cathedral town offering a wealth of historic and cultural connections, beautiful buildings, and a pleasantly relaxed atmosphere. The Gothic Münster, or cathedral, faces a busy pedestrian square with an open-air market held every weekday morning. Two other squares to visit are the Rathausplatz, site of the city hall, and Oberlinden, with its medieval burgher houses, the 13th-century Swabian Gate, and one of the oldest inns in Germany, Zum Roten Bären (the Red Bear).

The tourist office organizes a variety of tours in and around Freiburg, and also promotes a number of special interest package deals, such as golf—there's a newly opened 18-hole course in nearby Dreisamtal—wine-tasting, or just plain sightseeing. Write them for their brochure *Ferien und Freizeit Ideen.*

GETTING THERE. Freiburg is just off the main Frankfurt–Basel highway (E4). Trains run from Dortmund, Munich, and Hamburg en route to Basel. The T67 Frankfurt–Munich long-distance bus service calls at the town, and there's an extensive network of local streetcars and buses. The tourist office sells one or four day "Rover" passes, which cover all forms of local transport.

TOURIST OFFICE. Verkehrsamt, Rotteckring 14, 7800 Freiburg-im-Breisgau, (tel. 0761–216 3289).

WHERE TO STAY. Kuhler Krug (M), Torplatz 1 (tel. 0761–29103). Small hotel in the Gunterstal district. 7 rooms with bath/shower; a garden terrace; good-value menus in the restaurant, and a comfortable old-style wine tavern.

Markgräflicher Hof (M), Gerberau 22 (tel. 0761–32540). Centrally located in the Old Town by Martinstor Gate, the hotel is at the top range of our price range. 21 rooms with bath in an historic building, with notable French restaurant and wine tavern.

☞Zum Schiff (I), Basler Landstr. 35–37 (tel. 0761–443378). Friendly family-run hotel-restaurant established in 1818, with its own vineyard. The 41 rooms have been recently renovated and all have bathrooms. Hearty local dishes at good-value prices in the restaurant.

Zur Bischofslinde (I), Am Bischofskreutz 15 (tel. 0761–82688). Quietly located in Betzenhausen district, this comfortable hotel has 22 rooms with bath; no restaurant, but generous breakfasts.

WHERE TO EAT. Weinstube Karcher (M), Eisenbahnstr. 43 (tel. 0761–22773). Easy-to-find wine tavern near the main train station, serving a straightforward menu of local dishes in cheerful surroundings.

Zähringer Burg (M), Reutenbachgasse 19 (tel. 0761–54041). An attractive 18th-century Badener tavern in the suburb of Zähringen, with mid-price menus and plenty of atmosphere.

☞Zur Tanne (M), Altgasse 2, Opfingen district (tel. 07664–21810). Another appealing 18th-century hostelry with a few rooms, as well as good-value menus and house wines. From mid-April to mid-June, the restaurant specializes in asparagus dishes.

MAJOR ATTRACTIONS. Augustiner Museum, Augustinerplatz. *Open year-round, Tues. and Thurs. to Sun. 10–5, Wed. 10–8; closed Mon. Guided tours Wed. 6 P.M., and Thurs. 4 P.M.* A superb collection of religious art displayed most effectively in a former Augustine monastery near the cathedral. Exhibits include beautiful 13th and 16th century stained glass and statuary removed from the cathedral for protection, and also a panel from the delightful Grünewald altarpiece "St. Mary of the Snows" (see also Bad Mergentheim entry).

Münster (Cathedral), *Münsterplatz. Open Mon. to Sat. 10–6, Sun. 1–6; tower Tues. to Sat. 10–5, Sun. 1–5. Guided tours daily.* Founded in 1200, the cathedral was not finished until some three centuries later, and is topped by a striking lacework steeple 112-meters (370-ft.) high containing eight bells, including the five-ton 13th-century "Hosanna" bell. The treasures within number works by Cranach the Elder, and Holbein the Younger; precious 17th-century Gobelin tapestries; and the early-16th-century high altar by Hans Baldung-Grien.

Universität (University). Founded in 1457, the University of Freiburg is one of the most important in Germany, and a vital cultural center. You'll find the old university building, and Jesuit church, in Bertoldstrasse (town center), and the new Albert Ludwig department in Humboldstrasse. American visitors may be interested to know that the name "Amerika" was first placed on the map by the cartographer Martin Waldseemüller, a native of Freiburg!

OTHER ATTRACTIONS. Kaufhaus. (City Chambers), *Münsterplatz.* Facing the Münsterplatz, opposite the cathedral, is the intriguing medieval Kaufhaus. Supported by four great vaulted arches over the sidewalk, the facade reaches steeply to the sky decorated with four statues of Hapsburg rulers, flamboyant pointed towers, and cunningly-shaped windows.

Neues Rathaus (New City Hall), *Rathausplatz.* The Neues Rathaus was opened in 1901, and is housed in two adjoining 16th-century patrician houses with Renaissance gables and splendid bay windows. In summer an open-air theater plays in the pretty, flower-bedecked square, and the **Glockenspiel** rings out daily at noon.

Stadtmuseum (City Museum), *Wenzingerhaus, Münsterplatz. Check with tourist office for opening times.* Located in the charming 18th-century town house built by artist and sculptor Christian Wenzinger, the recently opened museum traces the rich and varied history of Freiburg.

Heidelberg

Heidelberg, the ancient university town on the banks of the fast-flowing river Neckar, immortalized in *The Student Prince*, typifies the Romantic spirit at the heart of German folklore and literature.

Dominated by the architectural hodge-podge of its castle, the historic area is a maze of drunken-angled Baroque houses rebuilt on original medieval and Renaissance foundations after the sacking of the town by the French under Louis XIV and the Great Fire of 1693. The fire also saw the departure of the Palatinate Electors, who had ruled from the castle in a remarkably enlightened fashion for five centuries.

There are walking tours, organized by the tourist office, departing daily from Bismarkplatz and the Hauptbahnhof (main train station) at 10 and 2, as well as bus trips farther afield, and boat trips on the Neckar. July and August are the festival months, with open-air drama productions and international organ concerts in the Heiliggeistkirche (Church of the Holy Ghost). Check the dates of the castle illuminations and firework displays in June and September; also the Old Town Autumn Festival. Students represent a sixth of the population, so you'll find many inexpensive eating places. For good-value accommodations, check out the suburbs, away from the over-popular castle and Old Town.

GETTING THERE. Heidelberg lies on the Bergstrasse (B7), and Burgenstrasse (B37) tourist routes, and the Frankfurt–Basel highway (A5). Inter-City train connections run from all parts of Germany. Route 189 Mannheim–Rothenburg long-distance bus also makes a stop here.

TOURIST OFFICE. Hauptbahnhof, 6900 Heidelberg, (tel. 06221–10821). Room reservation service (tel. 06221–21341/27735).

WHERE TO STAY. Diana (M), Rohrbacher Str. 152–154 (tel. 06221–31243). Located on the edge of town, near the Alt Bergfriedhof cemetary, with 45 quiet and comfortable rooms. No restaurant, but residents can choose from a small snack menu.

Monpti (M), Friedrich Ebert Anlage 57 (tel. 06221–23483). Small, attractively furnished hotel in the town center. 14 rooms with own bath; no restaurant, but plenty of eating places in the vicinity.

Haus Sedlmayer (I), Gerhart-Hauptmann-Str. 5 (tel. 06221–412872). Nine rooms (some with bath or shower) in a quiet location on the north side of the Neckar. No restaurant.

Jeske (I), Mittelbadgasse (tel. 06221–23733). Excellent-value hotel a few minutes' walk from the town center.

WHERE TO EAT. Hirschgasse (M), Hirschgasse 3 (tel. 06221–49922). Long-established tavern-restaurant dating back to 1472. It also contains the more exclusive (and expensive) Gaudeamus Igitur restaurant.

⊖ **Weinstube Schloss Heidelberg** (M), at the castle (via Neue Schlossstr.) (tel. 06221–20081). Popular restaurant with a friendly atmosphere, and good-value set-price menus at the top of our price range.

Sole d'Oro (I), Hauptstr. 172 (tel. 06221–21480). Good-value Italian-style dining in a colorful atmosphere.

Schnookeloch (I), Haspelgasse 8 (tel. 06221–22733), and **Zum Roten Ochsen** (I), Hauptstr. 217 (tel. 06221–20977), are a couple of historic student taverns for a rip-roaring night out. The Schnookeloch has been doing its thing since 1407!

MAJOR ATTRACTIONS. Schloss (Heidelberg Castle). *Open year-round, daily 9–5. Guided tours of interiors 9–12 and 1:30–4.* Home of the electors of the Palatinate from the 13th to the 17th centuries, the castle is an eclectic mix of architectural styles, from Gothic through Renaissance with one or two early Baroque elements. A complete tour of the interiors is quite a lengthy business, but there are two sights which can, and should, be visited separately. First, the enormous 49,000-gallon **Grosses Fass** (Great Vat), *(open daily 9–7 in summer, 9–6 in winter)* once guarded by the legendary dwarf-jester, Perkeo, and where the electors' subjects deposited one-tenth of their wine in the form of tax! Second, the fascinating, if slightly hair-raising, **Deutsches Apotheken-Museum** (Pharmaceutical Museum), *(open daily 10–5 in summer)*.

Universität (University). The university, founded by Ruprecht I in 1386, celebrated its 600th anniversary in 1986. However, the present main building was built in 1931 with contributions collected in the United States by J.G. Schurman, a former student and one-time American ambassador to Germany. The **Universitätsbibliothek** (Library) in Plöck, possesses some beautiful medieval illuminated manuscripts displayed in the exhibition galleries. On a more down-to-earth level, you can visit the old **Studentenkarzer** (Students' Jail) in Augustinergasse *(open Mon. to Sat. 9–5)*, and try to decipher the graffiti scribed by generations of rowdy youths left to cool their heels for a couple of days!

OTHER ATTRACTIONS. Heiliggeistkirche (Church of the Holy Ghost), *Marktplatz.* The 14th-century Gothic church was one of the few buildings to escape the Great Fire. Originally, it was used as the burial site of the prince-electors, but only the graves of Ruprecht III and his queen, Elisabeth of Hohenzollern, remain. The uniform height of the ceilings in both the nave and aisles is typical of the barn-like "hall" style of some German medieval churches.

Königstuhl Cablecar, *lower station in the Kornmarkt (tel. 06221–22796). Open mid-Mar. through mid-Oct., daily, 10–6.* Stopping at the castle, Molkenkur terrace-restaurant, and the Fernsehturm TV tower at the summit of Königstuhl, this trip provides tremendous views over the town, and surrounding Neckar valley.

Kurpfälzisches Museum (Museum of the Electorate of the Palatinate) *Hauptstr. 97. Open year-round Tues. to Sun. 9–5, until 9 P.M. Thurs; closed Mon.* The collection is gathered in the Baroque Morass Palace, built in 1712 by the architect Breunig. Exhibits trace the history of the town all the way from 500,000 B.C. (represented by the jaw of the prehistoric "Heidelberg Man") through the Palatinate period; and there's a fine display of 19th-century paintings and drawings.

Heilbronn

An old imperial town and important wine center, Heilbronn lies between Heidelberg and Stuttgart in the Neckar valley. There are many interesting buildings dating from the high days of imperial patronage in the 16th century, though many were reconstructed following extensive bomb damage in World War II; that rebuilding program is symbolized by the hand-hammered iron phoenix at the top of the Baroque Hafenmarktturm (tower). There are two other towers which formed part of the original 14th-century town walls; the Bollwerksturm, and the Götzenturm, the latter named after Götz von Berlichingen, an outlaw knight with an iron hand. (see "Neckarzimmern" below for more details on this legendary figure).

The tourist office arranges a number of sightseeing tours in and around town, on foot or by bus, as well as an evening excursion taking in the available nightlife. Bicycles are a great way to get around, or you can take a boat trip on the Neckar (Easter through Oct.) from the landing stage at Friedrich-Ebert-Brücke near the Insel Hotel. Information from Personenschiffahrt-Stumpf, tel. 07131–85430.

GETTING THERE. Heilbronn is on the Burgenstrasse tourist route (the Castle Road), and just off the Nürnberg–Saarbrucken (A6) and Würzburg–Bodensee (A81) highways. Trains run from all parts of the country. Long-distance bus routes T21, from Stuttgart; T67, from Frankfurt; T91N, from Nürnberg; and T195S, from Dortmund also call at Heilbronn.

TOURIST OFFICE. Verkehrsamt, Marktplatz, 7100 Heilbronn, (tel. 07131–562270).

WHERE TO STAY. Café Beck (M), Bahnhofstr. 31 (tel.

07131–81589). 44 rooms near the rail station; snacks available in the cafe.

Grüner Kranz (M), Lohtor Str. 9 (tel. 07131–85633). Good-value hotel with 30 rooms, all with bath or shower. Centrally located near the Rathaus.

☙ **Kronprinz** (M), Bahnhofstr. 29 (tel. 07131–83941). 36 rooms with bath in a traditional hostelry. The restaurant is renowned for its high standard of cuisine and reasonable prices.

WHERE TO EAT. ☙ **Harmonie** (M), Allee 28 (tel. 07131–86890). Attractive restaurant with a lovely garden-terrace—a must in summer!

Haus des Handwerks (M), Allee 76 (tel. 07131–84628). Good-value restaurant with varied menu, and several local house wines.

Ratskeller (M), Marktplatz 7 (tel. 07131–84628). Excellent wine tavern in the historic Gothic-style Rathaus. Wholesome regional dishes form the basis of the menu; garden for *al fresco* dining.

ATTRACTIONS. Deutschordenshof and **Deutschordensmünster,** *Eichgasse.* The former residence and adjoining church of the Order of Teutonic Knights (see "Bad Mergentheim" above), the Deutschordenshof now houses the local museum, the **Stadtmuseum.**

Karlsruhe

A relative new town by European standards, Karlsruhe was founded by Karl Wilhelm, Margrave of Baden, in 1715, and is more widely recognised for its important industrial role than for its cultural and artistic connections. Seat of Germany's Supreme Constitutional Court, Karlsruhe also has an interesting architectural history. Designed in the shape of a fan, the main city throughfares angle away from the facade of the ducal palace at their apex; the pattern is repeated to the rear of the palace, but roads are replaced by pathways through open parklands. The general appearance of the city is neo-Classical and spacious, with many pedestrian malls and large areas of greenery.

Karlsruhe is also known as the "Gateway to the Black Forest," and is a good base for excursions into the northern region, the Palatinate Hills, and Baden-Baden. Accommodations come in a wide variety of guises, and the tourist office provides a room reservation service; there's also a youth hostel and campsite. A final note for beer-lovers: Karlsruhe is an important brewery town, brewing half-a-dozen leading brands of the stuff. So, a visit to the Bierakademie at Douglasstr. 10 (tel. 0721–27302) to sample a little local produce straight from the barrel is essential!

GETTING THERE. Karlsruhe is an international communications center with a domestic airport, and road, rail and bus connections with all major German cities.

TOURIST OFFICE. Verkehrsverein, Bahnhofplatz 6, 7500 Karlsruhe, (tel. 0721–387085).

WHERE TO STAY. Erbprinzenhof (M), Erbprinzenstr. 26 (tel. 0721–22190). Centrally located, and at the top end of our price bracket. 59 rooms (most with bath); no restaurant—breakfast only.

Fässle (M), Lameystr. 12 (tel. 0721–54433). 30 rooms (most with bath) outside the town center, en route to the Rhine harbor.

●**Hasen** (I), Gerwigstr. 47 (tel. 0721–615076). Good-value family-run hotel on the Durlach road, east of center city. 37 rooms, most with bath; varied restaurant menu and breakfast buffet.

WHERE TO EAT. Goldenes Kreuz (M), Karlstr. 21a (tel. 0721–22054). Popular local inn open daily until late. Long menu with something for everyone, and rapid service.

Harmonie (M), Kaiserstr. 57 (tel. 0721–374209). The "in" music-and-beer-tavern with live performances by well-known artists. Two fixed-price menus daily, plus an *à la carte* menu, and salad bar.

●**Unter den Linden** (M), Kaiserallee 71 (tel. 0721–849185). Wide-ranging menu from regional dishes to international cuisine; fish and game specialties in season; good-value fixed-price menus.

MAJOR ATTRACTION. Schloss und Badische Landesmuseum (Ducal Palace and Regional Museum of Baden). *Open year-round, Tues. to Sun. 10–5:30, Thurs. until 9 P.M.; closed Mon.* The palace was begun in 1715 by Margrave Karl Wilhelm in the wake of the chaos wrought by the French armies of Louis XIV. Surrounded by extensive parklands and formal gardens, the building was finally completed in gracious neo-Classical style by the architect Weinbrenner in 1781. The **Regional Museum** presents a wideranging collection of exhibits from the prehistoric period to the present day; particularly interesting are the military trophies and memorabilia amassed by Ludwig the Turk, Margrave of Baden, during the Turkish campaigns of 1683 and 1692.

OTHER ATTRACTIONS. Staatliche Kunsthalle (State Art Gallery), *Hans-Thoma-Str. 2–6. Main gallery open year-round, Tues. to Sun. 10–1 and 2–5; Orangerie gallery open 10–5; closed Mon.* An impressive regional collection, particularly strong on the medieval period, with a gallery devoted to Matthias Grünewald. The Orangerie houses the **Hans Thoma Collection,** and works by Impressionist artists, including Monet and Degas, as well as Franz Marc, co-founder of the powerful 20th-century Blaue Reiter (Blue Rider) school.

Stadtgarten (City Park), *Bahnhofstr. Open daily 9–7 in summer; 9–4 in winter. Glasshouses open Mon. to Fri. 9–4, Sat. and Sun. 9–12 and 1–5.* A pleasant wide-open space in the town center which offers a small zoo, a botanical garden, glasshouses guarding a vicious-looking host of cacti, a Japanese Garden, and a Rose Garden, in addition to carefully tended pathways and welcome bench seats for the footsore and weary!

Konstanz

Lake Constance, or Bodensee in German, covers an area of over 200 square miles on the Swiss-German border at the western tip of the Bavarian Alps. The main town of Konstanz (Constance) lies on the southern shore, at the mouth of the Rhine. A popular summer resort, and notable trading center from Roman times, Konstanz's greatest hour was the "Council of Constance" in 1414. The Council was convened in order to reunify the Catholic church, then laboring under the auspices of no less than three different popes. The matter was finally resolved with election of Pope Martin V in 1417.

Today the attractive Old Town and beautiful lakeside setting draw thousands of visitors every year. Extra encouragement is provided by the annual International Music Festival in June/July, and a wine festival in July/August. Watersports are a popular diversion on the lake. Other attractions include a casino for the well-heeled, and boat trips to the glorious gardens on Mainau Island, a must for every summer visitor.

The Bodensee Pass is a great way of exploring the lake; it entitles you to reduced rate travel on a variety of forms of local transportation,—in ferries, busses, and mountain railways. Hotels are pricey in the town center, but farther out you'll find good-value *gasthofs* and private accommodations; try suburbs such as Litzelstetten or Wollmatingen.

GETTING THERE. Between Munich and Zurich (in Switzerland) airports, Konstanz is well-served by road and rail connections from all major cities. The ships of the Weisse Flotte (White Fleet) provide regular services between all the Bodensee resorts. For details of timetables, and the Bodensee Pass, contact Bodensee Schiffsbetriebe, Hafenstr. 6, Konstanz, (tel. 07531–281389).

TOURIST OFFICE. Verkehrsamt, Bahnhofsplatz 13, 7750 Konstanz (tel. 07531–284376).

WHERE TO STAY. Deutsches Haus (M), Marktstätte 15 (tel. 07531–27065). Centrally located pension in 19th-century building, fully renovated with 42 rooms (most with bath). No restaurant.

Goldener Adler (M), Furstenbergstr. 70, in Wollmatingen district (tel. 07531–77128). 33 rooms with bath in the quiet suburb of Wollmatingen. Restaurant serving mixed menu at affordable prices.

Hotel-Restaurant Inselblick (I), Holdersteig 7, in Litzelstetten district (tel. 07531–44240). Small *gasthof* with 11 rooms, some with bath. Sauna and solarium, and good-value café-restaurant.

WHERE TO EAT. ●Capri Fischerstube (M), Neugasse 10 (tel. 07531–22950). Rustic-style restaurant specializing in locally caught fish accompanied by good-value house wines. Atmospheric ground floor wine tavern; also serves beer and inexpensive light snacks.

Casino Restaurant am See (M), Seestr. 21 (tel. 07531–63615). For a taste of the high-life head for the casino, which has its own restaurant overlooking the lake. There's an extensive *à la carte menu,* but try the good-value fixed-price menu.

Konzil Gastätten (M), Hafenstr. 2 (tel. 07531–21221). In the historic old Council Hall, the restaurant has a lovely terrace on the lakeside and features freshwater fish and local specialties.

MAJOR ATTRACTIONS. Mainau Island. *Open daily Apr. through Sept.* The highlight of any visit to the Bodensee, Count Lennart Bernadotte's spectacular island flower-gardens are accessible by boat or footbridge. Throughout the spring and summer Mainau is a riot of color and smells, climaxing in the glorious "Dahlia Show" in September. There's a pleasant terrace-café with views of the lake, and a **children's zoo** with irresistible dwarf pot-bellied Siamese pigs, but the flowers win the day.

Münster (Cathedral of Our Lady), *Münsterplatz.* The imposing bulk of the cathedral sits atop the narrow winding streets of the Old Town in a quiet square. The main body of the building is a mass of conflicting periods and styles, from the austere Roman crypt to the gilded Baroque chapels and brilliant stained glass. During a brief moment of unity at the "Council of Constance," the gathered ecclesiastics joined force to condemn Protestant reformer, Johannes Hus, to be burnt at the stake. As he was taken from the cathedral, Hus stopped to pray, and legend has it that the stone where he knelt will always be dry, whatever the weather.

OTHER ATTRACTIONS. Rathaus (City Hall). The Rathaus is located in a 14th-century guild house once owned by the Company of Linen Weavers. The delightful painted facade charts the town's early history, and the quiet courtyard is used for open-air concerts in summer. Other painted buildings include the beautifully restored **Rheintor** and **Schnetztor** city gates.

Rosgartenmuseum, *Zum Rosgarten, Rosgartenstr. 3–5. Open year-round,* Tues. to Sun. 10–5; closed Mon. Housed in a splendid Gothic-style guild house, the museum displays many examples of local history and culture from prehistoric and medieval times through to the 19th century.

Ludwigsburg

Ludwigsburg lies on the river Neckar, a short distance north of Stuttgart. Created by the Württemberg family in the 18th century, the town is largely incidental to the stupendous Baroque ducal palace, the largest of its kind in Germany, with a total of 452 rooms! The historic center is an impressive, if unimaginative, Baroque assemblage, and the attractive Marketplatz is brightened by a colorful open-air market on weekdays. From May to October, the Schloss Festspiel (Music and Drama Festival) attracts many visitors, but accommodations are limited and correspondingly expensive, so make this a daytrip from Stuttgart.

GETTING THERE. Ludwigsburg is on Route 327, just off A81 highway. It's easily accessible from Stuttgart on the S-Bahn (service every 20 mins.), and by rail or bus.

TOURIST OFFICE. Verkehrsamt, Wilhelm Str. 12, 7140 Ludwigsburg (tel. 07141–910252).

MAJOR ATTRACTION. Schloss Ludwigsburg. *Open Mar. through mid-Oct., daily 9–12 and 1–5. Guided tours.* Inspired by the glories of Versailles, and set amid rolling parkland and formally landscaped gardens, the Ludwigsburger Castle boasts its own theater, and an ornate Baroque and Roccoco-style chapel festooned with decorative stucco. The carefully restored interiors are furnished in the Empire-style, with superb collections of porcelain and silver, the whole recreating the stately elegance of court life.

OTHER ATTRACTIONS. Schiller National Museum, *Marbach am Neckar. Open year-round daily 9–5.* Created in the home town of the great 18th-century poet and dramatist, Schiller, the museum has amassed a fully representative collection of original manuscripts, first editions, and assorted memorabilia. You can also visit Schiller's unassuming birthplace, **Geburtshaus,** at Niklas-Tor-Str. 33 *(open daily 9–12 and 1–5, until 6 Mar. through Oct.).*

Meersburg

Located almost directly opposite Konstanz (see above), on the north shore of the Bodensee, Meersburg is a delightful resort town rising steeply from the lakeside surrounded by vineyards. The Unterstadt (lower town) is an area of tree-lined promenades and the busy little harbor; behind it there's a steep hill leading to the Oberstadt (upper town), a maze of narrow streets and half-timbered houses laden with window boxes and hanging baskets.

There's plenty to do: two castles to visit; watersports on the lake; and a variety of boat trips and tours into the surrounding country. For details, contact Meersburg Travel Agency at Unterstadtstr. 13, or the tourist office. The tourist office also has a useful and comprehensive list of good-value *gasthof* and private accommodations; hotels here can be expensive.

GETTING THERE. Meersburg is on Route 31, and there are good road connections with Munich and Stuttgart. Fast trains from Munich run via Ravensburg; and there are many other rail and bus links from around the country. Weisse Flotte ferries depart on regular services around the lake from the landing stage in the Understadt.

TOURIST OFFICE. Verkehrsverwaltung, Schlossplatz 4, 7758 Meersburg am Bodensee, (tel. 07532–82383).

WHERE TO STAY. Seehotel zur Münz (M), Seestr. 7 (tel. 07532–9090). Great location on the lakeshore, with a roof-terrace affording a panorama of the Bodensee. 18 comfortable rooms with bath; pleasant restaurant and sidewalk cafe.
🔴**Weinstube Löwen** (M), Marktplatz 2 (tel. 07532–6013). Traditional hostelry with tastefully modernized rooms, and a friendly restaurant plus wine tavern.
Zum Bären (M), Marktplatz 11 (tel. 07532–6044). Atmospheric old inn right in the center of town, with a good-value restaurant.

WHERE TO EAT. There are many good-value taverns where you can sample the delicious local wines. In addition to the hotel-restaurants mentioned above try:
🔴**Winzerstube zum Becher** (M), Höllgasse 4, (tel. 9009). Just by the Neuen Schloss, the Becher is the oldest wine tavern on the Bodensee. Reservations are recommended for the popular, good-value dining room.

ATTRACTIONS. Altes Schloss (Old Castle). *Open Mar. through Oct. daily 9–6; Nov. through Feb. 10–5.* The medieval Altes Schloss is the oldest inhabited castle in Germany, dating back to the 7th century. Within the sturdy walls you can visit 28 furnished rooms with magnificent furniture and a display of historic jousting equipment;

also, the dismal **"oubilettes"** (dungeons)—from the French "oublier," to forget.

Neues Schloss (New Castle). *Open Apr. through Oct., daily 10–1 and 2–6.* The Baroque "new" castle was built for the prince-bishops in the 18th century, and features a splendid staircase by the famous Roccoco architect, Balthasar Neumann. A Concert Festival is held in the Hall of Mirrors each summer, and there's an art gallery with exhibits of local crafts.

Neckarzimmern

The castle-fortress, Burg Hornberg, sits atop a small hill, surrounded by vineyards, one mile east of Neckarzimmern in the Neckar Valley. During the 16th century, Hornberg belonged to Götz von Berlichingen, a baron celebrated by Göethe in his play of the same name. Today, several parts of the castle are in ruins, but the remaining buildings harbor a museum and an historic hotel-restaurant, where medieval banquets are held amid all the feudal trappings. Special packages are arranged by the tourist office, or you can opt for a quiet night; an overnight stay in one of the 22 bedrooms, plus breakfast and the evening meal will cost around DM 140. Call Burghotel Hornberg—tel. 06261–4064.

GETTING THERE. Neckarzimmern is on the Burgenstrasse scenic road between Heidelburg and Heilbronn; it is also accessible by rail, or on the EB189 long-distance bus.

TOURIST OFFICE. Verkehrsamt, Rathaus, 6951 Neckarzimmern, (tel. 06261–2579).

ATTRACTIONS. Burgmuseum (Castle Museum), *Open Mar. through Apr., and Sept. through Oct. daily 9–5, May through Aug. daily 8–6; closed Nov. through Feb.* This is well worth a visit to see Götz's suits of armour, and catch up on some of his extraordinary history. Other exhibits include archeological finds; period weaponry; and the castle **chapel,** with some medieval stained glass.

Tauberbischofsheim

A picturesque medieval fortress-town on the Romantic Road (the Römantischestrasse), Tauberbischofsheim lies just south of Wertheim on the road to Rothenburg. Named for its position in the delightful Tauber valley, the town is surrounded by beautiful countryside—forests and vineyards—which make for pleasant excursions on foot or bike, or maybe on horseback. Little remains of the old fortress, but there are some attractive half-timbered houses and Baroque courtyards, as well as a range of events and festivals held in the town. There's a Spring Festival in May; the Old Town Festival in the first week of July; and wine festivals during September and October in the neighboring wine-growing districts. Also, fencing and show-jumping tournaments take place throughout the year. And there's more good news in the shape of accommodations, which are plentiful and affordable both in and around town.

GETTING THERE. The town is on the Römantischestrasse, and is also accessible from the Würzburg–Heilbronn highway (A81, exit Tauberbischofsheim). The nearest Inter-City rail station is Würzburg; and the long-distance Würzburg–Frankfurt (EB190) bus route runs through town.

TOURIST OFFICE. Verkehrsamt in Rathaus, Postfach 1405, 6972 Tauberbischofsheim (tel. 09341–8030).

WHERE TO STAY AND EAT. ☙Badischer Hof (I), Hauptstrasse 70 (tel. 09341–2385). Centrally located, and family-run for over 100 years, the hotel has cosy interiors and modern rooms. The restaurant features home-cooking, with daily specialties.

Henschker (I), Bahnhofstr. 18 (tel. 09341–2336). A family-run turn-of-the-century inn with 16 rooms all with bath/shower and modern facilities. Good-value restaurant serving generous breakfasts and hearty regional dishes.

ATTRACTIONS. Stadtkirche St. Martin (Parish Church). The church is a modern building dating from the beginning of the century, but it houses a number of treasures, including a fine side-altar attributed to the master woodcarver, Riemenschneider.

Tauberfrankisches Landschaftsmuseum (Tauber Valley and Franconia Rural Museum), *Kurmainz, Schlossplatz 7. Open Easter through Oct., Tues. to Sun. 2:30–4:30, also Sun. 10–12.* Located in the Gothic elector's castle, the collection ranges from archaeological finds to exhibits of rural life and culture. There is a good display of ecclesiastical art, including woodcarvings from the Riemenschneider school and Gothic panel paintings.

Tübingen

One of the great German centers of learning, Tübingen's historic university, founded in 1477, has an impressive list of alumnae: the Renaissance astrologer, Kepler; Melanchthon, theologian and author of the Protestant charter; poets Hölderin and Mörike; and philosophers Hegel and von Schelling. Today, the students represent one in four of the town's population, and contribute much to its character and atmosphere. The Old Town is the student quarter—a maze of narrow twisting streets crammed with artisan's boutiques and antique dealers, galleries and theaters, jazz cellars and taverns. The river Neckar is another center of student philosophy, as they patrol the embankments lost in discussion, or relax in the traditional black punts, hung with lanterns in the evening.

The best way to explore town is on foot; take the tourist-office arranged guided tours. The tourist office can also arrange renting of punts and buying theater tickets, and there's a room reservation service, plus information on events and excursions into the Neckar valley. For fresh air you can head off to the nature park at Schönbuch, just north of the town, where you'll find a wild animal reserve, bathing lakes and many sporting facilities.

GETTING THERE. In the heart of the Neckar valley, Tübingen is well served by main highways; the Munich–Karlsruhe (A8, exit Echterdingen or Vaihingen); Stuttgart–Singen (A81, exit Herrenberg or Rottenburg); B27 from Stuttgart; and B28 from Ulm. Trains run from Stuttgart, Munich, and Zurich among others.

TOURIST OFFICE. Verkehrsverein, An der Neckarbrücke, Postfach 2623, 7400 Tübingen, (tel. 07071–35011).

WHERE TO STAY. ●Hospiz (M), Neckarhalde 2 (tel. 07071–26002). Good value for the center of town (near the Marktplatz), with comfortable rooms, all with bath. Regional cooking in the dining room, and a friendly wine tavern.

Am Bad (I), Europastr. (tel. 07071–73071). Quietly located near the Municipal Park, well-kept hotel with a welcoming atmosphere; modern rooms; good food in the restaurant.

Gasthof Ritter (I), Am Stadtgraben 25 (tel. 07071–22502). Simple *gasthof* opposite the Botanical Garden, with 10 rooms, and a restaurant which serves game dishes in season.

WHERE TO EAT. Alte Weinstube Gohner (M), Schmiedtorstr. 5 (tel. 07071–22870). Old Swabian wine tavern where you'll find good-value lunches.

Ratskeller (M), Haaggasse 4 (tel. 07071–21391). Plenty of atmosphere in the cellar vaults of the old Rathaus, and hearty regional dishes on the menu.

●Waldhauser Hof (M), Waldhausen 9 (tel. 07071–64365). Country-house style restaurant in the suburb of Waldhausen. Rustic interiors and a varied menu offering such delicacies as freshly smoked trout and shellfish. The fixed-price menus are particularly good value.

Museum (I), Wilhelmstr. 3 (tel. 07071–22828). Large café-restaurant, with inexpensive fixed-price menus and delicious pastries from its own bakery.

Wein und Bierkeller La Cave (I), Kirchgasse 6 (tel. 07071–27571). Handy student tavern in the center of town between the Marktplatz and the Holzplatz. Small meals and snacks—a good place for lunch.

Weinstube Rebstock (I), Ammergasse 12 (tel. 07071–212552). An Old-Town tavern with an extensive wine list and good regional cuisine.

ATTRACTIONS. Hölderlin Turm, *Bursagasse 6. Open year-round Tues. to Fri. 10–12 and 3–5, Sat. and Sun. 2–5; closed Mon.* The tower room of a house built into the 13th-century town walls, and home of the poet Johann Friedrich Hölderlin from 1807 to his death in 1843. A memorial exhibit has been installed on the ground floor.

Hölzmarkt and **Stiftskirche.** Dominated by the Stiftskirche St. Georg, the Hölzmarkt is the rival center to the Marktplatz. To the southwest of the square you'll find the ancient **Bursa,** the former 15th-century students' hostel and lecture theater. Leading southeast is the busy pedestrian mall of **Neckarstrasse,** packed with street vendors and artists. The late-Gothic collegiate church of St. George contains the tombs of the Palatinate Princes, and a monument to Eberhardt the Bearded, founder of the university. There are some notable choirstalls, stained glass both ancient and modern, and a fine view of the town and surroundings from the church tower.

Marktplatz. The 15th century **Rathaus** (City Hall), or "town parlor," is the showpiece of the square. Originally a two-story half-timbered house, built in 1435, the building was extensively rebuilt in the Renaissance-style during the 16th century, while the intricate painted decoration on the facade is a 19th-century addition. During the week a colorful open-air **market** takes place around the Neptunbrunnen fountain.

Schloss Hohentübingen. The present 16th-century Renaissance castle was built on the foundations of an 11th-century fortress above the Neckar. It belonged to the Palatinate Princes of Württemberg, and boasts a richly carved portal bearing the family coat-of-arms. Part of the castle is now owned by the university. In the north wing you can see the second-largest wine barrel in Germany, constructed in the 16th century for Count Ulrich of Tübingen.

Städtische Sammlung, *Theodor Haering Haus, Neckarhalde 31.* The museum/archives contain a wealth of documentation about the famous philosophers, scientists, and literary figures who studied at the university, as well as the history, culture, and everyday life of the majority of students and the local townsfolk.

Ulm

The city of Ulm lies on the river Danube, the eastern boundary of Baden-Württemberg with Upper Bavaria. Ulm was badly damaged during the war and a new town, Neu-Ulm, has sprung up on the eastern banks of the river, but contains little of interest to the visitor. But you will be kept more than busy exploring the intriguing Fischviertel (Fisherman's Quarter), visiting the glorious cathedral, or catching up with a spot of shopping. Ulm's excellent main shopping district centers around Hirschstrasse, west of the cathedral, and, apart from the major department stores, there are souvenirs such as chocolate or pottery sparrows (the mascot of the city), and reproductions of the less-than-successful flying machine built by Albrecht Berblinger, the "Flying Tailor of Ulm", in 1811. Albert Einstein was born in Ulm in 1879 (too late to help Berblinger), and there's a fine sculpture of him by Max Bill, erected in his honor in Bahnhofstrasse.

If you tire of the busy downtown area, take a stroll in the Friedrichsau Park on the banks of the Danube. Laid out in 1811, there are many rare trees, as well as lakes, beer gardens, and a bear-pit.

Or perhaps you'd prefer a more cultural experience? Try the *Ulm Theater* in Neutorstrasse (tel. 0731–161–3265). It's a modern building, the successor to Germany's oldest theater, and hosts a glittering array of opera, ballet, and drama. The tourist office operates various guided tours (some in English); and there are boat trips on the Danube during summer, departing from the historic Metzgerturm tower (a former prison) Mon. to Sat. at 3, and hourly between 1 and 5 on Sun.

GETTING THERE. At the intersection of the Munich–Stuttgart (A8) and Aalen–Kempten (A7) highways, Ulm is a major road center. Inter-City trains connect to all parts of the country; and buses run throughout the area. In the city, the public transport system (SWU) is widespread; tickets for buses and trams are available from machines at stops, and can be bought for one-way or four separate journeys.

TOURIST OFFICE. Verkehrsbüro, Münsterplatz 51, 7900 Ulm, (tel. 0731–161–2036). Room reservation service available.

WHERE TO STAY. Prices in the city center are pretty steep, but there are plenty of good-value accommodations in the suburbs of Böfingen, Grimmelfingen, Lehr, and Söflingen; all are linked to the center by regular transport services.

Engle (M), Loherstr. 35, in Lehr district (tel. 0731–60884). 30 rooms all with bath/shower, in the northeast of town, near the university. Facilities include a sauna and solarium, plus attractive terrace.

Ibis (M), Neutorstr. 12 (tel. 619091). Modern hotel, centrally located opposite the Ulm Theater. Good restaurant with international cuisine and hotel-bar.

●**Ulmer Spatz** (M), Münsterplatz 27 (tel. 0731–68081). Quiet and comfortable hotel opposite the cathedral, with 45 rooms (most with bath). Rustic decor, and a garden-restaurant serving a mixed menu; also a wine tavern.

Sonnenhof (I), Eberhard-Finckh-Str. 17, in Böfingen district (tel. 0731–26091). Newly-built hotel with simple rooms, a restaurant serving generous portions of local dishes, and a small beer tavern.

WHERE TO EAT. **Forelle** (M), Fischergasse 25 (tel. 0731–63924). Situated in an old fisherman's house with a small terrace on the River Blau, and renowned for its fish specialties.

●**Pflugmerzler** (M), Pfluggasse 6 (tel. 68061). Good-value wine tavern in the Old Town district, serving a selection of delicious fixed-price menus in rustic surroundings.

There are two good-value self-service restaurants in the main department stores: **Hertie** (I), at Hirschstrasse 9; and **Horton** (I), at Bahnhofstrasse 5.

MAJOR ATTRACTIONS. **Fischerviertel** (Fishermen's Quarter). Enchanting Old-Town district once occupied by the local fishermen and tanners. Picturesque squares and medieval houses, such as the **Scheifes Haus** (Crooked House), a 15th to 16th-century half-timbered building, are still lived in today.

Münster (Cathedral), *Münsterplatz*. One of the most beautiful cathedrals in Germany, the 14th-century Münster also boasts the world's tallest spire 160-meters (530-ft.) high; it was erected in 1890. Above the main doorway is a carved frieze depicting the Creation, and a compelling statue, "Man of Sorrows," by Hans Multscher (1429). The highlight of the interior is the superb **choirstalls** by Jörg Syrlin the Elder (1469–71), decorated with hundreds of carved figurines of Biblical and secular characters. The massive organ (93 stops and 8,000 pipes!) is exercised at weekly concerts in the summer (Apr.–Nov. Sundays at 11:15); and the fit visitor can scale the spire to a height of 143 meters (469 ft.) for a magnificent view which extends to the distant Zugspitze peak on the Austrian border.

Rathaus (City Hall), Marktplatz. Originally a 14th-century storehouse, this delightful Renaissance building made the transition to town hall in 1419. The ornate facade, with its allegorical decoration, dates from 1540, and illustrates many of the town's traditional associations and commercial links. Above the interior staircase you'll find a replica of Berblinger's disastrous homemade "wings;" after his fatal ducking in the Danube, his wife sold the original wings to an umbrella maker who used the silk for umbrellas!

OTHER ATTRACTIONS. Ulmer Museum, *Marktplatz 9. Open Oct. through June, Tues. to Sun. 10–12 and 2–5, continuously during July and Sept; closed Mon. Guided tours available.* Displays trace the history and culture of Ulm and Upper Swabia from prehistoric times. The important fine art collection contains contributions from local masters, Multscher and Syrlin (whose work can also be seen in the cathedral), to 20th-century figures, Picasso and Kandinsky.

◆

S P L U R G E S

A Night in the Burghotel Hornberg, Neckarzimmern, 6951 Neckarzimmern (tel. 06261–4064). This is a hotel in an 11th-century castle, and you can't ask for anything much more historic than that. In fact, this was where Götz von Berlichingen lived, the Knight of the Iron Hand. His armor is displayed in the castle (parts of which are open to the public). Some have complained that the hotel lacks a certain style, but the sense of ages past is strong nonetheless. There's also a fantastic view over the vineyards that spread over the slopes below the castle. The original chapel is still in use, too. The restaurant is excellent, serving top-rate local specialties and wines. Expect to pay around DM 160 for a double room.

Scenic Rail Trip Through the Black Forest. Begin your ride on the Schwarzwaldbahn und Höllentalbahn at Offenburg. En route the train passes through Freiburg, Hinterzarten, Titisee, Donaueschingen, and Triberg. There are few better ways to get an overall appreciation of the Black Forest region. Prices start from around DM 42, making this an affordable as well as an enjoyable introduction to this marvelously scenic area.

◆

FRANCONIA

Franconia, the northern part of Bavaria, contains some of the most lovely and traditional-laden areas of all Germany; this really is the romantic heart of the country. It is a land of exquisite and intricate medieval cities; of myths and legends; of magnificent Baroque and Rococo palaces built by pleasure-loving, art-loving prince-bishops; of brooding hill-top castles and stately Gothic cathedrals; and of rich vineyards whose golden grapes mature to be pressed into pale, dry wines. Here the Minnesingers created Germany's lyric poetry in the early Middle Ages, and the Meistersingers later sang to the beat of the craftsmen's tools; and here Wagner built his great opera house, a fitting symbol of this, the epicenter of German mythology.

For all that Franconia is so rich in history and architecture, it's a remarkably good-value region, especially for lodging and dining. Similarly, bike hire is well developed throughout the area, and there are a series of bike vacations—lasting anywhere between two and seven days—offered by local tourist authorities. The vast areas of forests and the numerous nature parks also make Franconia something of a hiker's paradise. There are also specialty walking tours. How about fossil hunting in the limestone quarries around Solnhofen and Eichstätt in the Altmühl valley?

The whole region is easily visited by train and car. Nürnberg and Würzburg, the two main cities, are the nerve center of Franconia's road system, and both are easily reached from more or less anywhere in Germany. If you're planning to go direct to Franconia from the US, Frankfurt is the nearest international airport. The region also sees the start of the most famous specially designated tourist road in Germany, the Romantic Road. Rothenburg-ob-der-Tauber, Feuchtwangen,

Dinkelsbühl, Nördlingen, Harben, and Donauwörth are all on the Romantic Road. If you don't have a car, take the Europa bus (EB190). It runs the length of the great tourist trail. The Castle Road also runs through Franconia, entering the region at Rothenburg and continuing eastward to Nürnberg.

The symbol ⊜ represents our highly recommended selection.

Aschaffenburg

For those coming from Frankfurt, just 25 miles (40 kilometers) to the northwest, Aschaffenburg, on the river Main, is the gateway to Franconia and the streams and woods of the Spessart hills. It's a small town, which, despite a ring of factories around it—it's a major center for the manufacture of clothes—has retained its quiet, market-town atmosphere. The historic center has been carefully preserved, and much of it transformed into an elegant pedestrian mall.

GETTING THERE. Aschaffenburg is on A3 and A5 autobahns, the former linking it with Frankfurt. There are good train links, especially from Frankfurt.

TOURIST OFFICE. Fremdenverkehrsamt, Dalbergstr. 6, 8750 Aschaffenburg (tel. 06021–30426).

WHERE TO STAY. Aschaffenburger Hof (M), Frohsinnstr. 11 (tel. 06021–21441). 59 rooms, all with bath. Modern hotel located two minutes' walk from the train station. Rooms are functional but comfortable, and service is excellent. There's a good restaurant, though prices can be high.

Wilder Mann (M), Löherstr. 51 (tel. 06021–2155). 50 rooms, all with bath. The historic exterior of this old inn is not matched by the functional interior. It's located in the center of the historic area, five minutes' walk from the train station.

Dumpelsmühle (I), Gailbacherstr. 80 (tel. 06021–94449). 22 rooms, all with bath. Low prices, good wholesome specialties in the excellent restaurant (try the trout), and a country location two and a half miles (four kilometers) from the historic center.

WHERE TO EAT. Romantik Hotel and Restaurant Post (M), Goldbacherstr. 19–21 (tel. 06021–21333). The hotel here is expensive—it was originally a post inn—but the atmospheric restaurant is a must. Choose carefully from the immense menu if you want to stay within your budget.

Schlossweinstuben (I), Schloss Johannisburg (tel. 06021–12440). Wine cellar set in the castle, with a wide selection of local wines to complement the hearty food. The terrace, with a view over the Main valley, is unbeatable in the summer. Fixed-priced menus are available, as well as more expensive *à la carte* dishes. Pike can make for a memorably unusual choice.

ATTRACTIONS. Schloss Johannisburg, *Schlossplatz. Open Apr. through Sept., Tues. to Sun. 9–12 and 1–5, closed Mon.; Oct. through Mar., Tues. to Sun. 10–12 and 1–4, closed Mon.* This imposing Renaissance castle, built between 1605 and 1614, was the residence of the prince-electors of Mainz, hereditary rulers of Aschaffenburg. The outside of the doughty sandstone castle looks back to the Middle Ages—it's more of a fortress than a palace—with four massive corner towers guarding the inner courtyard. The interior, by contrast, is a much more gracious affair, with princely furnishings throughout. There are two small museums. The **Schloss Museum** charts the history of Aschaffenburg (and also contains a good collection of German glass). The **Staatsgalerie** (City Art Gallery) has a small section devoted to Lucas Cranach, the 16th-century German painter. Both museums are open the same hours as the castle. The grounds contain the **Pompeianum,** a replica of the temple of Castor and Pollux at Pompeii. It was built around 1840 by Ludwig I, king of Bavaria, father of "mad" King Ludwig II.

Schönbusch Park. The park lies across the river Main, about two miles from the historic area. The most enjoyable way to reach it, in good weather anyway, is on foot; start from the castle grounds. It was laid out in the 18th century by the prince-electors, and combines formal walks and flowerbeds with areas of landscaped parkland dotted about with temples, summer houses, and statues. A small neo-Classical palace overlooks the lake. Hire a row boat or have lunch at the café-restaurant.

Stiftskirche (Abbey Church of Sts. Peter and Alexander). The great abbey church stands on a small hill overlooking the town. Little remains of the original Romanesque buildings save the cloisters; most of the present building dates from the 16th and 17th centuries. But the real reason for coming here is to see the *Lamentation of Christ,* a gaunt and disturbing work by Renaissance painter Matthias Grünewald.

Bamberg

Bamberg is one of the great historic cities of Germany, filled with buildings and monuments that recall its glory days as the seat of one of the most powerful ruling families in the country. Though founded as early as the 2nd century A.D., Bamberg rose to prominence only in the 11th century, under the irresistible impetus provided by its most famous son, Holy Roman Emperor Heinrich II. His imperial cathedral still dominates the historic area.

The city lies on the river Regnitz, about 50 miles (80 kilometers) north of Nürnberg. The historic center stands on a small island in the river; to the west is the so-called Bishop's Town, to the east of Burghers' Town. Connecting them is the bridge bearing the Altes Rathaus, the old town hall, carefully positioned on neutral ground between ecclesiastical and secular strongholds. Though there are any number of attractions to see here, the preeminent pleasure of a visit is to stroll through the narrow, sinewy streets of old Bamberg, past half-timbered and gabled houses and formal 18th-century mansions. Peek into cobbled, flowered-filled courtyards or take time out in a waterside cafe, watching the little steamers as they chug past the colorful row of fishermen's houses that make up Klein Venedig, Little Venice.

GETTING THERE. There are excellent road and rail links to Bamberg. Both A73 and A3 autobahns pass right by the town. Buses link Bamberg with Bayreuth, Coburg, Ebrach, and Pommersfelden.

TOURIST OFFICE. Stadtisches Fremdenverkehrsamt, Haupwacherstr. 16, Postfach 110153, 8600 Bamberg (tel. 0951–21040).

WHERE TO STAY. Barock Hotel am Dom (M), Vorderer Bach 4 (tel. 0951–54031). 19 rooms, all with bath. Small and elegant Baroque town house right by the cathedral. Many original touches complement the solid modern comfort of rooms and the unusual cellar breakfast room.

●**Romantick Hotel Weinhaus Messerschmitt** (M), Lange Str. 41 (tel. 0951–26471). 12 rooms, all with bath. Onetime home of aircraft pioneer Willy Messerschmitt, and now an elegant and small hotel with an especially good restaurant. The handsome Baroque exterior prepares you for the intricate and atmospheric interior, with its antiques and heavy wood paneling, and carved headboards over many of the beds.

Hotel Garni Graupner (I), Lange Str. 51 (tel. 0951–26056). 28 rooms, most with bath. Simple accommodations at low rates in the heart of the historic area. There's no restaurant, but the cafe provides hearty breakfasts. A modern 10-room annex accommodates extra guests but lacks charm.

WHERE TO EAT. Michel's Kuche (M), Markusstr. 13 (tel. 0951–26199). Choose one of the fixed-price menus for exceptional value or splurge on the *à la carte* selections. This was once one of

Bamberg's many breweries, and the hearty beer-drinking flavour of the place is still much in evidence. Guests are seated at long wooden tables. Try the venison; other specialties are more nouvelle than German.

Historischer Brauereiausschank Schenkerla (I), Dominikanerstr. 6 (tel. 0951–56060). Authentic, mug-banging atmosphere and low prices make this beer-restaurant a longtime favorite. The rough-hewn wooden tables, plaster walls, and noisy smoky ambiance are perfect for beer drinkers and those in search of the beating heart of German after-hours' fun.

➡ **Würzburger Weinstube** (I), Zinkenwörth 6 (tel. 0951–22667). Fine wines and great-value food (ranging from hearty to nouvelle) complement the exposed-beam-and-plaster-wall atmosphere of this half-timbered inn. There's a courtyard where you can dine outside in the summer, and an amazing-value fixed-price menu.

MAJOR ATTRACTIONS. Dom (Imperial Cathedral), Domplatz. Open daily except during services. This is one of the most important of Germany's cathedrals, a building that tells not only Bamberg's story but that of much of Germany's, too. The first building here was begun by Heinrich II in 1003, and it was in the partially completed cathedral that he was crowned Holy Roman Emperor in 1012. In 1237 it was mostly destroyed by fire, and the present late-Romanesque/early-Gothic building begun. From the outside, the most dominant features by far are the four massive towers at each corner. Heading into the dark interior, you'll find one of the most striking collections of monuments and art treasures of any European church. The most famous is the **Bamberg Rider,** an equestrian statue, carved—no one knows by whom—around the year 1230 and thought to be an allegory of knightly virtue. The larger-than-life-size figure is incredibly realistic for the period, more like a Renaissance work than a Gothic piece. Compare it to the mass of carved figures huddled in the tympana, the semi-circular spaces above the doorways of the church; where these are stylized and awkward, though effective, the Bamberg Rider is poised and calm. In the middle of the nave you'll find another great sculptural work, the massive tomb of Heinrich and his wife, Kunigunde. It's the work of Tilman Riemenschneider, Germany's greatest Renaissance sculptor. Pope Clement II is also buried in the cathedral, in a great tomb under the main altar; he was the only pope to be buried north of the Alps.

Make an effort to visit the **Diözesan Museum** at Domplatz 5. *Open Apr. through Nov., Tues. to Fri. 10–5, Sat. and Sun. 10–3;*

closed Mon. It contains the Cathedral treasury, a collection that boasts a splinter of wood from the cross and the *heilige Nagel,* or holy nail, also supposedly from the cross. You can also see Heinrich's and his wife, Kunigunde's, skulls, mounted in elaborate metal supports. The buildings these ecclesiastical relics are housed in was built by Balthasar Neumann, Germany's leading Rococo architect, between 1730 and 1733.

Neue Residenz, *Domplatz 8. Open Apr. through Sept., daily 9–12 and 1:30–5; Oct. through Mar., daily 9–12 and 1:30–4.* This immense Baroque palace on the Domplatz, or cathedral square, was the home of the prince-electors. Their wealth and prestige are easily imagined as you tour the glittering interior. The standout is the **Kaisersaal,** or throne room, complete with giddy ceiling frescoes and complex stucco work around the walls. Be sure also to visit the **rose garden** in back of the building; there's a fine view from it over to the Benedictine abbey church of **St. Michael.** The palace houses the **Staatsbibliothek,** the state library. *It's open Sept. through July, Mon. to Fri. 9–5:30, Sat. 9–12, closed Sun.; Aug., Mon. to Fri. 9–12, closed Sat. and Sun.* Among the thousands of books and illuminated manuscripts are the original prayer books belonging to Heinrich and his wife, a 5th-century manuscript of works by Roman historian Livy, and handwritten manuscripts by 16th-century painters Dürer and Cranach.

OTHER ATTRACTIONS. Alte Hofaltung, *Domplatz 7. Open May through Oct., Tues. to Sat. 9–12 and 2–5, Sun. 10–1; closed Mon. and Nov. through Apr.* This was the imperial and episcopal palace until the Neue Residenz was built. It's a sturdy and weather-worn half-timbered Gothic building on the cathedral square. Today, it contains the **Historisches Museum,** a collection of documents and maps charting Bamberg's history that will probably appeal most to avid history buffs and/or those with good German.

Altes Rathaus. You can't actually visit this, the old town hall, but you can at least pay your respects to the exterior of what is among the most bizarrely sited municipal buildings in Europe. It stands on a little island in the river Regnitz, connected to both halves of the town by a stone bridge. Half the building is Renaissance; half is Gothic; between them is an ornate Baroque gateway topped by a tapering spire. While here you'll get just about the best view in town of the fishermen's houses of Klein Venedig.

Fränkisches Brauereimuseum (Franconian Beer Museum), *Michaelsberg 10. Open year-round, Mon. to Fri. 1–4; closed Sat. and Sun.* All beer lovers and/or parents with kids in tow should make a bee line to this museum. Bambergers have the distinction of consuming more beer per head of the population than the inhabitants of any other part of Germany—a startling 50 gallons each year. The most famous local beer is Rauchbier, a distinctive, smoky-flavoured product. The museum charts its history and that of beer-swilling Bamberg in graphic style.

Hoffmann-Haus, *Schillerplatz 26. Open Apr. through Sept., Mon. to Fri. 9:30–5:30, Sat. and Sun. 9:30–10:30.* Hoffmann was a Romantic writer and poet who lived in this little house between 1809 and 1813. Unusually, he is best remembered not for one of his own works but for an opera written about him by composer Jacques Offenbach, *The Tales of Hoffmann.* The house has been preserved much as it was when Hoffmann lived here, and will appeal to those with a taste for genteel life in early-19th-century Germany as much as to anyone specifically interested in Hoffmann.

Stephanskirche, *Stephansberg.* This is one of Bamberg's major architectural treasures, and its spire one of the most distinctive landmarks of the city skyline. It was built originally by Heinrich II, but remodeling and reconstruction over the centuries have produced today's essentially Baroque structure. It is the city's chief Protestant church.

EXCURSIONS. Vierzenheiligen and **Banz Abbey.** Lovers of Baroque and Rococo church architecture won't want to miss the trip to this astounding pair of buildings 19 miles (32 kilometers) north of Bamberg. The larger of the two, though in some ways the less impressive, is Banz Abbey, standing high above the river Main on what some call the "holy mountain of Bavaria." There has been a monastery here since 1069, but the present set of buildings—now home to a lucky group of senior citizens—dates from the end of the 17th century; they were completed in 1772. Highlight of the complex is the **Klosterkirche,** the abbey church, the work of architect and stuccoist Johann Dientzenhofer. *It's open Apr. through Sept., daily 8:30–11:30 and 1–5:30; Oct. through Mar., Mon. to Sat. 8:30–11:30 and 1–4:30, closed Sun.* Two massive onion-dome towers soar over the restrained yellow sandstone facade. Note the animated statues of saints set in niches. Inside, the church shimmers and glows with gorgeous Rococo decoration.

From the terrace there's a striking view over the Main to Vierzenheiligen. It's probably the single most ornate Rococo church in Europe, not that you'd know it from the exterior. There are those same onion-dome towers, and a lively curving facade, but little suggests the incredible array of painting, stucco, gilt, statuary, and rich rosy marbles inside. It was built by Balthasar Neumann between 1743 and 1772 as a pilgrimage church (it was here, in 1445, that a vision of the Christ Child and 14 saints appeared to a shepherd). Your first impression will be of the richness of the decoration and the brilliance of the coloring, the whole more like some fantastic pleasure palace than a place of worship. Notice the way the whole building seems to be in motion—almost all the walls are curved—and how walls and ceiling are alive with putti and delicate stucco. Much as the builders of Gothic cathedrals aimed to overwhelm through scale, so Neumann wanted to startle worshippers through beauty, light, color, and movement. Anyone who has seen the gaunt Romanesque cathedrals of Protestant northern Germany will have no difficulty in understanding why it was that the Reformation was never able to gain more than a toehold in Catholic southern Germany. There are few more uplifting buildings in Europe.

Bayreuth

Bayreuth (pronounced "Bay-roit") means Wagner. This small north Bavarian town was where 19th-century composer Richard Wagner finally settled after a lifetime of rootless shifting through Europe, and where he built his great theater, the Festspielhaus, as a suitable setting for his grandiose and heroic operas. The annual Wagner Festival, first held in 1876, regularly brings the town to a halt as hordes of Wagner lovers descend on Bayreuth, pushing prices skyhigh and filling hotels to bursting point and beyond. The festival is normally held in July, so, unless you've come to Bayreuth specifically for it—in which case you can forget about finding value for money anywhere—that's the time to stay away. (See "Splurges" at the end of the chapter for more information on the Wagner Festival.) Likewise, those whose tastes do not include opera and the theater will not find much here to divert them. Bayreuth is no picture-postcard town, and there is little or nothing that is not connected in some way or another with music, specifically Wagner's.

GETTING THERE. Bayreuth is well served by trains from all parts of the country. The A9 Nürnberg–Berlin autobahn also passes by the town. The "Bayern Express" Berlin to Munich bus calls at Bayreuth.

TOURIST OFFICE. Fremdenverkehrsverein, Luitpoldplatz 9, 8580 Bayreuth (tel. 0921–22011).

WHERE TO STAY. Accommodations are limited year-round, so advance reservations are essential. If you plan to stay during the festival, make reservations several months in advance. Check into staying in a hotel in the country around town and traveling in by bus; rates are much lower. The tourist office has details of all hotels in and around Bayreuth.

●**Am Hofgarten** (M), Lisztstr. 6 (tel. 0921–69006). 18 rooms, 9 with bath. Delightful small hotel more like a private home than a hotel. Rooms are all decorated differently, and with many personal touches. There's an appealingly rustic bar, and a pretty garden out back. No restaurant. Composer Franz Liszt lived in the house opposite.

●**Goldener Anker** (M), Opernstr. (tel. 0921–65500). 29 rooms, all with bath. No question about it—this is the place to stay in Bayreuth; *and,* rates are low. The hotel is located right by the Festspielhaus and has been entertaining composers, singers, conductors, and players for over 100 years, as the signed photographs in the lobby and the guestbook make all too clear. Rooms are small but individually decorated with many antique pieces. The restaurant is justly popular.

WHERE TO EAT. Annecy (M), Gabelsbergerstr. 11 (tel. 0921–26279). Stick to the fixed-price menus for best value; ordering *à la carte* may prove pricey. Food is French and simple.

MAJOR ATTRACTIONS. Festspielhaus, *auf dem Grünen Hügel.* Contact the tourist office for details of tours of the interior. This plain plaster building, standing above the northern edge of Bayreuth on a low hill, is the high temple of the cult of Wagner. The building was conceived, planned, and built by the great man specifically as a setting for his epic operatic productions. Today, it plays host to the annual Wagner festival, still put on by descendants of the compelling romantic genius. The spartan look of the building is mostly explained by Wagner's perpetual financial crises. Equally, inside at least, it also stems from his efforts to achieve perfect acoustics. Thus, the plain wooden seats have no upholstering, while the walls are similarly bare of ornament. One of the more striking features of the building is the huge size of the stage, capable of holding the immense casts required for even Wagner's largest operas.

Markgräfliches Opernhaus (Margrave's Opera House), *Opernstr. 14. Guided tours daily, except Mon., Apr. through Sept. from 9–12 and 1:30–5; Oct. through Mar. from 10–11:30 and 1:30–3.* If Wagner's immense opera house is plain to the point of austerity, the same can hardly be said of this Rococo jewel. Intriguingly, it was this tiny, 500-seat theater that drew Wagner to Bayreuth in the first place. Searching for a theater to stage his operas, he toyed with the idea that this might be it. In fact, while it may be the perfect place to hear Mozart, it's hard to imagine a less suitable setting for Wagner. The theater was built by Margravina Wilhelmina, sister of Frederick the Great of Prussia and wife of the Margrave, or Marquis, of Brandenburg, an otherwise altogether unremarkable minor German ruler of the mid-18th century. Catch a performance here if you can; otherwise take one of the tours around the gilt and red-velvet interior, with its rows of little boxes and fanciful Rococo decoration.

OTHER ATTRACTIONS. Altes Schloss Ermitage (Old Castle and Hermitage). *Open Apr. through Sept., Tues. to Sun. 9–11:30 and 1–4:30, closed Mon.; Oct. through Mar., Tues. to Sun. 10–11:30 and 1–4:30, closed Mon.* This early 18th-century palace, three miles (five km) north of Bayreuth, also displays the Rococo taste of Margravina Wilhelmina, or at least the delicate interior, alive with light and color, does; the exterior is plain and almost fortress-like. The building was put up around 1718 by Margrave Georg Wilhelm as a summer palace, and was remodeled some 20 years later by Wilhelmina. The standout is the extraordinary Japanese room, filled with Oriental treasures and Chinoiserie furniture. The park and gardens, partly formal, partly natural, are enjoyable for idle strolling in summer.

Neues Schloss, *Ludwigstr. 21. Guided tours daily from 10–12 and from 1:30–5:30.* The Margravina Wilhelmina's distinctive touch is much in evidence at this mid-19th-century palace, built to replace the Baroque castle that had been destroyed by fire. The palace stands in the heart of the old part of town. Anyone with a taste for the wilder flights of Rococo decoration will love it. The **Staatsgalerie,** with a representative collection of mainly 19th-century Bavarian paintings, is housed in the palace (and is open same hours).

Richard Wagner Museum, Haus Wahnfried, *Richard Wagner Str. 48.* Open year-round, daily 9–5. This was where Wagner and his wife, daughter of composer Franz Liszt, lived; and here, too, they are buried. The house has naturally become something of a shrine to Wagner, but even those who are not normally moved by him will find it an intriguing and educational place to visit. Standout exhibits are the original scores for a number of his operas, including *Parsifal, Tristan, Lohengrin, The Flying Dutchman,* and *Götterdämmerung.* But you can also see designs, some dating back to the last century, for productions of his operas; his huge library; and a host of many other objects owned by him.

Coburg

The small town of Coburg in northern Franconia, close to the East German border, is known primarily not for any amazing sights or historical monuments so much as for having been the home of the Saxe-Coburgs. They were a remarkable family. Superficially just one among dozens of small German ruling families, they managed to establish themselves as what some people have uncharitably called "a royal stud farm." During the 18th and 19th centuries they provided a seemingly inexhaustible supply of blue-blooded marriage partners to ruling houses the length and breadth of Europe. The most famous of these royal mates was Prince Albert, husband of Queen Victoria; their children, married off among more of Europe's kings, queens, and emperors, helped spread even farther afield the tried-and-tested Saxe-Coburg stock. There's a statue of the high-minded prince in the main square. His birthplace at nearby Schloss Rosenau can be visited.

GETTING THERE. There are excellent train links to Coburg from all parts of Germany. No autobahns pass close to the town, but A9 Munich–Berlin autobahn and A7 Hamburg–Würzberg autobahn both provide reasonably convenient access, backed up by good local roads. Buses run to Coburg from Fulda, Würzberg, Bamberg, and Hof.

TOURIST OFFICE. Fremdenverkehrsamt Stadt Land Coburg, Herrngasse 4, Postfach 666, 8630 Coburg (tel. 09561–95071).

WHERE TO STAY. Goldener Anker (M), Rosengasse 14 (tel. 09561–95027). 55 rooms, all with bath. Centrally-located and comfortable hotel right by the marketplace. A swimming pool and sauna are unexpected bonuses in this class of hotel.

WHERE TO EAT. Klosterschänke (M), Nägleinsgasse 4 (tel. 09561–92665). For a taste of old Coburg atmosphere, make for this historic vaulted cellar in the center of town. Coburg grilled sausages are a specialty, and there is a wide range of chilled local wines.

MAJOR ATTRACTION. Veste Coburg (Coburg Fortress). *Open Apr. through Oct., Tues. to Sun. 9–12 and 2–4, closed Mon.; Nov. through Mar., Tues. to Sun. 9–12 and 2–3:30, closed Mon.* This is Coburg's castle, one of the largest and most impressive in Germany. Its brooding bulk stands on a small hill above the town, between the Thüringian Forest and the Upper Main valley. The first buildings here went up around 1055, but, with progressive rebuilding and remodeling down the centuries, today's predominantly late-Gothic/early-Renaissance edifice bears little resemblance to the original rude fortress. It contains a number of separate museums (all open same hours as the castle itself). See the **Fürstenbau,** or Palace of the Princes, where Martin Luther stayed for six months in 1530. Among the main art treasures here are four paintings by Cranach. Cranach, Dürer, and Rembrandt are all represented at the **Kunstsammlungen,** the art museum in the fortress, as are many examples of German silver, porcelain, arms and armor, and furniture. Finally, there's the **Herzoginbau,** the duchess' building, a sort of 18th-century transportation museum, with carriages and sledges.

OTHER ATTRACTIONS. Naturwissentschaftliches Museum (Natural History Museum), *Hofgarten. Open Apr. through Oct., daily 9–6; Nov. through Mar., daily 9–5.* This is just about Germany's leading natural history collection, with over 8,000 exhibits of flora and fauna, and geological, ethnological, and mineralogical specimens. The museum is located in the **Hofgarten,** a sprawling park laid out in the 18th century, linking the Veste with the ducal palace (see below).

Schloss Ehrenburg (Ducal Palace), *Schlossplatz. Open year-round, Tues. to Sun., closed Mon.; tours at 10, 11, 1:30, 2:30, 3:30, and 4:30.* This was the boyhood home of Prince Albert, a vast, rambling Renaissance palace much altered in the 19th century. Some of the formal rooms have been carefully preserved. See the throne room, the great hall, and the white hall.

Dinkelsbühl

Dinkelsbühl has been described as a medieval town that has drifted off to sleep. While that may be an exaggeration, it does at least give some idea of what you can expect to find in this pretty little walled town. It owes its survival largely to the uncharacteristic decision of Swedish troops, marching south into Germany in the Thirty Years' War of the mid-17th century, not to lay waste to it. The story runs that the children of the town persuaded the Swedes to spare them and Dinkelsbühl. At all events, the major event on Dinkelsbühl's calendar is still the Kinderzeche, or Children's Tribute, held every July, with dances and an historical play in remembrance of the town's salvation. You won't find any outstanding treasures here, but those in search of romantic Germany without the tourist hype of Rothenburg, say, will not be disappointed.

GETTING THERE. Dinkelsbühl lies on the Romantic Road (route B2/B25), the scenic highway from Würzburg to the Alps. The long-distance Romantic Road buses 190 and 190A pass through the town. Dinkelsbühl is not on any main train lines, but a local line from Augsburg and Donauwörth calls at the town.

TOURIST OFFICE. Verkehrsamt, Marktplatz, 8804 Dinkelsbühl (tel. 09851–3013).

WHERE TO STAY AND EAT. Blauer Hecht (M), Schweimarkt 1 (tel. 09851–811). 31 rooms, all with bath. A 17th-century former brewery-owned gasthof, now a comfortable and well-run small hotel. Rooms are individually decorated, some more successfully than others.

☛**Deutsches Haus** (M), Weinmarkt 3 (tel. 09851–2346). 11 rooms, most with bath. Half-timbered inn dating from 1440 and exuding the romantic atmosphere of Old Germany. Nicely decorated rooms, an excellent restaurant serving Franconian dishes, and a richly painted and carved facade make the Deutsches Haus somewhere special.

Weisses Ross (I), Steingasse 12 (tel. 09851–2274). 14 rooms, 5 with bath. Simple and good-value guesthouse offering reasonable comfort and excellent local specialties.

WHAT TO SEE. Touring Dinkelsbühl is not so much a matter of taking in specific sights—museums, palaces, parks, and churches, say—so much as of simply wandering around the historic area, pausing to admire a facade or a shop window or the juxtaposition of architectural styles, from Gothic through Baroque, that make this little town memorable and so very German. Altrathausplatz, Seringerstr., Bahnhofstr., Marktplatz, and Turmgasse will all reward lovers of cutesy, picture-postcard Teutonic townscapes. The one standout sight for many is:

St. Georg's Kirche, *Marktplatz. Open-year-round, daily 9–12 and 2–6*. Big enough, at 235-feet (72-meters) long, to be a cathedral, St. George's is among the best examples of the late-Gothic in Bavaria. Note especially the complex fan-vaulting that spreads sinuously over the ceiling. If you can face the climb, head up the 200-foot (60-meter) tower for amazing views over the jumble of Dinkelsbühl's rooftops.

Nordlingen

Nordlingen, another little town on the Romantic Road, likes to call itself "the living medieval city." It's not a bad description for this picturesque old walled town. In fact, it's not only the buildings here that have been preserved; at night the watchman's call still echoes through the narrow streets as it has done for centuries. The city's buildings hark back to medieval times, too. The Anno 1643 pageant, for example, commemorates Nordlingen's troubles in the Thirty Years' War. The Scharlachrennen, or Scarlet Derby, held in July, is the oldest horse race of its kind in the country.

Nordlingen provides one curious geological statistic. The town lies in the center of a gigantic crater, formed by an immense meteorite 15 million years ago, measuring 16 miles (25 km) across. The crater, known as the Ries, is said to be the most intensively studied in the world.

GETTING THERE. Nordlingen lies midway between Dinkelsbühl and Donauwörth on the Romantic Road, Route B25. The train station has regular services from Stuttgart and Munich. The nearest mainline station is Donauwörth.

TOURIST OFFICE. Städtisches Verkehrsamt, Marktplatz 15, 8860 Nordlingen (tel. 09081–4380). (As well as the regular tour guides organized by most German tourist offices, you can book a two-hour trip around the city with a guide sporting 16th-century garb; tours are given in English and German.)

WHERE TO STAY AND EAT. Am Ring (M), Bürgermeister-Reiger-Str. 14 (tel. 09081–4028). 39 rooms, all with bath. Functional but efficiently-run modern hotel near the train station. Try the restaurant for good-value local and international foods.

◗ Sonne (M), Marktplatz 3 (tel. 09081–5067). 40 rooms, all with bath. For a real taste of old Nordlingen, this 15th-century inn hard by the cathedral and Rathaus is the place to stay. Combines the best of the past with modern comfort, and not a little elegance. Hefty German specialties are available in the moderately-priced restaurant.

WHAT TO SEE AND DO. Rathaus, *Marktplatz. Tours Tues. to Sat. from 9–12 and 2–5, Sun. 10–12 and 2–4; closed Mon. and all Nov.* Though partially rebuilt in 1934, the Renaissance town hall still gives off a strong sense of ancient Nordlingen. Note especially the Freitreppe, the exterior stairs, a typical Franconian motif. Inside, you'll find the **Stadtmuseum,** the municipal museum (open same hours). It charts the history of the town, with a special section on the Ries, the crater in which the town stands.

St. Georg's Kirke, Marktplatz. As at Dinkelsbühl, this church of St. George dates from the 15th century and is what the Germans call a *hallenkirche,* meaning a "hall" church. It's a descriptive name for a relatively simple structure. The emphasis here, as at all late-Gothic churches, is to provide large areas of glass to light the interior. Note also the fine fan-vaulting. You can climb up the 300-foot (92-meter) tower—it's called the **Daniel**—for a predictably fine view.

Nürnberg

Nürnberg is the principal city of Franconia, and second in size and significance in Bavaria only to Munich. Its origins date back at least to 1040. It's among the most historic and visitable of Germany's cities; the core of the old town, through which the river Pegnitz flows, is still surrounded by its original medieval walls. Nürnberg has always taken a leading role in German affairs. It was here, for example, that the first "diet," or meeting of rulers, of every Holy Roman Emperor was held. And it was here, too, that Hitler staged the greatest and most grandiose of Nazi rallies. (Here, as well, that the war trials were held by the Allies.) War-time bombing destroyed much of medieval and Renaissance Nürnberg, though faithful reconstruction has since done much to re-create the city's pre-war atmosphere.

The city grew because of its location at the meeting point of a number of medieval trade routes. With prosperity came a great flowering of the arts and sciences. Albrecht Dürer, the first indisputable genius of the Renaissance in Germany, was born here in 1471, and returned to see out his days in 1509. (His house is about the most popular tourist shrine in the city.) Other leading Nürnberg artists of the Renaissance included woodcarver Michael Wolgemut and sculptors Adam Kraft and Peter Vischer. Earlier the Minnesingers, medieval poets and musicians, chief among them Tannhäuser, had made the city a focal point in the development of German music. In the 15th and 16th centuries their traditions were continued by the Meistersingers. Both groups were celebrated much later by Wagner. Among a great host of inventions, about the most famous were the pocketwatch, gun casting, the clarinet, and the geographical globe (the first of which was made before Columbus discovered the Americas).

Nürnberg is rich in special events and celebrations. By far the most famous is the Christkindlmarkt, an enormous pre-Christmas market that runs from November 27 to Christmas Eve. Highlight is the December 10 candle procession, in which thousands of children march through the city streets. 1988 sees the International Organ Weeks, to be held from June 23 to July 4. Concerts by internationally known organists will be held at various locations throughout the city, including the Meistersingerhalle.

GETTING THERE. Nürnberg lies at the meeting point of a transportation network. It has an international airport, just five miles (eight km) outside the city (though few flights from the US land here). Three

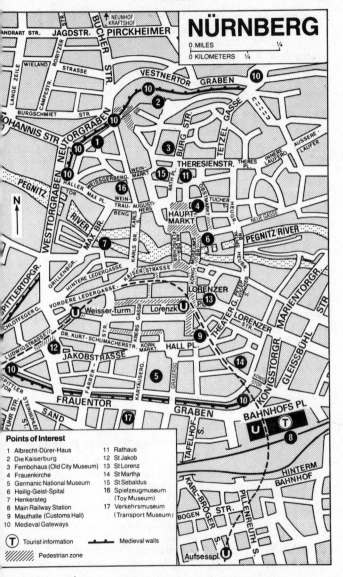

NÜRNBERG

0 MILES ¼
0 KILOMETERS ¼

Points of Interest

1 Albrecht-Dürer-Haus
2 Die Kaiserburg
3 Fembohaus (Old City Museum)
4 Frauenkirche
5 Germanic National Museum
6 Heilig-Geist-Spital
7 Henkersteg
8 Main Railway Station
9 Mauthalle (Customs Hall)
10 Medieval Gateways

11 Rathaus
12 St Jakob
13 St Lorenz
14 St Martha
15 St Sebaldus
16 Spielzeugmuseum
   (Toy Museum)
17 Verkehrsmuseum
   (Transport Museum)

Ⓣ Tourist information
////// Pedestrian zone

━ ● ━ Medieval walls

autobahns converge on the city: A3 (Frankfurt–Passau); A6 (Stuttgart–Nürnberg); and A9 (Berlin–Munich). In addition, it lies at the eastern end of one of the country's leading scenic routes, the Castle Road. Europabus 189 runs about two-thirds of it, from Mannheim to Rothenburg ob der Tauber, where you can catch the Bahnbus on to Nürnberg. There are excellent train links to major cities throughout Germany.

TOURIST OFFICE. Verkehrsverein Nürnberg, Eilgutstr. 5 (tel. 0911–23360). Other offices at the Rathaus and the train station; latter operates an accommodations service (tel. 0911–23360).

WHERE TO STAY. Burghotel Grosses Haus (M), Lammgasse 3 (tel. 0911–204414). 44 rooms, all with bath. Right at the top end of the budget range, but worth it for the central location, tastefully "rustic" decor, and the view over the old town. No restaurant, but good café-bar, and a sauna. Avoid the smaller and less conveniently placed annex at Schildgasse 16.

●**Weinhaus Steichele** (M), Knorrstr. 2 (tel. 0911–204378). 54 rooms, all with bath. Historic, centrally-located small hotel, owned and run by the same family for three generations. Rooms are plain but cheerful. Small annex next door is modern but with something of the same red-checked mood. The wine tavern is full of Nürnberg atmosphere, and offers an excellent-value fixed-price menu, as well as a wide range of Franconian dishes.

Drei Raben (I), Königstr. 63 (tel. 0911–204583). 50 rooms, all with bath. Though it's simple, you'll find comfort and hospitality in this small hotel. No restaurant.

Gasthof Schlötzer (I), Loher-Hauptstr. 118 (tel. 0911–345718). 38 rooms, about half with bath.

WHERE TO EAT. Bammes (M), Bucher Hauptstr. 63 (tel. 0911–391303). Head here for a great combination of wholesome and heavily German food with, at night, nouvelle touches. Rustic wood paneling and friendly service set the mood in this long-time Nürnberg favorite. Try the trout or, if you're feeling adventurous, the pike.

●**Heilig-Geist-Spital** (M), Spitalgasse 12 (tel. 0911–221761). Heavy wooden furnishings and more than 100 wines are the reasons for visiting this authentic wine tavern in the historic center by the river. Food is simple (and inexpensive) or more fancy (and more expensive) according to taste. The venison makes for a rich and filling main course. Try for a table overlooking the river.

Bratwurstglöcklein (I), Am Konigstor. Nürnberg is famed for its grilled sausages, *Bratwürste*, and, among the many inexpensive restaurants and stand-up counters all over the city that serve it, this is among the best. It's located in the modern "medieval" shopping mall near the train station. Sauerkraut and potato salad are the traditional accompaniments. Wash it all down with a glass of beer.

MAJOR ATTRACTIONS. Albrecht Dürer Haus, *Albrecht-Dürer-Str. 39 (opposite Tiergargärtner gate). Open Mar. through Oct. and Christkindlmarkt, Tues. to Sun. 10–5 (10–9 Wed), closed Mon.; Nov. through Feb. except Christkindlmarkt, Tues. to Fri. 1–5 (1–9 Wed.), closed Mon., Sat., and Sun.* This was the home of the great German painter, Dürer, from 1509 to his death in 1528. It is also about the best-preserved late-medieval house in the city, typical of the type of prosperous merchants' homes that once filled Nürnberg. Admire the half-timbering of the upper stories, and the tapering gable, before stepping into the building. Dürer was an extraordinary man, a German Leonardo, the Renaissance man incarnate, bursting with curiosity. Artistically, his greatest achievement was in the field of woodcuts, a notoriously difficult medium to use but which he raised to new heights of technical sophistication, combining great skill with a haunting, immensely detailed drawing style and complex allegorical subject matter. A number of original prints can be seen on the walls. Those who remain unmoved by Dürer himself may well enjoy simply visiting the house for the convincing sense of life in early 16th-century Germany it conveys.

Die Kaiserburg (The Imperial Castle), *Burgstr. Open Apr. through Sept., daily 9–12 and 12:45–5; Oct. through Mar., daily 9:30–12 and 12:45–4.* This immense cluster of ancient buildings, standing just inside the city walls at the north end of the historic area, was the residence of the Holy Roman Emperors. Impressive rather than beautiful, the complex comprises three separate groups of buildings. The oldest, dating from around 1050, is the **Burggrafenburg,** the Burgraves' Castle, with a craggy, ruined seven-sided tower and bailiff's house. It stands in the center of the complex. To the east is the **Kaiserstallung,** the imperial stables. It was originally built in the 15th century as a granary, and was converted into a youth hostel after the war. The real interest, however, centers on the Imperial Castle itself, the westernmost part of the fortress. The standout feature here is the strange Renaissance **Doppelkappelle,** or double chapel. The lower part of the building was used by the castle minions, and is accordingly austere; the adjoining upper part, correspondingly richer, larger, and more ornate, was where the emperor and his family worshipped. But visit also the **Rittersaal** and the **Kaisersaal,** the knights' hall and the throne room. Their heavy oak beams, painted ceilings, and sparse interiors have changed little since they were built in the 15th century.

Germanisches Nationalmuseum (Germanic National Museum), *Kornmarkt. Open year-round, Tues. to Sun. 9–5 (Thurs. 8–9:30); closed Mon.* You could easily spend an entire day visiting this vast and fascinating museum—stamina permitting, of course. This is the largest museum of its kind in Germany, and about the best arranged. The setting gets everything off to a flying start; it's located in what was once a Carthusian monastery, complete with cloisters and monastic outbuildings. The museum's brief is, simply, German culture, and there are few fields, from the Stone Age to the 19th century, that are not covered. Quantity and quality are evenly matched. For some, highlights may be the superb collection of Renaissance German painting (with Dürer, Cranach, and Altdorfer well to the fore). Others may prefer the exquisite medieval ecclesiastical exhibits—manuscripts, altarpieces, statuary, stained-glass, jewel-encrusted reliquaries—or the collections of arms and armor, or the scientific instruments, or even the toys. Few will be disappointed.

OTHER ATTRACTIONS. Frauenkirche (Church of Our Lady), *Hauptmarkt.* The interest here is not so much the church, a small 14th-century building, as the **Männleinlaufen,** a clock dating from 1509 set on the church's facade. It's one of those colorful, mechanical marvels the Germans have long excelled at, in which a love for punctuality and ingenuity are perfectly matched. Every day at noon, the Electors of the Holy Roman Empire glide out of the clock to bow to Emperor Charles IV before sliding back under cover. It's worth scheduling your morning to catch the display if you can.

St. Lorenz Kirche, *Königstr.* Opinions are divided as to the most beautiful church in Nürnberg, though most agree that St. Lorenz and St. Sebaldus are the front-runners. See them for yourself and make up your own mind. St. Lorenz was begun around 1220 and completed by about 1475. It's a sizeable church, with two towers flanking the main entrance, itself covered with a forest of carving. In the lofty interior, note those works by sculptors Adam Kraft and Veit Stoss. The great stone tabernacle to the left of the altar by Kraft and the wooden *Annunciation* at the east end of the nave by Stoss are considered their finest works. There are many other carvings throughout the building, a fitting testimony to the artistic richness of late-medieval Nürnberg.

St. Sebaldus Kirche, Sebaldkircheplatz. Though it lacks the quantity of art treasures boasted by rival St. Lorenz, the lofty nave and choir of this 13th-century church are among the purest examples of Gothic ecclesiastical architecture in Germany, elegant, tall, and airy. Veit Stoss carved the crucifix at the east end of the nave, while the elaborate brass shrine, containing the earthly remains of St. Sebaldus himself, was cast by Peter Vischer around 1520.

Schöner Brunnen (Beautiful Fountain), *Hauptmarkt*. This is very much the symbol of the city. It's a 60-foot-(18-meter-)high fountain, carved around the year 1400, and decorated with 30 or so figures arranged in tiers. They include prophets, saints, local noblemen, electors of the Holy Roman Empire, and one or two strays such as Julius Caesar and Alexander the Great. It stands outside the Frauenkirche.

Spielzeug Museum (Toy Museum), *Karlstr. 13. Open Tues. to Sun. 10–5, closed Mon.* There are few places where a toy museum seems more appropriate. Nürnberg likes to call itself the toy capital of the world, and the museum here does its best to prove why. One or two of the exhibits date back to Renaissance times; most, however, are from the 19th century. Simple dolls vie with the complex mechanical toys, even a little Ferris wheel.

Tucherschlösschen (Tucher Castle), *Hirschelgasse 9. Open year-round, Mon. to Fri. 2–4, Sun. 10–11; closed Sat.* A small but select collection of art treasures competes for your attention with the mid-16th-century patrician family home—built for the Tucher family—in which it is housed.

Verkehrsmuseum (Museum of Transportation), *Lessingstr. 6. Open Apr. through Sept., Mon. to Sat. 10–5, Sun. 10–4; Oct. through Mar., daily 10–4.* December 7, 1835, saw the first ever train trip in Germany, from Nürnberg to nearby Fürth. A model of the epoch-making train is here at the Museum of Transportation, along with a series of original 19th- and early-20th-century trains and stage coaches. Stamp-lovers will also want to check out some of the 40,000-odd stamps in the extensive exhibits on the German postage system.

Rothenburg-ob-der-Tauber

Rothenburg is the kind of gem-like medieval town that even Walt Disney might have thought too good to be true. The reason for its survival is simple. Rothenburg (the ob-der-Tauber means "on the Tauber," the little river that flows through the town) was a small but thriving 17th-century town. It had grown up around the ruins—themselves destroyed in an earthquake—of two 12th-century churches. Then, it was laid low economically by the havoc of the Thirty Years'

War, the cataclysmic religious struggle that all but destroyed Germany in the 17th century. Its economic base devastated, the town slumbered, an all-but-forgotten backwater, until modern tourism rediscovered it. And here it is, milking its "best-preserved-medieval-town-in-Europe" image to the full, undoubtedly something of a tourist trap, but real enough for all that. You'll find, as a consequence, that prices here are appreciably steeper than in most other small German towns, but it's hard to visit this part of Germany and miss out on Rothenburg. There really is nowhere else quite like it.

GETTING THERE. Rothenburg is 25 miles (45 km) south of Würzburg. It sits astride both the Castle Road and the Romantic Road (of course). The long-distance Europa buses 190 and 189 both call at Rothenburg; likewise A3/A7 (Frankfurt–Feuchtwangen) and A6/A7 (Heilbronn–Würzburg) autobahns pass close by. Main line trains don't call at Rothenburg, though there's a limited local service from Steinach.

TOURIST OFFICE. Kur-und-Fremdenverkehrsamt, Marktplatz, 8803 Rothenburg-ob-der-Tauber (tel. 09861–40492).

WHERE TO STAY. Adam (M), Burggasse 29 (tel. 09861–2364). 13 rooms, all with bath. Small and welcoming, and simply oozing that peculiarly German fresh-faced, hand-carved atmosphere. The restaurant is reserved for hotel guests only.

Gasthof Glocke (M), Am Plönlein 1 (tel. 09861–3025). 30 rooms, all with bath. Better known as a cheerfully rustic and spic-and-span wine restaurant (complete with obligatory beams and rough plaster walls), the Glocke nonetheless has a number of comfortable, modern rooms. Not the most atmospheric place to stay, but a good bet for all that.

Mittermeier (M), Vörm Würzburger Turm 9 (tel. 09861–2259). 15 rooms, all with bath. American-style comfort rather than old Rothenburg charm is the order of the day here. But for those who feel the need for an indoor pool, a sauna, and a solarium to help unwind after a day in the Rothenburg time-capsule, this is the place to make for.

●Gasthof Greifen (I), Obere Schmiedgasse 5 (tel. 09861–2281). 22 rooms, most with bath. Great helpings of authentic Rothenburg atmosphere are available at this modest 14th-century inn. You won't find great luxury, but the sunny garden (perfect for early-morning coffee and rolls) and central location, plus a distinctly better-than-average restaurant, make Gasthof Greifen great all-round value.

WHERE TO EAT. ❥ **Baumeisterhaus** (M), Obere Schiedgasse 3 (tel. 09861–3404). Tops for good value and atmosphere. The Baumeister, located right by the Marktplatz, with its carved figures, looks as though it's come straight out of *Hansel and Gretel*. The courtyard of this late-16th-century building is especially appealing for summer dining. Prices are surprisingly affordable given not only the toy-maker-type setting but the high quality.

Ratsstube (M), Marktplatz 6 (tel. 09861–3404; note that the phone number is the same as that of neighboring Baumeisterhaus). Some find the relentless diet of wholesome but cute German restaurants in Rothenburg—beams, heavy wood furniture, scrubbed floors, frilly curtains, and the like—hard to swallow after a while. Those who like it should feel very much at home here. But note that it's a place for foaming beer mugs rather than appreciative wine sipping.

❥ **Tilman Riemenschneider** (I), Georgengasse 11 (tel. 09861–5061). Choose carefully, and dinner in this old wine tavern can be one of the best buys in Rothenburg. The food is resolutely hearty, and makes no attempt to mimic the nouvelle touches that have invaded so much German cooking.

WHAT TO SEE AND DO. With practically the whole of Rothenburg one large open-air museum, sightseeing here means first and foremost wandering around the historic area and just seeing where you end up. There are few outstanding sights as such. Be sure to walk along the city walls—they are about the most complete in Europe, and give great views of the historic area. Other standouts include:

St. Jacobs Kirche, *Geigengasse*. This large Gothic church, built between 1336 and 1448, is as famous for its Altar of the Holy Blood, carved by Tilman Riemenschneider in the early-16th century, as for its soaring architecture. The front panel of the altar has a complex wood carving of the Last Supper—Judas is the only figure not carved from the same piece of wood. Above it is a lump of crystal, held in a gold cross and said to contain drops of Christ's blood.

Kriminal und Foltermuseum (Museum of Crime and Torture), *Burggasse 3. Open Apr. through Oct., daily 9–6; Nov. through Mar., daily 12–4.* A large and gruesome collection of mainly medieval instruments of torture delights or appalls, though kids generally love it.

Alt Rothenburger Handwerkerhaus (Museum of Old Rothenburg Crafts), *Alter Stadtgraben. Open Apr. through Oct., daily 9–6 and 8 P.M.–9 P.M.* See how a Rothenburger craftsman and his family lived in the Middle Ages. An historic half-timbered home, dating back to 1270 (and which really was inhabited by a variety of craftsmen), has been lovingly restored to show just what life was like in those far-off times. It's a fair bet it wasn't half so hygenic as it seems here.

Rathaus, *Marktplatz. Open Apr. through Oct., daily 9–6.* The Rathaus, the town hall, stands in the main square, the logical place to begin your exploration of the town. Half the building is Gothic, built from 1240, the other half Classical, built from 1572. Originally, the whole structure was Gothic, but a fire in 1501 destroyed part of it, hence the newer, Renaissance, half which faces onto the main square. Go inside to see the **Historiengewölbe,** a museum housed in the vaults below the building and charting Rothenburg's role in the Thirty Years' War. Great prominence is given to the Meistertrunk, the Master Drink. This was an event that will follow you round Rothenburg. Upstairs, you can see the room in which it took place. It came about when Protestant Rothenburg was captured by Catholic forces. During the victory celebrations, the conquering general was embarrassed to find himself unable to drink a great tankard of wine in one go, as his manhood demanded. He volunteered to spare the town further destruction if one of the city councillors could drain the mighty draught. The mayor, a man by the name of Nusch, took up the challenge and succeeded, and Rothenburg was preserved. The tankard itself is on display at the Reichsstadtmuseum (see below). As it contains fully three and a quarter litres, the wonder is not so much that the conquering general was unable to knock it back but that he should have ever thought to try in the first place. An annual pageant celebrating the prodigious feat, with townsfolk parading the streets dressed in 17th-century garb, also helps keep alive the legend. The festival begins in the town hall, in the court room upstairs, the room in which the legendary feat is said to have occurred.

Ratsherrenstuben (City Councillors' Tavern), *Marktplatz.* This old tavern is opposite the town hall. Originally, it was a sort of up-market wine tavern, where only the town's leading families were allowed to drink. Today, the major interest is provided by the clock overlooking the square. At 11, 12, 1, 2, 9, and 10 the Master Drink is reenacted by the little figures that glide out of the clock's inner workings.

Reichsstadtmuseum (Imperial City Museum), *Klosterhof 5. Open Apr. through Oct., daily 10–5; Nov. through Mar., daily 1–5.* Two attractions in one: This is the **city museum,** containing a reasonable sampling of artifacts charting Rothenburg and its history, including the great tankard of Die Meistertrunk. It's housed in a onetime convent, the oldest parts of which date from the 13th century. Tour the old buildings—cloister, kitchens, and dormitory—and then see the collection.

Würzburg

Würzburg, the northernmost city of the Romantic Road, is a city of Rococo, a heady example of what can sometimes happen when great genius teams up with great wealth. The genius was provided by a German architect, Balthasar Neumann, and a Venetian painter, Giovanni Batista Tiepolro; the wealth by the pleasure-loving ruler, both spiritual and temporal, of Würzburg, Prince-Bishop Johann Philipp Franz von Schönsorn. Together, in the early 18th century, they built the Residenz, a glittering Rococo palace for the Prince-Bishop. Afterwards, the city became one of the most celebrated and spectacular in 18th-century Europe as a stream of kings, queens, emperors, princes, and aristocrats came to Würzburg to admire this high temple of the Rococo.

Of course Würzburg was a town of consequence before the 18th century. It had been ruled by prince-bishops since the 10th century—they lived in the grim bulk of the Marienburg Fortress, which you can still visit—and, standing on two major medieval trade routes, the city had prospered and grown fat. But it is the Residenz that is the main reason for visiting this appealing city on the river Main.

GETTING THERE. Würzburg stands at the junction of Germany's most important autobahns, making it easy to reach from just about any point in the country, and from a great many in the rest of Europe, too. The autobahns are: A3/A9 (Köln–Munich); A3 (Regensburg–Passau); A7 (Hamburg–Fussen); and A81/A98 (Würzburg–Basel). In addition, it is also the northern end of the Romantic Road. If you want to take the Romantic Road bus from the city, be sure to make reservations in advance (enquire at the tourist office). There are excellent train links to Würzburg from all parts of Germany.

TOURIST OFFICE. Fremdenverkehrs-und Kulturamt, Würzburg-Palais am Congress Centrum, 8700 Würzburg (tel. 0931–37335). There is also a branch at the train station (tel. 0931–37436); open Mon. to Fri. only, 8–8.

WHERE TO STAY. Franziskaner (M), Franziskanerplatz 2 (tel. 0931–50360). 46 rooms, all with bath. Though sited in a turn-of-the-century building, renovations in 1983 have transformed the Franziskaner into a bright and comfortable modern hotel. Better-than-average and moderately priced restaurant.

Walfisch (M), Am Pleidenturm 5 (tel. 0931–50055). 41 rooms, all with bath. Head here for comfort, no little style, the excellent wine tavern, and the great view of the Marienburg Fortress. Located near the river Main.

●**St. Josef** (I), Semmelstr. 39 (tel. 0931–53155). 35 beds, no rooms with bath. You won't find many more atmospheric places to stay in Würzburg than in this mid-15th-century gasthof. The carved and garlanded facade sets the mood. Inside, rooms are rather plain but comfortable. The restaurant offers exceptional value.

WHERE TO EAT. Ratskeller (M), Langgasse 1 (tel. 0931–13021). Atmosphere by the ton and hearty German food make this an absolutely typical town-hall restaurant. In summer, eat on the terrace.

Schiffbäuerin, Katzengasse 7 (tel. 0931–42487). Lovers of fish—try the trout or the pike—will find this old half-timbered restaurant irresistible. Wash your meal down with some of the excellent local wines. Choose carefully to stay within your budget.

●**Zum Stachel** (M), Gressengasse 1 (tel. 0931–52770). The oldest wine tavern in the city dates from 1413 and is every bit as atmospheric as you might expect, with heavy tables, exposed beams, and dark wooden paneling. Don't come expecting haute cuisine; the food is nothing if not heartily wholesome.

Juliusspital (I), Juliuspromenade 19. This is the wine tavern of the 18th-century Julius hospital. It's long on traditional decor, hearty foods, and great-value local wines.

MAJOR ATTRACTIONS. Marienburg Fortung. *Open Apr. through Sept., daily 9–5; Oct. through Mar., daily 10–4.* This was the heart of Würzburg from the mid-13th century to the early 18th, the residence of the prince-bishops of the city. The oldest buildings—note especially the **Marienkirche,** the core of the complex—date from even earlier, from around 700. In addition to the rough-hewn medieval fortifications, there are a number of fine Renaissance and Baroque apartments. But the real reason for visiting is to see the Mainfränkische Museum (the Main-Franconian museum), *open Apr. through Oct., daily 10–5; Nov. through Mar., daily 10–4.* The rich and varied history of Würzburg is brought alive by this remarkable assembly of art treasures. The number-one standout is the gallery devoted to Würzburg-born Renaissance sculptor Tilman Riemenschneider, but see also the paintings by Tiepolo and Cranach, and the collections of porcelain, firearms, and antique toys. Wine-lovers won't want to miss the old wine presses, some of them of stupendous size, and other exhibits charting the glorious history of Franconian wine. For those who prefer not to make the stiff climb up to the castle, there's a bus every half-hour from 9:45 from the Old Main bridge.

Residenz, *Residenzplatz. Open Apr. through Sept., Tues. to Sun. 9–5, closed Mon.; Oct. through Mar., Tues. to Sun. 10–4, closed Mon.* This is the highpoint of Bavarian Rococo, a palace of dazzling beauty containing a quite remarkable number of treasures. Anyone harboring doubts as to whether the prince-bishops of 18th-century Würzburg were bishops first and princes only incidentally will have them swept aside once and for all. The Residenz is irrefutable evidence of the worldly power of these glamorous rulers and men of God. It was built between 1719 and 1744 by a team led by Balthasar Neumann. The majority of the internal decoration was entrusted to the Italian stuccoist, or plaster-worker, Antonio Bossi and the Venetian painter Giovanni Batista Tiepolo. But the man whose spirit infuses the palace is von Schönborn, the luxury-loving prince-bishop of Würzburg. Sadly, he did not live to see his gorgeous new home finished.

Your tour of the building starts with a bang. As you enter, the largest Baroque staircase in the country—the **Treppenhaus**—stretches away from you. Halfway to the second floor, it divides in two and turns through 180 degrees. Above it is Tiepolo's giant fresco of *The Four Continents,* a gorgeous exercise in blue and pink with allegorical figures at the corners representing the continents. America boasts a contemplative Indian brave, Africa languorous camels and crocodiles. Make your way to the **Weisersaal,** the White Room, and from there to the grandest of the state rooms, the **Kaisersaal** or throne room. The Baroque/Rococo ideal of *Gesamtkunstwerk*—the fusion of the arts—is illustrated to perfection here. Architecture melts into stucco, stucco invades the frescoes, the frescoes extend the real space of the room into their fantasy world. Nothing is quite what it seems; and no expense is spared to make it so. Tiepolo's frescoes actually show the visit of the Emperor Frederick Barbarossa to Würzburg in the 12th century to claim his bride. That the characters all wear 16th-century Venetian dress is of no account. There are few great interiors anywhere in the world that use such startling opulence to such effect: The room is airy, magical, intoxicating. You'll find more of the same heady brew in the **Hofkirche,** the chapel, further proof that the prince-bishop saw no conflict between his love of ostentation and the service of God. Among the lavish marbles, rich gilding, and delicate stuccowork, note the Tiepolo altarpieces, ethereal visions of *The Fall of the Angels* and *The Assumption of the Virgin.*

Finally, tour the palace garden, the **Hofgarten;** the entrance is by the chapel. The 18th-century European taste for formal gardens, with trim, ankle-high shrubs outlining geometrical flowerbeds and gravel walks, plus stately gushing fountains, is illustrated here as well as anywhere else in the country.

OTHER ATTRACTIONS. Dom (Cathedral of St. William), *Domstr*. This is the fourth-largest Romanesque church in Germany, built from 1045. Step inside and you'll find yourself, disconcertingly enough, in a shimmering Rococo treasure house. This is, perhaps, only fitting; Prince-Bishop von Schönborn, instigator of the Residenz, is buried here, and it's hard to imagine him slumbering amid the dour weightiness of a Romanesque edifice.

Marienkapelle, *Marktplatz*. Those whose tastes run to the Gothic rather than the Rococo will find this slim, late-15th-century church an oasis of calm after the exuberant excesses of the 18th-century Würzburg. They won't escape completely, however: architect Balthasar Neumann is buried here.

Neumünster, *Schönbornstr*. Originally an austere 11th-century basilica, this onetime abbey church has also been transformed into a Baroque/Rococo wonder. In the cloister you'll find the tomb of Walter von der Vogelweide, one of the Minnesingers of Nürnberg, who spent his final years at Würzburg.

------------------- ◆ -------------------

S P L U R G E S

A Night at the Eisenhut Hotel, Rothenburg, Herrngasse, 8803 Rothenburg-ob-der-Tauber (tel. 09861–2041). It seems appropriate that the prettiest small town in Germany should have the prettiest small hotel in the country. It stands in the center of the town and is located in what were originally four separate town houses—the oldest dating from the 12th century, the youngest from the 16th. Inside, there's a riot of antiques and other unique decoration, the whole fusing to create a distinctively Bavarian, yet classy, quality. There's a fine restaurant with a good choice of wines, including a good-value "wine of the week." Prices start at around DM 210 for a double room.

A Performance at the Festspielhaus, Bayreuth. Opera-lovers cheerfully admit that there are few more instense operatic experiences to be had than at the annual Wagner Festival in Bayreuth. This is the Holy Grail. The festival is held in June, but write long, long before that if you want tickets (at least 12 months), and be prepared for much higher rates at all hotels and restaurants. Tickets are available from **Theaterkasse,** Luitpoldplatz 9, 8580 Bayreuth (tel. 0921–69001). If you can't get seats for the Wagner festival and/or prices seem too dauntingly high, remember that the Bavarian State Opera also performs in Bayreuth every year at the end of May. Prices are a little lower and tickets not quite so scarce. Full details of all performances are available from Theaterkasse.

◆

THE RHINE AND MOSELLE

The Germans like to call it "Vater Rhein," Father Rhine. The rest of the world knows it simply as the Rhine. It's the longest river in Europe, extending 1,355 km (840 miles) from eastern Switzerland to Holland and the North Sea. En route, it passes through or borders six countries: Switzerland, Liechtenstein, Austria, Germany, France, and Holland. Throughout recorded history it has been the most important river in Europe; a natural frontier and a great highway.

Of all the many and varied reaches of the Rhine, none has quite the same array of scenery, history, architecture, and natural beauty as that contained in the 129 km (80 miles) between Koblenz and Mainz—the Mittel Rhein. It is a land of steep and thickly wooded hills, of terraced vineyards rising step by step above the river banks, of massive hilltop castles, of tiny villages hugging the shore. And it is a land of legend and myth. The Lorelei, a steep mountain of rock jutting out of the river, home of the beautiful and bewitching maiden who lured boatmen to a watery end in the swift currents, is perhaps the most enduring. There are the Nibelungs, too, a Burgundian race said to have lived on the river banks around whom Wagner wove no fewer than four of his epic operas.

The most famous tributary of the Rhine is the Moselle,

which joins the river at Koblenz. This is another great wine-producing area, and contains scenery almost as striking as that along the Rhine. At its western end is Trier, once one of the great cities of the Roman Empire.

The Rhine—specifically the Mittel Rhein—is one of Germany's major tourist regions, drawing visitors from around the world. As a result, prices here for just about everything are high, often a good deal more so than elsewhere in the country. This doesn't mean that you have no choice but to forget about your budget and splurge, splurge, splurge. Follow a few simple rules and you'll be surprised how far you can make your money go. Rule number 1: Avoid hotels in towns and villages actually on the Rhine; the nearer the river you get the higher the cost. No more than two or three miles from the Rhine prices fall appreciably. Check out farmhouse accommodations especially—the German National Tourist Office at home and local tourist offices on the spot can give you full details. Rule number 2: Make reservations as far in advance as you can; don't wait till you arrive. That's the way to make sure you stay in the place you want and can afford. Rule number 3: Take full advantage of one of the most comprehensive networks of public transportation in Germany and save yourself dollars. The whole of the Moselle, for example, is served by German Railroads' great-value *Moseltalbahn*, a bus calling at every major place of interest along the river. One ticket allows you to get on and off the bus wherever you want, just so long as you don't go back on your route. Similarly, Rhine river boats operated by the KD line have a combined rail-boat ticket that lets you alternate as many times as you like between boats and trains. Their ferries ply up and down the river at frequent intervals during the summer, and no trip to the area is complete without at least one river journey. So take the boat out and the train home, and save yourself money.

Our ● symbol represents our Highly Recommended Selection. The German National Tourist Office and local offices have full details of all services. Otherwise, contact the KD line at Frankenwerft 15, 5000 Köln 1 (tel. 0221–20880).

Bacharach

Bacharach is the sort of tiny old wine village, complete with 15th-century encircling walls and hilltop castle, that has made the Rhine a tourist magnet. Not that it's especially spoilt; the town seems somehow to have avoided the crass overdevelopment that can so easily destroy what it seeks to exploit. Its name comes from the Latin "Baccaracum," meaning the altar of Bacchus, a reference to a great stone that stood on the river bank until it was dynamited in the last century during engineering work on the river. The name of course also makes clear that this is wine country. Wine tasting in and around Bacharach can be arranged via the tourist office. The first weekend in October sees a colorful wine festival.

GETTING THERE. The most romantic way to get to Bacharach is by river boat; all KD boats call in here. Bacharach is on Rheingoldstrasse—Rhine Gold Road—which runs from Boppard to Bingen. There is no train station.

TOURIST OFFICE. Fremdenverkehrsamt, Oberstr. 1, 6533 Bacharach (tel. 06743–2968).

WHERE TO STAY. Im Malerwinkel (M), Blücherstr. 41 (tel. 06743–1239). 20 rooms, most with bath. This historic half-timbered inn dates back to 1696. Located right in the center of town, it is excellent value. No restaurant.

ATTRACTION. Burg Stahleck. *Visitors may tour the exterior only.* Some people will be visiting this 12th-century fortress high above the town to stay in what must be the youth hostel with the most romantic setting in Germany. Others will come simply to admire the buildings and the view over the Rhine. The castle was built from 1135 for the bishops of Köln; in 1190 it was presented by Holy Roman Emperor Barbarossa to his brother, Conrad. Thereafter, it passed into the hands of the Wittelsbachs, the Bavarian ruling dynasty, before falling into ruins at the end of the 17th century. In this century it was taken over by the Rhineland Historic Monuments Association, who rebuilt it and opened it as a youth hostel.

Bernkastel-Kues

Bernkastel-Kues is a twin town on the Moselle, located about midway between Trier and Koblenz; the north bank is Bernkastel, the south bank is Kues. Wine has long been the lifeblood of the town. The vineyards clinging to the steep slopes around the town produce some of the best vintages in the Moselle. Visit in the first week in September and Bernkastel-Kues will have given itself over to its heady Mittelmosel wine festival, complete with fireworks and colorful processions. But you'll find many other activities year-round, especially in summer. There are indoor and outdoor pools; rowboats and canoes to rent; waterskiing; and river trips. Those in search of history and architecture will not be disappointed either. The historic area around Marktplatz is among the most appealing of all the Moselle wine towns.

GETTING THERE. Coming by train change at Wengerohr—it's on the main Köln–Trier route—for the half-hour ride to Bernkastel-Kues. The Moseltalbahn and express buses T81 and T82 all stop at Bernkastel-Kues. The town is also on Moselweinstrasse—Moselle Wine Road—Highway B53.

TOURIST OFFICE. Am Gestade 5, 5550 Bernkastel-Kues (tel. 06531–3588). Tours of the town leave Thurs. in summer at 3:30 from St. Michael's Church, Marktplatz.

WHERE TO STAY. For low rates and as much local color as you'll ever want, stay at one of the vineyards around town. Two to try are: **Manfred Bohn,** Goldbachstr. 7 (tel. 06531–8443), 4 rooms, located in the Andel suburb by the river, with wine tasting and bike rental; **Fritz and Else Schneider,** Goldbachstr. 12 (tel. 06531–8438), stay here for more than six days and all wine tasting is offered free. Both are open Apr. through Oct. only.

    ● **Hotel Burg Landshut** (M), Gestade 11 (tel. 06531–3019). 30 rooms, all with bath. The riverside location alone is enough to single out the Burg Lanshut—try for a room with a balcony. The light and spacious rooms, and the traditional wine cellar, make the hotel a particularly good buy.

    Zur Post (I), Gestade 17 (tel. 06531–3001). 40 rooms, all with bath. More traditional Moselle hospitality is found in this early 19th-century inn. It was originally a post inn and some half-timbered interior walls have been carefully preserved. The restaurant offers a good-value fixed-price menu.

WHERE TO EAT. Doctor-Weinstuben (M), Hebegasse 5 (tel. 06531–6081). An atmospheric hotel restaurant whose building dates from the mid-17th century and has been an inn since 1830. Garlands of carved vines and flowers abound, plus heavy exposed beams, sturdy tables, and half timbering. Fixed-price menus are available, plus a wide range of local wines.

    ● **Ratskeller** (I), **Am Markt** (tel. 06531–2423). Hearty food, frothing giant-sized mugs of beer, and golden Moselle wines make this dark and appealing wine cellar in the Renaissance town hall a must for those in search of traditional German food and drink.

ATTRACTIONS. Burg Landshut. The ruins of this once-commanding 13th-century fortress tower above the town. Visit it for the amazing view of the Moselle and to wander around its flower-strewn remains. There's a little open-sided bus up to the castle from the parking lot by the river; it runs on the hour in the summer.

Geburtshaus des Nikolaus von Kues (Birthplace of Nicolaus Cusanus), *Nikolausfer 49, Kues. Open Apr. through Oct. Tues. to Sat. 10–12 and 2:30–5, Sun. 10–12; closed rest of year.* Nikolaus von Kues was a German Renaissance man—a philosopher and theologian, and later a cardinal. He is buried in the chapel (except for his heart, which was taken to Rome). His birthplace contains an exhibit on his life as well as changing art exhibits. Among his many good works was founding the **St. Nikolaus Hospital** in 1447, which is now open to visitors (tel. 06531–2260).

Marktplatz (Market Square). This is the heart of Bernkastel-Kues, and about as authentic a small-town German market square as you could wish for. The majority of the buildings are great late-medieval/early-Renaissance half-timbered structures, their facades a maze of intricately carved beams. The Renaissance **Rathaus,** the town hall, strikes a more restrained, Classical note. In the center of the square is the **Michaelsbrunnen,** or Michael's Fountain, a graceful 17th-century work. During the wine festival, wine replaces the water jetting out of the fountain.

Cochem

Cochem is an old wine town on the north bank of the Moselle, located about 48 km (30 miles) west of Koblenz and 85 km (55 miles) east of Trier. It's a typical Moselle riverside town, overlooked by vineyards and the bulk of the Reichsburg, the imperial castle, the town's major attraction. You can hire boats or take a river trip from the landing stage. Wine tasting and visits to vineyards can be arranged at the tourist office.

GETTING THERE. Cochem is on the main Koblenz–Trier railroad. It's also on Moselweinstrasse, Moselle Wine Road, Highway B53. The Moseltalbahn bus calls here.

TOURIST OFFICE. Verkehrsamt, Enderplatz, 5590 Cochem (tel. 02671–3971).

WHERE TO STAY. ✆ Brixiade (M), Uferstr. 13 (tel. 02671–3015). 40 rooms, all with bath. Despite a surprisingly modern exterior, the Brixiade has been welcoming guests—including Kaiser Wilhelm II—for more than a century. Ask for a room with a view over the town and the river. The restaurant offers a fixed-price menu and magnificent local wines. Dine on the terrace in summer.

Am Rosenhügel (M), **Valwiger Str. 57** (tel. 02671–1396). 23 rooms, all with bath. The emphasis here is on solid comfort and value for money rather than Teutonic atmosphere. Those who appreciate sturdy German hospitality will feel at home. Some rooms have great views over the river. No restaurant.

Thul (M), Brauselaystr. 27 (tel. 02671–7134). 27 rooms, most with shower. Modern and rather functional family-run hotel offering traditional German comforts. The restaurant is better than average if lacking in atmosphere.

WHERE TO EAT. ◒ Weissmuhle (M), Endertal (tel. 02671–8955).
You'll want to eat here as much to see the charmingly rustic village of Endertal just outside of Cochem as to sample the fare offered by the restaurant. It's decorated in that inimitable German gingerbread style, with carved beams and lace curtains galore. Try the trout, freshly caught from the Moselle, or the spit-roasted kebabs.

Noss (I), Moselpromenade 17 (tel. 02671–3612). There's no better place to soak up the atmosphere of old Cochem than in the cavernous wine cellars of the Noss. The food is reasonable rather than memorable, but it's the atmosphere that counts.

ATTRACTION. Reichsburg (Imperial Castle). *Open mid-Mar. through mid-Nov., daily 9–6. Guided tours on the hour between 9 and 5.* This is one of the largest and most impressive castles in Germany. It's located on the rise behind the town and can be reached in about 20 minutes on foot. The views over Cochem and the river are predictably sensational. Much of the castle is actually 19th century (there are also some post-World War II renovations), but the oldest parts of the building, notably the octagonal **central tower,** date back to 1030. Louis XIV destroyed a good part of the fortress in 1689, and it remained in ruins until its 19th-century rescuers moved in.

Koblenz

Koblenz stands at the confluence of the Moselle and the Rhine. The heart of the historic area is close to the point where the rivers meet at the Deutsches Eck; literally, the "corner of Germany." The city's strategic location helps explain both its significance and its age. The first settlement was Roman, founded in A.D. 9. The Romans called it Castrum at Confluentes, "the castle at the confluence," which was later corrupted to Koblenz. It was a powerful city in the Middle Ages, controlling trade on both rivers. Despite appalling war-time bomb damage that saw 85% of the Old Town destroyed, conscientious restoration has done much to re-create the atmosphere of old Koblenz.

It's an excellent base from which to explore both the Moselle and the Rhine. All KD ferries call in here, so stop off for a day or two if you're taking a cruise on the Rhine. The city offers a wide range of low-cost entertainment, from walking along the miles of paths that run through the surrounding forests and meadows, wine tasting in one of the numerous vineyards around the city, or just a visit to one of the wine taverns in the Weindorf, the wine "village" overlooking the Rhine. The last weekend in September sees the Koblenz wine festival, one of the country's most uproarious (though make reservations well in advance if that's when you plan to visit). On the second Saturday in August there's a superb firework display in Ehrenbreistein Fortress.

GETTING THERE. Koblenz stands at the hub of a dense road and rail network. It's easy to reach by train from just about anywhere in Germany. A3, A48, and A61 autobahns pass close to Koblenz; B9 Rhine Valley Highway runs through the city. All KD, Moselle, and Lahn river boats stop at Koblenz.

TOURIST OFFICE. Press und Fremdenverkehrsamt der Stadt Koblenz, Verkehrspavillon, 5400 Koblenz (tel. 0261–31304). There is also an information office on Konrad-Adenauer-Ufer (tel. 0261–33134) on the Rhine promenade (the Rheinanlagen).

RIVER TRIPS. There are trips from May through Sept. at 11, 2:15, 3, and 5 to the castles at Braubach, Stolzenfels, Lahheck, and Marnsburg. You can interrupt your trip at any of the landing stages en route. Fares are between DM 6 and DM 12 per person. Call Merkelbach Shipping Company (tel. 0261–76810) for further details.

Round trips to the Lorelei, calling in St. Goar and St. Goarshausen en route, depart daily at 2, May through Oct. Call 0261–37744 for further details.

WHERE TO STAY. Though Koblenz has a wide range of accommodations at all prices, the best budget-bets are those in the suburbs, north and south of the center of town. Central hotels, especially those in the Old Town and along the Rhine, are tops for atmosphere, but are more expensive.

Hamm (M), St.-Josef-Str. 32 (tel. 0261–34546). 30 rooms, most with bath. Stay here for adequate overnight accommodations rather than great comfort or atmosphere; the building is modern and nondescript. Rail travelers will appreciate the location: It's a five-minute walk from the train station. No restaurant.

➛ Trierer Hof (M), Deinhardplatz (tel. 0261–31060). 28 rooms, all with bath. A terrific location right by the Koblenz Theater and behind the palace makes this 18th-century building a good bet for those who want to be in the heart of things. Rooms are large, if plain. There's a reasonable restaurant serving Yugoslavian specialties.

Union (I), Löhrstr. 73 (tel. 0261–33003). 48 rooms, most with bath. The Union is no more than a two- or three-minute walk from the historic area. Functional comfort sets the tone. No restaurant.

WHERE TO EAT. ● **Weinhaus Hubertus** (M), Florinsmarkt 54 (tel. 0261–31177). This is about the most atmospheric restaurant in town. The flower-strewn half-timbered exterior gives a good idea of the country-style mood inside. Antiques and dark wood predominate. Food is ample and served with gusto.

Weindorf. You'll find an unbeatable combination of atmosphere and low prices in the little wine taverns that make up the wine village (it was purpose-built in 1925 for the German Wine Exhibit). It stands by the Rhine at the west end of Pfaffendorfer Bridge. Visit in good weather if you can and sit outside. Music and dancing—and all of it free—add to the heady atmosphere.

MAJOR ATTRACTIONS. Deutsches Eck. This is the point where the Rhine and the Moselle meet. Climb the steps to the viewing platform for the terrific view over Ehrenbreitstein Fortress on the other side of the Rhine. There used to be a statue of Wilhelm I here; now there's a memorial, unveiled in 1953, to German unity. About the most enjoyable way to get to the Deutsches Eck is along the Rheinanlagen, the Rhine promenade. Then walk down to the Alte Stadt, the Old Town, along the Moselanlagen, the Mosel promenade. Standouts in the Old Town include the **Kastor Kirche** and the **Liebfrauenkirche** (see below), and the **Rheinmuseum** (Ehrenbreitstein) *open Easter through Oct., daily 9–5,* which charts the history of the Rhine.

Festung Ehrenbreitstein (Ehrenbreitstein Fortress). *Open year-round, daily 9–5.* This is among the largest and most commanding fortresses in Germany, a vast complex of military buildings on a 400-ft.-high rock on the east bank of the Rhine. The views alone justify a visit. The earliest buildings date from around 1100 but the bulk of the fortress was constructed in the 16th century. In 1801 Napoleon more or less managed to blow the entire structure to pieces. Then in the mid-19th century the whole thing was rebuilt, making it one of the largest fortresses in Europe. The U.S. Army took it over after World War I and stayed here almost 10 years. In addition to containing the largest youth hostel in Germany, the fortress is also home to the **Museum für Vorgeschichte und Volkskunde,** the Museum of Pre-history and Ethnography. The most dramatic way to get to the fortress is to take the cablecar (the *sesselbahn*). If you suffer from vertigo, walk up, though the climb is steep.

Liebfrauenkirche (Church of Our Lady), *Am Plan*. This venerable church is the focal point of the Old Town. It stands on the foundations of a Roman building at the highest point of the historic area. The bulk of the church is Romanesque—austere and weighty—but the **choir** is late 15th-century Gothic, and generally held to be among the finest and most ornate examples of its type. Rising somewhat incongruously above the west front are two Baroque **towers** topped by onion domes. They were put up between 1693–4.

St. Kastor Kirche, *Kastorstr*. Like the Liebfrauenkirche, the Kastor Kirche contains elements from many different periods, the earliest—the bases of the west towers—dating back to the Carolingian period in the 8th century. It was here that the Treaty of Verdun was signed in 843, the treaty that formalised the division of Charlemagne's great empire between his sons and in effect led to the creation of Germany and France as separate states. Inside, there's a striking combination of Romanesque—the **nave columns** especially—and Gothic styles—the complex and decorative **fan vaulting** of the nave.

OTHER ATTRACTIONS. Mittelrhein Museum, *Florinsmarkt 15. Open year-round, Tues. to Sat. 10–1 and 2:30–5:30, Sun. 10–1; closed Mon.* The building in which the museum is housed—it was originally the Merchants' Hall and dates from 1419—is as interesting as the exhibits. These trace the development of Koblenz and the Rhineland, with examples from pre-historic times through the present day.

Rüdesheim

Rüdesheim may only be a small town but it is about the most important tourist destination on the Rhine. It's in the Rheingau, that stretch of the Rhine between Wiesbaden and Bingen where the river bends west for about 24 km (15 miles). The south-facing slopes of the Rheingau produce the finest of Germany's wines—legend has it that the first vines here were planted by Charlemagne—and at the heart of the Rheingau is Rüdesheim.

Three million visitors annually testify to the enduring popularity of the town, and one look is enough to tell you why. It's a town of winding streets and hidden courtyards, of ancient half-timbered and gabled buildings decked out with geraniums, presenting that sort of Brothers Grimm atmosphere you only find in Germany.

The heart of the place is Drosselgasse, a narrow street lined with wine taverns. Visit in June, July, or August—'88 dates for the Rüdesheim wine festival are August 12–15—and you can barely fight your way through the crowds surging in and out of the taverns. Some people love it; others find it all rather tacky.

With prices peaking in the summer for all hotels, consider staying in nearby Assmanshausen where prices are marginally lower and the wine flows just as freely, or try Bingen on the opposite bank of the Rhine, where prices are appreciably lower. Alternatively, come in spring or fall. Most hotels are still open, while the wine taverns never close.

While wine provides the *raison d'etre* of Rüdesheim, there are some interesting excursions in the area, notably to the castles of Burg Ehrenfels and Boosenburg. One of the major attractions—expect crowds—is the annual "Rhine in Flames" firework display ('88 date is July 2) held at Bingen Loch immediately opposite Rüdesheim.

GETTING THERE. Most express trains from Frankfurt and Köln stop at Rüdesheim. The town has equally good road links. B42 Rhine Valley Highway goes through the town, while A66 (Wiesbaden–Frankfurt) and A61 (Köln–Bingen) autobahns pass close by. There is a regular ferry service from Bingen on the west bank of the Rhine.

TOURIST OFFICE. Stadtische Verkehrsamt, Rheinstr. 16, 6220 Rüdesheim (tel. 06722–2962).

WHERE TO STAY. Alte Bauernschänke Nassauer Hof (M), Niederwaldstr. 18 (tel. 06722–2332). 67 rooms, all with bath. This old wine tavern dates from 1408, and, though modernized and comfortable, the rustic carved-wood atmosphere has been carefully preserved. There's both a wine tavern and a beer tavern, plus a noisy and bustling restaurant, but choose carefully to stick to your budget. It's located in Assmanshausen.

Gasthof Krancher (M), Eibinger Oberstr. 4 (tel. 06722–2762). 75 rooms, all with bath. Wine is the dominant theme in this new two-building complex. It's located a 10-minute walk from the historic area next to vineyards owned by Herr Krancher himself, who will arrange wine tasting and visits to his vineyards.

❺Hotel und Weinhaus Febenkeller (M), Oberstr. 64 (tel. 06722–2094). 64 rooms, all with bath. A combination of age and fresh modern comfort makes this a standout among Rüdesheim hotels. The building dates from the early 18th century and comes complete with a carved and painted exterior—vine leafs predominate—and a delightful room for wine tasting. It's located round the corner from Drosselgasse.

WHERE TO EAT. Prices are high, so cost-conscious visitors should aim to snack at one of the many wine taverns along the Drosselgasse. Typical Rhineland specialties offer the best value. Try *Sauerbraten* (marinated beef), *Himmel un Äd* (a potato-based dish), or *Döppekooche* (a sort of sausage and mashed potato hash). It's hard to recommend individual wine taverns; most offer similar food and wine. But try:

Drosselhof, perhaps *the* Drosselgasse wine tavern, with swaying crowds and singing and dancing all night long.

Rüdesheimer Schloss, atmosphere and reasonable food compete with an immense wine list—it includes some 19th-century vintages which will probably cost you more than your entire vacation—in this cavernous 18th-century haunt.

ATTRACTIONS. **Niederwaldenkmal** (Niederwald Monument). Standing high above the Rhine and reached either by cablecar from Assmanshausen or on foot from Rüdesheim (head up Oberstr., then follow the signs) in about 30 minutes, is this mammoth Classically-inspired statue of Germania. It was built at the command of Bismarck to commemorate the unification of Germany in 1871. At the unveiling in 1883—held in the presence of the Kaiser and Bismarck—an anarchist attempted to blow up the statue and assembled dignitaries. In true comic-opera style a shower put out the fuse on his bomb. The statue is impressive, if pompous, and the views from its site are remarkable. You can continue along the path to **Niederwald Park,** laid out in the 18th century by Count Carl Maxilian von Geisenheim as the grounds for his sumptuous hunting lodge—today an even more sumptuous hotel—to the Rittersaal view point and the mock ruined castle at Rossel. From here the view is even more astounding. The walk from and to Rüdesheim takes about two hours.

Museum für die Geschichte des Weines (Wine Museum), *Rheinstr. 2, Brömserburg. Open year-round, daily 9–12 and 2–5.* Two thousand years of wine growing are charted in this extensive collection. Drinking vessels, bottles, winepresses, even corkscrews, bring the world of Rhine wine to life. It's located in Brömserburg Castle.

St. Goarshausen

St. Goarshausen, on the east bank of the Rhine below Koblenz, is of interest chiefly as the nearest point to the Lorelei, the great craggy rock that rises nearly 400 feet above the Rhine, home, so the legend goes, of a water nymph who lured sailors to their death by her bewitching singing. In fact the river is particularly treacherous here, so there's some substance to the story. The high rocky cliffs that overlook the river, allied to a slight narrowing of the channel, produce rapid and dangerous currents that can still send smaller craft spinning out of control. The town itself will please those who feel unhappy at the rampant commercialization and overcrowding of Rüdesheim and the other tourist traps of the Rhine. There are no outstanding sights, but the medieval heart of St. Goarshausen is attractive and relatively unspoilt. The town can also make a good base from which to strike out down lovely Lorelei Burgen Strasse, Lorelei Castle Road.

GETTING THERE. The main Frankfurt–Köln train route passes through St. Goarshausen, though not all trains stop here. A61 (Koblenz–Ludwigshafen) autobahn passes by St. Goarshausen on the opposite (west) bank of the Rhine, from where a regular ferry runs across to St. Goarshausen. Rhine Valley Highway B42 passes through the town. KD steamers also stop at St. Goarshausen.

TOURIST OFFICE. Verkehrsamt, Bahnhofstr., 5422 St. Goarshausen (tel. 06771–427).

WHERE TO STAY. Restaurant-Pension Hermann's Muhle (M), Forchbachstr. (tel. 06771–7317). 8 rooms, all with bath. Small guest house about three-quarters of a mile outside town on the road to the Lorelei. Those who value peace will feel at home. Rooms are functional but comfortable.

Colonius, Bahnhofstr. 35 (tel. 06771–604). 34 rooms, most with bath. Convenience rather than atmosphere is the reason for staying here; but the central location and low prices are hard to ignore.

ATTRACTIONS. Lorelei. You can either take one of the regular ferries that make the trip to the Lorelei—though the rock is curiously less impressive from the water—or drive up the road that winds around the river bank (there are frequent buses) and walk up the footpath to the viewing point.

Burg Katz and Burg Maus. These twin castles—Burg Katz located just to the north of St. Goarshausen, Burg Maus to the south—were long rivals in the lucrative matter of the collection of river taxes. Burg Katz was built in 1371 by Count Wilhelm II von Katzenelnbogen, literally "cat's elbow", hence the name. It was the count who nicknamed the rival up-stream Burg Maus Castle, meaning "mouse castle." The games of cat and mouse have long since come to an end. Neither castle is open to the public, but both can be seen from the outside.

Trier

Trier claims to be the oldest town in Germany, founded, some say, by the Assyrian Prince Trebata around 2000 B.C. What's beyond dispute, however, is that around 2,000 years later the Romans settled here and made Trier—Augusta Trevorium—one of the leading cities of their empire, briefly promoting it at one stage to Roma Secunda, the Second Rome. It rapidly grew to become a powerful administrative capital, adorned with all the noble and powerful civic buildings of a major Roman settlement—public baths, palaces, barracks, an amphitheater, and temples. Later Roman emperors, Diocletian (who made it one of the four joint capitals of the empire) and Constantine especially, lived in Trier for years at a time.

Trier survived the Roman collapse to become an important early Christian center, and later one of the most powerful archbishoprics in the Holy Roman Empire. The city thrived throughout the Renaissance and Baroque periods, taking full advantage of its location at the meeting point of major east–west, north–south trade routes to grow fat on the commerce that passed through it. It also became one of Germany's most important wine-exporting centers. A later claim to fame is as the birthplace of Karl Marx.

Trier is located at the western end of the Moselle, and makes an excellent base from which to explore the snaking course of the river. It will take about two days to make the trip by boat along the Moselle to Koblenz and the Rhine, calling in at various little wine towns en route. '88 dates for the Trier Wine Festival are July 31 to Aug. 3.

GETTING THERE. The nearest international airport is in neighboring Luxembourg. If you plan to start your German vacation at Trier it's significantly easier to fly directly to Luxembourg and cross over the frontier into Germany than to fly to Frankfurt. Otherwise, there are train links with almost all major German cities. There are bus connections with Aachen and Frankfurt. A1, A48, and A602 autobahns all pass through Trier.

TOURIST OFFICE. Tourist-Information, An der Porta Nigra, Postfach 3830, 5500 Trier (tel. 0651–48071). Stop in here to pick up a **Tageskarte Trier,** a go-as-you-please transit ticket good for the entire public transportation network for any 24-hour period. Cost is DM 5. Up to three children under 15 can ride free if accompanied by an adult holder of the card. If you'll be in the city over a weekend, get a **Wochenende Familienkarte,** a weekend family pass. For DM 6 three adults and three children are entitled to unlimited travel on all buses.

WHERE TO STAY. Am Hugel (M), Bernhardstr. 14 (tel. 0651–33066). 25 rooms, all with bath. Comfort and quiet are guaranteed in this small hotel; it's located in a park near the center of town. No restaurant, but there's an attractive wine terrace where you can eat breakfast in the summer.

Deutschherrenhof (M), Deutschherrenstr. 32 (tel. 0651–48308). 13 rooms, all with bath. It's central location, close to the Porta Nigra, and rather understated decor add up to a reasonable, if not outstanding, place to lay your head for the night.

☛**Petrisberg** (M), Sickingenstr. 11 (tel. 0651–1181). 31 rooms, all with bath. Striking views through immense windows onto forests and vineyards provide the most compelling reason to stay in this medium-sized hotel. Antiques abound, and there's a good wine tavern in the basement. It's located about a seven-minute walk from the amphitheater. No restaurant.

Klosterschenke (I), Klosterstr. 10 (tel. 0651–6089). 9 rooms, all with bath. Simple rooms in a historic building, plus a good-value restaurant; eat in the garden in summer.

WHERE TO EAT. Europa Park Hotel Mövenpick (M), Kaiserstr. 29 (tel. 0651–71950). Eat in the excellent-value restaurant of this otherwise expensive modern hotel. Sunday brunch is an especially good buy.

Lenz Weinstuben (M), Viehmarkt Platz 4–5 (tel. 0651–45310). This wine tavern is right in the center of town, in the old cattle market. An immense choice of wines is available to wash down the regional specialties, but choose carefully to stick to your budget.

☛**Zum Domstein** (M), Hauptmarkt 5 (tel. 0651–74490). This is the place to make for if atmosphere and wine rate high as priorities. It's located in a series of interlinking rooms in an old house, and offers the very best kind of hearty German welcome. You can splurge on the *à la carte* menu or snack on simple fare. But it's the wine that counts; wine tasting can be arranged for as little as DM 5 per person, with six different wines lined up for you to sample.

MAJOR ATTRACTIONS. If you plan on visiting all the Roman monuments, buy the combined entry ticket from the tourist office. Cost is DM 6.

Amphitheater, *Olewiger Str.* Open Jan. through Mar., Tues. to Sun. 9–1 and 2–5, closed Mon.; Apr. through Sept. daily 9–1 and 2–6; Oct., daily 9–1 and 2–5; Nov., Tues. to Sun. 9–1 and 2–5, closed Mon.; closed Dec. Once 20,000 people could be accommodated here—all of them seated—to watch gladiatorial combats and games.

Today, weeds, grass, and flowers grow over and around the formerly massive building. It's actually the oldest Roman structure in Trier, built around A.D. 100. You can climb down into the cellars beneath the arena to see the machinery that was used to change the scenery and the cells where lions and other wild animals were kept before being unleashed to devour maidens and do battle with gladiators.

Kaiserthermen (Imperial Baths), *southern end of Kürfürstliche Palace Gardens. Open same hours as amphitheater*. These were once the third largest public baths in the Roman empire; only Diocletian's baths in Yugoslavia and the baths of Caracalla in Rome were bigger. They covered an area 270 yards long and 164 yards wide. Today, only the weed-strewn fragments of the **Calderium**, the hot baths, are left, but they are enough to give a fair idea of the original splendor and size of the complex. When the Romans pulled out, the baths were turned into a fortress and then became a church before becoming a fortress again. Don't confuse them with the much smaller Barbarathermen (open same hours) in Kaiser-Friedrich-Str.

Dom (Trier Cathedral), *Domplatz. Open year-round, daily 7–12 and 2–6; guided tours daily at 2*. If you want a potted history of Trier, visit the cathedral. There is practically no period of the city's past that is not represented here. It stands on the site of the Palace of Helen of Constantine, mother of the Emperor Constantine. This was knocked down by Constantine in A.D. 326, who put up a large church in its place, which in turn burned down in 336, when a second and even larger church was built. Parts of the foundations of this third building can be seen in the east end of the present structure, itself begun in about 1035. Today's cathedral is a weighty and sturdy edifice, with small round-headed windows, rough stonework, and asymmetrical towers, the whole as much like a fortress as a church. Inside, Gothic styles predominate—the result of remodeling in the 13th century—though there are also many Baroque tombs, altars, and confessionals. This architectural jumble—Romanesque, Gothic, and Baroque—gives the whole place the air of an up-market antique shop. Make sure you visit the **Domschatzmuseum**, the treasury, site of two extraordinary objects. One is the 10th-century **Andreas Trag Altar,** the St. Andrew's altar, made of gold by local craftsmen and supposedly portable, as indeed it must be in comparison, say, to the main altar in the cathedral; otherwise, only a superman would be able to lift it so much as an inch. The other is the **Holy Robe,** the garment supposedly worn by Christ at the time of his trial before Pontius Pilate and gambled for by Roman soldiers. The story goes that it was brought to Trier by Helen of Constantine, a tireless collector of holy relics. It is so delicate—whatever it may in fact be, there's no doubting its extreme age—that it is displayed only once every 30 years. The next time is 1989. Otherwise, it lies under a faded piece of 9th-century Byzantine silk.

Porta Nigra, *Porta-Nigra-Platz. Open same time as amphitheater.* This is by far the best-preserved Roman structure in Trier, and one of the grandest Roman buildings in northern Europe. It's a city gate, built in the 4th century when the Romans extended Trier. Its name—the Black Gate—is misleading; it's not actually black but a light, although discolored, sandstone. Those with an interest in Roman construction techniques should look for the holes left by the original iron clamps that held the whole thing together. There's a kind of awful grim efficiency about the Porta Nigra, eloquent proof of the sophistication of Roman military might and ruthlessness. Attackers, for example, would have been lured into the two apparently innocent-looking arches only to find themselves in a courtyard and at the mercy of the defending forces. To one side are the remains of the Romanesque Simeonskirche, today the **Stadtsiches Museum Simeonstift** *(open same hours).* The church was built by Archbishop Poppo in honor of the early medieval hermit Simeon, who, for seven years, shut himself up in the east tower of the Porta Nigra. Collections of art and artifacts produced in Trier from the Middle Ages to the present day now commemorate Simeon.

Römische Palastula (Basilica), *Konstantinstr. Open Jan. through Mar. and Nov. through Dec., Tues. to Sat. 11–12 and 3–4, Sun. 11–12; closed Mon. Apr. through Oct., Mon. to Sat. 9–1 and 2–6, Sun. 11–1 and 2–6.* Today, this is the major Protestant church of Trier. When first built by the Emperor Constantine around A.D. 300 it was the Imperial Throne Room of the palace. At 239 feet long, 93 feet wide, and 108 feet high, it gives some idea of the astounding ambition of its Roman builders and of their remarkably advanced building techniques. It's also the second largest Roman interior in existence; only the Pantheon in Rome is larger. Despite the rough stone walls—these would have been plastered and painted in Roman times—the overwhelming impression is of great lightness and spaciousness. Look up at the deeply coffered ceiling; more than any other part of the building it conveys most powerfully the opulence of the original building.

OTHER ATTRACTIONS. Bischöfliches Museum (Episcopal Museum), *Windstr. Open year-round, Mon. to Fri. 10–12 and 2–5, Sat. and Sun. 10–1.* Excavations around the cathedral have unearthed most of the treasures here; they include a rare 4th-century ceiling painting that is believed to have come from Constantine's palace. Other finds trace the ecclesiastical history of Trier.

Karl-Marx-Haus (Karl Marx's Birthplace), *Brückenstr. 10. Open year-round Tues. to Sun. 10–1 and 3–6, Mon. 3–6.* Serious social historians will feel at home. Marx was born here in 1818, and the building has since been turned into a little museum exploring his life and the development of socialism round the world. A signed first edition of *Das Kapital* may be the highlight for some.

Rheinisches Landesmuseum (Rhineland Archeological Museum), *Ostallee. 44. Open year-round, Mon. to Fri. 9:30–4, Sat. 9:30–2, Sun. 9–1.* The largest collection of Roman antiquities in Germany is displayed here. The chief treasure is a 3rd-century A.D. stone relief of a wine ship on the Rhine, proof that this area of Germany has been in the wine business for almost 2,000 years. If your tastes run to broken fragments of ancient pottery and cracked mosaics—there are over 150—this is the place to make for. Admission is free.

Zell

Zell, like Cochem (see above), is a typical Moselle wine town. It's located about midway between Trier and Koblenz on the south bank of the river. If you have a yen to stay in a small and historic town where wine rules, this is a fine place to try. Stroll around the medieval core of the town—it's dominated by the twin towers of Schloss Zell, now an exclusive hotel—and down to the river. The rolling hills and woods around Zell are ideal for walks. Splurge on a bottle of Zeller Schwarze Katz, the ''Black Cat,'' Zell's most famous wine. Experts think it one of Germany's best.

GETTING THERE. The main Trier–Koblenz rail line passes close to Zell, stopping at Bullay; take the bus from there for the 10-minute ride into town. The main highway through town is B49. Moselle ferries call at the Zell landing stage.

TOURIST OFFICE. Verkehrsamt, Rathaus, 5583 Zell/Mosel (tel. 06542–4033).

WHERE TO STAY. Great-value and atmospheric accommodations are available in vineyards around Zell. Prices are about 10%–20% less than those in town. Try: **Gästehaus Anni Gibbert,** (tel. 06542–41284), 3 rooms, bed-and-breakfast only; **Paul Haas-Lenz,** Planterstr. (tel. 06542–4420), 3 rooms, wine tasting can be arranged; **Albertine Schawo-Weber,** Römerstr. 2 (tel. 06542–41297), 2 rooms.

⊖ **Zur-Post** (M), Schlossstr. 8 (tel. 06542–4084). 16 rooms, all with bath. The riverside location and the wine tavern, complete with intricately carved wooden beams and obligatory rough plaster walls, make this a delightful place to stay. Rooms are spacious and all have balconies.

WHERE TO EAT. Winehaus Mayer (M), Balduinstr. 15 (tel. 06542–4530). Stop by the restaurant of this small hotel for good-value local specialties and wines from their own vineyard.

◆

S P L U R G E S

Cruises on the Rhine. In addition to the regular day or half-day trips you can take on both the Rhine and the Moselle, you can take an overnight or even a two-day cruise. For example, a two-day cruise on the KD line's superbly appointed *Lorelei Deck* from Köln to Frankfurt, with all meals and excursions, costs DM 515 per person. An overnight cruise, leaving in the evening and with entertainment on board, costs DM 275 per person. There's no better way to see the river, and KD have established an enviable record for magnificent food and their supremely comfortable boats. Contact the German National Tourist Office or KD at Frankenwerft 15, 5000 Köln 1 (tel. 0221–208 8277).

A Night at Schloss Zell, Schlossstr. 8, 5583 Zell/Moselle (tel. 06542–4084). Germany is renowned, and rightly, for the quality of her castle-hotels, castles that have been converted with style and flair into luxurious and atmospheric hotels. And there is none better than this magnificent specimen in the little town of Zell. The building itself dates from 1220 and is filled with priceless family heirlooms and antiques. There are only seven rooms, however, so, if this is one of your splurges, be sure to make reservations well in advance. Dine in the magnificent restaurant and order a bottle of Schwarze Katz wine, the celebrated "Black Cat" wine, whose curious name comes from a black rock shaped like a cat in the vineyard.

◆

FRANKFURT

Frankfurt-am-Main, to give the city its full name, was transformed more radically than perhaps any other German city by the destruction of World War II. Before the war, Frankfurt was a charming, largely medieval town. A 20th-century Rip van Winkle revisiting Frankfurt today would find it almost unrecognizable.

Other German cities, pummeled by Allied bombing, made immense efforts to re-create their ancient buildings. Frankfurt, on the other hand, was rebuilt in an aggressively modern manner. The hope was that it would be chosen as the new capital of West Germany. In the event, it was Bonn that was selected, leaving Frankfurt's city fathers shame-faced as they contemplated the high rises and apartment blocks that now stood where once there had been medieval guild halls and Baroque town houses. It was really only in the early '80s, by which point Frankfurt had acquired an unenviable reputation as a graceless and hard-headed center given over entirely to commerce, that efforts were made to restore Frankfurt's heritage. The results have been spectacular. The Romer, the square at the heart of the city, now boasts six painstakingly restored 15th- and 16th-century town houses opposite the city hall, itself a wonder of stepped gables and Gothic archways. Likewise, the 19th-century Alte Oper, the opera house, though a high-tech showpiece inside, has been re-stored on the outside to its full 19th-century opulence. The high rises and the banks, the huge hotels and the convention centers are still very much in evidence, of course, but at last Frankfurt is beginning to slough off its image as a city devoted simply to balance sheets.

Nonetheless, in many ways Frankfurt would have an excellent capital of West Germany. Located almost in the dead

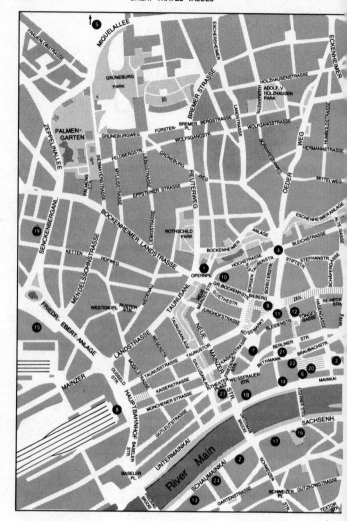

FRANKFURT

0 miles ½
0 kilometers ½

Points of Interest

1 Alte Oper
2 Deutsches
Architekturmuseum;
Deutsches Filmmuseum;
Deutsches Postmuseum
3 Dom (Cathedral)
4 Eschenheimer Turm
5 Fernmeldeturm
6 Historisches Museum
7 Goethe Haus und
Goethemuseum
8 Hauptbahnhof
9 Hauptwache
10 Heinrich Hoffmann
Museum
11 Katharinenkirche
12 Liebfrauenkirche
13 Liebieghaus
14 Leonhardskirche
15 Messe
16 Museum für
Kunsthandwerk
17 Museum für
Völkerkunde
18 Museum für Vor und
Frühgeschichte
(Karmeliterkloster)
19 Naturmuseum
Senckenberg
20 Nikolaikirche
21 Paulskirche
22 Römer
23 Schauspielhaus
24 Städelsches
Kunstinstitut und
Städtische Galerie
25 Zoo

▨ Pedestrian zone

center of the country, it has always been a major crossroads. Today, it stands at the heart of the autobahn network. Similarly, its airport is one of the biggest and busiest in Europe. There are no fewer than five train stations, connecting the city with the whole of the Continent, and three harbors, which together comprise the largest inland port in Europe.

It's because it's a crossroads that Frankfurt has always been a city of trade, ever since the Romans first built a bridge across the river Main 2,000 years ago. The first customs house was built in the 11th century; it provided a regular flow of revenue to the city coffers. By the following century, Frankfurt had become a major trading center. Its first Autumn Fair, attracting merchants from every corner of the Continent, was held in 1240. In 1330 the Spring Fair was inaugurated. Both are still going strong.

Hand in hand with trade went finance. Frankfurt established its Stock Exchange back in 1595. Banking became an important concern, as indeed it still is. Frankfurt's Jewish community, though confined to a ghetto in the Old Town, was to produce some of the world's greatest financiers, among them the Rothschilds, who opened their first bank in 1798.

It's not just businessmen who visit Frankfurt these days. The city is at last developing a thriving tourist trade, attracting those who just a few years ago would have shuddered at the very mention of the place. The downtown area has been transformed into a colorful and busy mall. The river banks are dotted with dazzling museums. The old quarter of Sachsenhausen, on the south bank of the river, is a model of sensitive restoration; visit one of the traditional Apfelwein taverns here and sample Frankfurt's curious cider (it's very much an acquired taste). Make an excursion out to the surrounding areas of the Taunus, Spessart, Odenwald and Rhön, or head down to the Rhineland.

Our ● symbol represents our highly recommended selection.

PRACTICAL INFORMATION

GETTING IN FROM THE AIRPORT. Frankfurt boasts the largest airport in central Europe, with over 700 plane movements daily. By far the easiest way to get into the city is by train; the station is actually in the airport building. (You can get trains to every part of the country, too; likewise, Germany's most important autobahn junction is here, the Frankfurter Kreuz, or Frankfurt cross.) There are trains every 10 minutes to the Hauptbahnhof, the main train station, in Frankfurt; the ride takes 11 minutes. A one-way ticket costs DM 3.10 (DM 4.20 during rush hours).

Facts and Figures

USEFUL ADDRESSES. Tourist Offices. The main tourist office (Informationsburo Verkehrsamt) is in the Hauptbahnhof (main train station) opposite track 23 (tel. 069–212 8849/51). It runs a hotel reservations service and can arrange sightseeing tours of the city as well as excursions. Opening times are Mon. to Sat. 8 A.M.–10 P.M. (8 A.M.–9 P.M. Nov. through Mar.), Sun. and public holidays 9:30 A.M.–8 P.M.

There is another information office in the center of the city underneath the Hauptwache train station (tel. 069–212 8708/09), open Mon. to Fri. 9–6 and Sat. 9–2. There are a further three offices at the airport; they are open all day and are located in the Departure Lounge, Arrival Hall B, and Transit Hall B.

Consulates. American Consulate General, Seismayerstr. 21 (tel. 069–740071); British Consulate General, Bockenheimer Landstr. 51–53 (tel. 069–72046/09/720400).

Lost and Found. Fundbüro Stadt, Mainzer Landstr. 323 (tel. 069–750 02403); Fundbüro Bahn, at the train station, opposite track 24 (tel. 069–265 5831); Fundbüro Flughafen, at the airport (tel. 960 2413).

Emergencies. Medical (tel. 069–792 0200); Dental (tel. 069–660 7271); Pharmacies (tel. 069–11500); Police (tel. 110).

Post Offices. Main Post Office (Hauptpost), Zeil 108 (tel. 222/1). Open Mon. to Fri. 8–6, Sat. 8–noon, late counter open Mon. to Fri. 6 P.M.–9 P.M., Sun. 9 A.M.–9 P.M. The post offices at the main train station (tel. 069–261 5120) and the airport are open round the clock.

Car Hire. Avis, Mainzer Landstr. 170 (tel. 069–230101/730505); Hertz, Mainzer Landstr. 139 (tel. 069–233151); InterRent, Hanauer Landstr. 334 (tel. 069–423025). All have desks in Arrivals Hall A at the airport.

Taxis. Tel. 069–250001/230023/545011.

Getting Around

Frankfurt and environs within a radius of 40 km (25 miles) of center city boast a complex and ultra-reliable interlinked network of public transportation, the whole operated by FVV, the city transit authority. The system comprises city and suburban buses, streetcars, subways (U-Bahn), and suburban trains (S-Bahn). Fares within each constituent area are uniform, and tickets bought in one area may be used in any other. Buy tickets from the blue machines at stations and streetcar stops, or from bus drivers. Best buy of all is the **24-hour tourist ticket.** It gives unlimited travel on all public transport and costs DM 7. It's available at the tourist office.

Where to Stay

With a host of businessmen and -women descending on Frankfurt almost year-round and numerous trade fairs and conventions, downtown hotels especially are both expensive and often booked up well in advance. This doesn't mean that good value and low rates are an impossible dream, but it does mean that some pretty careful thought has to be given to find an affordable place to stay. Consider staying in an inn or pension in the suburbs; getting into town is easy and fast on all public transportation and rates are significantly lower. Alternatively, write the tourist office long before you plan to come and inquire about discounted hotel rates at weekends and in the off-season. Many business hotels offer reductions of up to 50% at slack periods.

Moderate

Admiral, Holderlinstr. 25 (tel. 069–448021/23). 70 beds, all rooms with bath. This is a small, simply-furnished hotel close to the Zoo and within easy reach of center city. Ample breakfasts are available, but no other meals.

Arcade, Speicherstr. 3–5 (tel. 069–273030). 410 beds, all rooms with bath. Located close to the main train station, overlooking the river Main, this recently-opened functional hotel offers all modern comforts. Restaurant and bar.

Liebig, Liebigstr. 45 (tel. 069–727551). 29 beds. A small and clean hotel with large rooms; try for one at the rear of the building. Centrally located.

Mühlberg, Offenbacher Landstr. 56 (tel. 069–613063). 100 beds, most rooms with bath. Located on the other side of the river Main in Frankfurt-Sachsenhausen, but within easy reach of downtown Frankfurt on public transport. Quiet and clean hotel with large rooms, but no restaurant. Inquire about special weekend rates.

Neue Kräme, Neue Kräme 23 (tel. 069–284046). 29 beds, all rooms with bath. Small and modern hotel located right in the heart of the city in the pedestrian mall.

Palmengarten, Palmengartenstr. 8 (tel. 069–752041). 28 beds, some with bath. Small, family-run pension located opposite the main entrance to the famous Palmengarten; the quiet location is a real plus.

Inexpensive

Diana, Westendstr. 83 (tel. 069–747007). 32 beds, some rooms with bath. This quiet, attractive, and efficiently-run hotel is centrally located in the city's heart. No restaurant, but hearty breakfasts.

●**Maingau,** Schifferstr. 38–40 (tel. 069–612 7001/610751). 160 beds, most rooms with bath. Situated in Frankfurt-Sachsenhausen a 10-minute walk from center city. Rooms are comfortable and clean and there is an excellent, good-value restaurant.

Waldhotel Hensels Felsenkeller, Buchrainstr. 95 (tel. 069–652086). 30 beds, some rooms with bath. An immaculately clean hotel providing quiet, personal service located in the residential area of Frankfurt-Oberrad near the woods of the Frankfurter Stadtwald. Reached easily by public transport, it has a small restaurant, a café, and an indoor pool.

Youth Hostel

Haus der Jugend, Deutschherrenufer 12 (tel. 069–619058).

Camping

There is no campsite in Frankfurt itself. The closest is the **Campingplatz des Wassersportvereins** in Offenbach-Burgel (tel. 069–862949), which is easily accessible by car, streetcar, and bus. Open Apr. through Oct.

Where to Eat

As with hotels, so with restaurants: There's no shortage of places to eat in Frankfurt, but the accent in most is on expense-account haute cuisine. The trick, as in most other German cities, is to make for taverns serving local specialties in huge portions and offering that authentic German atmosphere. So head across the river Main to Sachsenhausen and the Apfelwein—literally, "apple-wine"—taverns. For quick and nourishing meals on the run at low prices, go to the Kleinmarkthalle in central Frankfurt. A number of stalls here sell a variety of sausages in bread rolls at affordable prices.

Frankfurt specialties include: *Frankfurter Würstchen,* sausages (frankfurters) served with bread and mustard; *Grüne Sauce* (green sauce), made from seven different herbs and served with boiled eggs or beef; *Handkäs mit Musik,* small pieces of cheese with oil, vinegar, and onions; *Haspel,* smoked pork; *Leberknödel,* liver dumplings with sauerkraut and mashed potatoes; *Leiterchen,* smoked spare ribs; and *Schäufelchen,* smoked pork shoulder.

Frankfurt's favorite drink is *Apfelwein,* a tasty but strong cider (processed in the same way wine is made from grapes), served in patterned glasses, or *Schobbe,* or in blue-gray stone jugs known as *Bembel.* Henninger and Binding beer are sold throughout the city.

Moderate

⊖ **Atschel,** Wallstr. 7 (tel. 069–619201). Located near the Sachsenhausen Altstadt (Old Town), this former *Apfelwein*-only restaurant is great value for local specialties; try one of the daily specials chalked up on the blackboard in the corner. There's a garden for summer-time eating.

Buchscheer, Schwarzsteinkautweg 17 (tel. 069–645121). (Streetcar stop: Louisa). This is the ideal place to start or end a walk through the Stadtwald Woods. Order up a glass of *Apfelwein* and one of the wide choice of Frankfurt specialties.

Dippegücker, Eschenheimer Anlage 40 (tel. 069–551965). **Also at:** Hauptbahnhof 4 (tel. 069–284947). Both restaurants offer an excellent-value international menu with fresh seasonal dishes. They are likely to be packed with office workers at lunchtime.

Green Hill, Gutzkowstr. 43 (tel. 069–626301). A friendly vegetarian restaurant in a small house in Sachsenhausen not far from Schweizer Platz. Try the stroganoff made of *tofu* (oriental soyabean cheese).

Wagner, Schweizer Str. 71 (tel. 069–614559). Attracts all age groups with its rustic atmosphere, home-made cider, and salted pork chops *(Rippchen)* served with sauerkraut.

Inexpensive

Apfelwein Klaus, Meisengasse 10 (tel. 069–282864). Situated in a quiet side street off the Fressgasse pedestrian mall, this restaurant offers local specialties, a daily-changing lunchtime menu, and international dishes. There are sidewalk tables in the summer.

Fichtekränzi, Wallstr. 5 (tel. 069–612778). The carved pine wreath which gave its name to this *Apfelwein* tavern was once a universal sign indicating fresh cider on sale for thirsty hikers. This restaurant still offers cider, of course, as well as local specialties in a traditional and original setting.

Fisch Franke, Domstr., corner of Berliner Str. (tel. 069–283560). Traditional fish restaurant located close by the cathedral; stop in for excellent-value fresh fish and potato salad, the traditional accompaniment.

Gutsausschank des Weingutes der Stadt Frankfurt am Main im Haus Limburg, Römerberg (tel. 069–291331). Does this place have the longest restaurant name in the world? Maybe. In fact, it's just the Ratskeller, a typical town-hall restaurant. Local specialties, lashings of Teutonic atmosphere, and good-value wines—try Hochheimer, reputedly Queen Victoria's favorite—abound.

Klaane Sachsehäuser, Neuer Wall 11 (tel. 069–615983). A family-run Apfelwein tavern; try the *Schaufelchen,* salted pork shoulder.

Naturbar, Oeder Weg 26 (tel. 069–554486). Open weekdays only. Recommended as an inexpensive spot for a quick bite of fresh salad at lunchtime.

➡ Zum Rad, Leonhardstrasse 2 (tel. 069–479128). (Take U-Bahn line 4 to Seckbacher Landstr., and bus 43/12). Dating back to 1806, this rustic tavern in Seckbach, a small, half-timbered village with great views of the city, is a terrific place for a good-value meal (changing specialties are a feature) and a glass of cider. You sit outside in the summer in the spacious courtyard framed by tall trees.

Wine Taverns

Abtskeller, Abtsgasse, corner of Schifferstr. (tel. 069–626832). Open daily 8–1. Various German wines can be enjoyed by candlelight in this cellar.

Dünker, Berger Str. 265. Open Mon. to Fri. 11:30–2 and 4–9, Sat. 10–2; closed Sun. For four decades inexpensive wines have been sold here; today, it is moving sharply up-market, and a´wide range of fine wines is available.

Fabrik, Mittlerer Hasenpfad 1, corner of Morfelder Landstr. (tel. 069–624406). This cellar, located in a one-time brick factory is an ideal spot for good-value steaks, vintage wines, and conversation round the open fireplace.

Frankfurter Bierhaus, Schutzenstr. 10, corner of Fischerfeldstr. (tel. 069–283977). Choose from 44 different sorts of beer in this vaulted cellar.

Hahnhof, Berliner Str. 64 (tel. 069–287833). Try the "Wine of the Month" on special offer, as well as dishes and wines of the Rhineland Palatinate.

Rheinpfalz-Weinstuben, Gutleutstr. 1, corner of Theaterplatz.

(tel. 069–283870). One of the best, reasonably-priced traditional wine restaurants in town. It's a great favorite for after-theater meals.

Cafés

Frankfurt, like all German cities, boasts innumerable cafés, scattered throughout the city. Here you'll find natives and visitors alike congregating (especially in the afternoons) to have coffee, cakes, and pastries. Frankfurt specialties which can be sampled in any café in town are *Frankfurter Kranz* cakes (filled with jam and cream and topped with nuts), and *Bethmännchen* (marzipan cakes). Three likely spots to try are:

Café Hauptwache, An der Hauptwache. 250-year-old building overlooking the busy square of the same name in the heart of the city, with a summer terrace.

Café Laumer, Bockenheimer Landstr. 67 (tel. 069–727912). Traditional cafe situated in the West End of the city; recommended for excellent cakes and light lunches. There is another branch in the Filmmuseum.

Café Schwille, Grosse Bockenheimer Landstr. 50 (tel. 069–284183). Just off the Hauptwache square, this café in the hotel of the same name serves breakfast from 6 A.M.

What to See and Do

MAJOR ATTRACTIONS. Dom (Cathedral of St. Bartholomew). *Open year-round daily 9–12 and 3–6:30.* Located on the Domplatz cathedral square. Built over the remains of a 9th-century chapel and enlarged in Gothic style between the 13th and 15th centuries, the cathedral has been added to several times after fire damage, and most recently after bomb damage sustained during the war. Its most impressive exterior feature is its tall Gothic tower. Excavations in front of the main entrance in 1953 revealed the remains of a Roman settlement and the foundations of a Carolingian imperial palace. The cathedral treasury *(Domschatz)* and the election chapel can be visited upon prior application to the Cathedral Office, Domplatz 14.

Goethehaus und Goethemuseum (Goethe's House and Museum), *Grosser Hirschgraben 23 (tel. 069–282824). Open Mon. to Sat. 9–6 (Oct. through June 9–4), Sun. 10–1.* Located near the Hauptwache. It was here that Goethe (1749–1823) was born. The building is furnished with original pieces that belonged to his family, while the adjoining museum contains a permanent collection of manuscripts, paintings, and memorabilia documenting the life and times of Germany's most outstanding poet.

Höchster Schloss *Bolongarostrasse, Höchst. (Reached by buses 51, 53, 55, 57, 58, and 70).* Built in 1360 as seat and Customs House of the Archbishops of Mainz, the palace was destroyed and rebuilt several times during its history; all that remains today is the medieval keep, the northeast wing, and one section of the living quarters. While in Höchst take the opportunity to see the picturesque **Altstadt** (Old Town), with its market and timbered houses.

Naturkundermuseum Senckenberg (Natural History Museum), *Senckenberganlage 25. Open year-round Mon., Tues., Thurs. and Fri. 9–5, Wed. 9–8, Sat. and Sun. 9–6. Free tours on Wed. at 8 P.M. and Sun. at 10:30 A.M.* This is the largest natural history museum in Germany, with Europe's most impressive collection of giant dinosaurs and prehistoric whales. Fossils, animals, plants, and geological exhibits are all displayed in an exciting, "hands-on" environment. The most important single exhibit is the only complete specimen in Europe of a **diplodocus** (actually, it was sent here from the States).

Palmengarten und Botanischer Garten (Tropical Garden and Botanical Gardens), *entrance in Seismayerstr. (Reached by streetcars 17, 21, and 22 from Theater- and Goetheplatz). Open year-round, daily 9–7. No entrance fee.* The large hothouses enclose a variety of tropical and sub-tropical flora, while the surrounding park offers numerous leisure facilities. Standing between the Palmengarten and the adjoining Grüneburgpark, the Botanical Gardens contain a wide assortment of flora from around the world.

Römerberg. This square marks the historical focal point of the city. On the west side is the Town Hall, the **Römer,** Frankfurt's traditional symbol. The most distinguishing feature of this beautiful edifice is its gabled Gothic facade. (In fact, it's actually three buildings in one: the **Alt-Limpurg,** the **Romer** itself, and the **Lowenstein).** Opposite, is a row of 15th- and 16th-century town houses, faithfully reconstructed following war-time damage. On the south side of the square stands the 13th-century church of **St. Nicholas,** formerly the chapel of the City Council. Inside the Römer is the **Kaisersaal,** the throne room, where, between 1566 and 1792, no fewer than 10 Holy Roman Emperors staged lavish coronation banquets. It now contains a portrait gallery of 52 emperors from 768 to 1806.

Städelsches Kunstinkstitut und Städische Galerie (Städel Art Institute and Municipal Gallery), *Schaumankai 63. Open year-round, Tues. to Sun. 10–5, Wed. 10–8.* This is one of the most significant art collections in Germany, with fine examples of Flemish, German, and Italian old masters, plus a sprinkling of French Impressionists.

Zoologischer Garten (Zoo), Alfred-Brehm-Platz. (Reached by streetcars 13 and 15 from Theaterplatz and the Römer). *Open mid-Mar. through Sept. daily 8–7; Oct. through mid-Nov., daily 8–6; mid-Nov. through mid-Mar., daily 8–5.* Founded in 1858, this ranks as one of the most important zoos in Europe, indeed one of the most advanced of its kind in the world, with about 5,000 animals and 600 different species. Visit the nocturnal animal house and **Exotariam** to see exotic animals in their natural habitat.

OTHER ATTRACTIONS. Alte Opera (Old Opera House), *Opernplatz.* Built between 1873 and 1880, this is one of the most splendid opera houses in Europe. Gutted by fire in 1944, it has been lavishly restored, and was reopened in 1981 as a concert and congress hall.

Deutsches Architekturmuseum (German Architectural Museum), Schaumankai 43. *Open year-round, Tues. to Sun. 10–5, Wed. 10–8; closed Mon. No entrance fee.* Built as a house within a house, this modern museum charts the progress and development of German architecture through the ages. There are five floors of drawings, models, and audio-visual displays as well as special exhibits.

Deutsches Filmmuseum (German Cinema Museum), *Schaumankai 41. Open year-round, Tues. to Sun. 10–5, Wed. 10–8; closed Mon. No entrance fee.* Germany's first museum of cinematography houses an imaginative collection of film artifacts, plus a special exhibit of drawings by Italian filmmaker Federico Fellini.

Eschenheimer Turm, Eschenheimer Tor. This is the finest of the original 42 city towers. It dates from the 14th century.

Fernmeldeturm (Telecommunications Tower), *Wilhelm Epstein Str.* Known locally as "Ginnheimer Spargal" (Ginnheim's Asparagus), at 331 meters high (1,085 ft.) this is the fourth-highest tower in the world. Take the elevator up to the revolving restaurant and the observation platform.

Goetheturm, *Wendelsweg.* Come down to earth and visit the highest wooden tower in Germany, 43 meters (137 ft.) high. It's located on the Sachsenhauser Berg hill on the edge of the Stadtwald. If you're feeling fit, climb the 196 steps leading up to the observation platform. There's a café at the foot of the tower where you can recuperate.

Museum für Kunsthandwerk (Museum of Applied Arts), *Schaumankai 17. Open year-round, Tues. to Sun. 10–5, Wed. 10–8; closed Mon.* This award-winning building by American architect Richard Meier contains a collection of 30,000 objects of European and Asian handicraft.

Schirn Kunstalle Frankfurt (Art Gallery), *Am Römerberg 6a.*

Open year-round, Tues. to Sun. 10–5, Wed. 10–8; closed Mon.
Frankfurt's most modern museum, located opposite the cathedral,
houses a fine collection of 20th-century art. There is a pleasant café.

St. Leonhardskirche, *Alte Mainzer Gasse.* This Gothic, single-
roofed church with five naves is the second oldest in the city, dating
back to 1219. Of particular interest are fragments of old stained glass,
an impressively carved altarpiece, and an immense hanging keystone.

Stadtwald (Public Woods). *Reached by bus 36 from Konstabler
Wacher to Hainer Weg.* Frankfurt is the proud owner of the largest
publicly-owned forest in Germany. With its innumerable parks and
trails, it is used by citizens and visitors alike for recreation, sport, and
relaxation. Of particular interest is the **Waldlehrpfad**—a trail leading
past a series of rare trees, each identified by a little sign.

Tours

Sightseeing tours in English and German are organised by the
tourist office located in the main train station opposite track 23 (tel.
069–212 8849/51). Tours leave from the north side of the station and,
in about three hours, take in the Römer town hall; Sachsenhausen; the
Goethehaus; the Hauptwache (the old city guardhouse); the
Eschenheimer Turm city gate; the Stock Exchange; the Old Opera
House; the West End and banking district; the Palmengarten park and
Botanical gardens; the University and the fair grounds. Tours are daily,
Mar. through Oct. at 10 A.M. and 2 P.M., Nov. through Feb. on Sat.
only at 2 P.M. and Sun. 10 A.M.. Cost is DM 26 (children and old-age
pensioners half-price). The tourist office also offers city tours which
include a trip into the nearby Taunus hills, a picturesque and scenic
region with small medieval towns along the route. Tours are available
daily from Jan. through Nov. at 11 A.M., last about two hours, and cost
DM 34.

A trip on Frankfurt's "Ebbelwei Express"—an old colorfully-
painted streetcar that will take you round the city and Sachsenhausen—
is not to be missed. It departs every 40 minutes on Sat. and Sun.
between 1:30 P.M. and 5:30 P.M., from Danziger Platz (Ostbahnhof).

Shopping

Frankfurt is a shoppers' paradise, with the main shopping area
located on and around **Rossmarkt, Goetheplatz, Rathenplatz,** and
in the **Hauptwache** (a square at the center of the city with shops and
boutiques on two levels). Along the **Zeil,** which runs east, is
Frankfurt's so-called "shopping mile," one of Germany's busiest and

best shopping streets, with the highest sales turnover in the country. It has recently been transformed into a pedestrian mall with a total of 18 department stores, as well as a wealth of shoe and clothing stores, restaurants, and cafés. To the right, using the Neue Krame or the Hasengasse, you reach **Kleinmarkthalle,** an indoor fresh-produce market, where you can buy or just admire the variety of fruit, vegetables, flowers, spices, cheese, meats, and sausages from all over the world.

Back at the Hauptwache, you can either walk through the **Goethestrasse,** with its exclusive stores, or take parallel **Grosse Bockenheimer Strasse,** nicknamed "Fresgasse," and lined with many wine dealers, delicatessens, and butchers. At **Opernplatz** choose from a variety of restaurants and cafés to have a snack or meal. Going west from the Hauptwache is the **Rossmarkt,** which leads to the **Kaiserstrasse.** It passes the BfG skyscraper which has three floors of expensive shops, boutiques, and restaurants, and connects the downtown area to the Hauptbahnhof. The Kaiserstrasse is known for its especially large selection of stores selling clothing, leather, hi-fi and photographic equipment, and stainless steel. The heart of the fur trade in Frankfurt is the **Düsseldorfer Strasse** opposite the Hauptbahnhof.

Not to be missed is the **Frankfurt Flea Market** which takes place every Saturday on Sachsenhauser Ufer, between Alte Brucke bridge and Untermain-Brucke bridge along the Main. Open from 8–4, there are almost 600 stalls selling objects d'art, bric-a-brac, antiques, and souvenirs.

Should you wish to take home a few bottles of German wine, stop at **Limpurger Gasse 2,** next to the Römer, where wine produced in the municipal vineyards is for sale. Open Mon. to Fri. 7:30–4, this is the place to buy a genuine bottle of Hochheimer for no more than a few marks.

Other typical Frankfurt souvenirs to look for are: *Apfelwein,* which can be purchased by the bottle in most supermarkets or taverns; *Bethmännchen und Brenten* (marzipan cookies); *Frankfurter Kranz* (creamy cakes); or a *Struwelpeter* puppet or doll, named after the famous children's book character invented by Heinrich Hoffman.

Entertainment and Nightlife

Frankfurt, for all its unashamed internationalism and sophisticated expense-account living, is unlikely to win many votes as Germany's foremost afterhours town. Whatever you do, avoid the streets around the main train station (Kaiserstrasse, Munchener Str. etc.); they're no more than a red-light district, and a tacky one at that.

For atmosphere and great value, head over the river to Sachsenhausen's Altstadt (Old Town) where the bars, discos, clubs, and beer and wine restaurants are concentrated around a few small streets. But the best bet for affordable entertainment are either the *Apfelwein* taverns or the large number of music spots, details of which can be found below.

Frankfurt has been one of the leading jazz centers of Europe for decades and plays host to the German Jazz Festival every fall. There are hundreds of jazz venues, from smoky backstreet cafés to concert halls, the most interesting of which are listed below. And rock music is equally at home in Frankfurt, too.

Information about what's on in town is available at the ticket office, **Kartenkiosk Sandrock,** under the Hauptwache.

Jazzkeller, Kleine Bockenheimer Str. 18a (tel. 069–288537). Open 9–3; closed Mon. This smoky cellar has been a well-known venue for live jazz for more than three decades.

Opernkeller (in the Old Opera House), Opernplatz (tel. 069–134 0320). Dixieland jazz and swing on Fridays only at 8 P.M.

Schlachthof, Deutschherrenufer 36 (tel. 069–623201). Every Sun. at 11:30 A.M. A sure bet for rock or hot jazz in a great atmosphere.

Jazzica, Holzgraben 9 (tel. 280244). Open 9–2. Cellar-disco.

Music-Hall, Voltastr. 74 (tel. 779041). Open 9–3. Hot music and all the latest hits; up to 2,000 people can be crammed in.

Music-Hall, Voltastr. 74 (tel. 069–624053). Open 5–2 (dancing from 8 P.M.), Sun. 11:30–1. Closed Mon., except during trade fairs. Restaurant with old-time dancing; not recommended for disco-fans.

THEATERS AND CONCERTS. Frankfurt has the largest budget for cultural expenditure in Germany. The city manages its own production company, the Städtische Bühnen (Municipal Theaters), with two avant-garde theaters and the Municipal Opera, all of which enjoy outstandingly high reputations.

Tickets can be purchased at the tourist office in the Hauptwache or from theaters themselves. For information about concerts, call 069–11517.

Alte Oper (Old Opera House), Opernplatz (tel. 069–13400). The elegant surroundings of the sumptuously renovated old Opera House make a perfect venue for classical concerts, light opera, musicals, and ballet, as well as jazz, rock, and pop concerts.

Festhalle (on the fair grounds), Ludwig-Erhard-Anlage 1 (tel. 069–7575/0). and **Jahrhunderthalle Hoechst,** Pfaffenwiese (tel. 069–3601/213; box office tel. 069–3601/240), open Mon. to Fri. 10–2. Two substantial concert and convention halls with changing programs.

Playhouse, Hansaallee 152 (tel. 069–151 8326). (Reached on subway line U1–U3, Dornbusch stop). English-language plays.

◆

S P L U R G E S

A Night at Hessischer Hof, Friedrich-Ebert-Anlage 40 (tel. 069–75400). You are unlikely to find many classy hotels in Frankfurt that aren't aimed fair and square at businessmen, and the Hessischer Hof is no exception. But unlike most of its rivals, the emphasis here is on style, elegance, and tradition rather than soulless high-rise efficiency. With prices beginning at around DM 300 for a double room, you may feel that this is one splurge that can be hard to justify. But if you stay here during a weekend when there are no trade fairs or conventions (admittedly a rare occurrence), you may just find that prices fall significantly.

Dinner at Erno's Bistro, Liebigstr. 15 (tel. 069–721997). For a city that has given itself over so wholeheartedly to modernity and high-tech living, it's a surprise to find that about the best restaurant in town is a small, distinctly French bistro. Erno himself takes personal charge of the cooking, and the results are generally spectacular. Prices are high, so order one of the house wines, however much the immense wine list tempts. Reservations are essential.

◆

KÖLN, BONN, AND DÜSSELDORF

No visitor to Germany can afford to miss the three great cities of the northern Rhineland—Köln, Bonn, and Düsseldorf. Each is an important and historic center, though while Köln and Düsseldorf are major industrial and trade centers, Bonn, capital of West Germany, is preeminently a city of politics and government. This chapter explores the budget possibilities of these three major metropolises.

KÖLN

Historic Köln (Cologne) is the largest city in the Rhineland and the fourth largest in Germany. Famous throughout the world for its scented waters, Eau de Cologne, the city is today a major commercial and cultural center.

At the heart of Köln stands the magnificent cathedral, the Dom, which largely escaped the bombing that destroyed 90% of the city in World War II. Complementing the cathedral's Gothic splendor are some striking new structures: the Wallraf-Richartz/Museum Ludwig, which houses the gigantic, circular Philharmonic Hall; the ultra-modern Opera House; and the Chamber of Commerce.

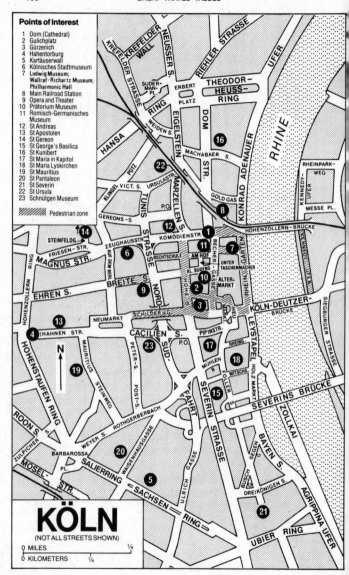

Points of Interest

1 Dom (Cathedral)
2 Gulichplatz
3 Gürzenich
4 Hahentorburg
5 Kartäuserwall
6 Kölnisches Stadtmuseum
7 Ludwig Museum;
  Wallraf -Richartz Museum;
  Philharmonic Hall
8 Main Railroad Station
9 Opera and Theater
10 Prätorium Museum
11 Romisch-Germanisches
  Museum
12 St Andreas
13 St Apostolen
14 St Gereon
15 St George's Basilica
16 St Kunibert
17 St Maria in Kapitol
18 St Maria Lyskirchen
19 St Mauritius
20 St Pantaleon
21 St Severin
22 St Ursula
23 Schnütgen Museum

///// Pedestrian zone

KÖLN
(NOT ALL STREETS SHOWN)

0 MILES ¼
0 KILOMETERS ¼

Köln's history dates back as far as Celtic times, but it was the Romans who first encircled it with walls and, in A.D. 50, founded Colonia Claudia Ara Agrippina, from which its name derives. Many traces of the 400-year Roman occupation have been discovered, from towers to burial grounds. Findings since the war have also revealed the city's importance during the early Christian era.

But it was during the Middle Ages that the city really grew, becoming a major center for international trade. Its medieval prosperity is reflected not only in the cathedral, but in the fact, for example, that there are no fewer than 12 Romanesque churches.

The rich intellectual life of the city is also much in evidence: the University, founded in 1388; the impressive range of museums; the large number of theaters, concert halls, and technical colleges; and the headquarters of the West German Radio.

Köln has much to offer the visitor, from its great historical heritage to its many cafés, restaurants, drinking haunts, and shops. The city possesses a vibrant and cosmopolitan atmosphere, epitomized by the Köln Carnival when, for five days in February, the city hums with processions and celebrations that attract over one million visitors every year.

Our ● symbol means highly recommended.

PRACTICAL INFORMATION

GETTING IN FROM THE AIRPORT. Köln/Bonn International Airport is about 16 km (10 miles) from center city. It takes about 15 minutes to get into the city on the autobahn. Bus 170 departs from the main airport building and stops at the bus station behind track 4A of the main train station. The journey takes about 20 minutes and costs DM 6 one way and DM 9 round-trip. Buses leave the main station for the airport every 20 minutes from 7 A.M., although there is one earlier bus at 6 A.M. En route, the bus also stops at the Köln-Deutz station.

There is no train connection from the airport, though the Lufthansa "Airport Express" train links the airport with the airports of both Düsseldorf and Frankfurt. Fares on this service are expensive (Köln–Frankfurt is DM 173 one way).

InterCity and Fern Express (FD) train routes intersect at Köln, with six IC trains leaving every hour (including one directly to Frankfurt airport). The city is also well-connected to the rest of the Rhineland, the Ruhr, Westphalia, and the south.

Facts and Figures

USEFUL ADDRESSES. Tourist Offices. The tourist office, located opposite the main entrance to the cathedral, is Verkehrsamt der Stadt Köln, Unter Fettenhennen 19, 5000 Köln 1 (tel. 0221-221 3345). Open Mon. to Sat. 8–9 P.M., Sun. and public holidays 9:30–7 P.M. They produce a monthly program of events, the *Monatsvorschau*. They also provide tourist guides, handle queries, and run an accommodations service (tel. 0221-221 3311), open Mon. to Sat. 8–10:30 P.M., Sun. and public holidays 9–10:30 P.M. (during winter from 2 P.M.). The service is free of charge, but reservations can only be made three days in advance, and are compulsory.

Cultural Contacts. Amerika-Haus, Apostelnkloster 13–15 (tel. 0221-210366); British Council, Hahnenstr. 6 (tel. 0221-236677).

Lost and Found. Fundbüro der Stadt Köln (city), Herkulesstr. 42 (tel. 0221-221 6312), open Mon. to Fri. 7:30–12, closed Sat. and Sun.; *KVB* (public transport), Scheidtweilerstr. 38 (tel. 0221-547 3672), open Mon. to Thurs. 7–3:30, Fri. 7–1, closed Sat. and Sun.; main train station, (tel. 0221-141 5172), open Mon. to Thurs. 8–4, closed Fri., Sat., and Sun.

Emergencies. Medical (tel. 0221-720772); Pharmacy, including dental and veterinary care (tel. 0221-11500); Police (tel. 110).

Post Office. The post office in the main train station is open 24 hours.

Car Hire. Avis, Clemensstr. 29 (tel. 0221-234333), at the airport (tel. 02203-402343); Hertz, Bismarckstr. 19–21 (tel. 515084/7), at the airport (tel. 02203-40251); InterRent, Luxemburger Str. 181 (tel. 0221-441047), at the airport (tel. 02203-53080).

Taxis. Tel. 2882.

Getting Around

The Köln transportation system (KVB) consists of an integrated network of buses, subway (U-Bahn), and streetcars. The streetcar network extends far out into the suburbs and surrounding areas. Fares can be difficult to work out, as they depend on both distance and time of day. Buy the **Tagesnetzkarte** which is valid for 24 hours and can be used on all forms of transport. It costs DM 6 (or DM 8 to include Bonn as well). There is also a three-day combined ticket **(Grüne Karte)** for Köln and Bonn costing DM 15. For information about public transport and tickets, contact KVB (tel. 0221–547 3672), or the tourist office.

Where to Stay

Moderate

Ahl Meerkatzen, Mathiasstr. 21 (tel. 0221–234882). 54 beds, all rooms with bath. Behind the historic facade of this hotel are comfortable, well-furnished rooms. Snacks are served in the bar. The building dates from 1264 and, is conveniently close to the center of town.

Alter Römer, Am Bollwerk 23 (tel. 0221–212385/216290). 24 beds, all rooms with bath/shower/WC. Just a short distance from the cathedral, in a lively part of the city, especially at night. Modern and comfortable rooms, some of which overlook the Rhine. Also has the Alte Römerschänke restaurant.

Casa Colonia, Machabäerstr. 63 (tel. 0221–132284). 25 beds, all rooms with bath. Elegantly furnished and comfortable hotel which offers attentive service in peaceful surroundings. A breakfast-buffet is served. Located close to the center of the city.

◒ Im Stapelhäuschen, Fischmarkt 1–3 (tel. 0221–213043). 57 beds, some with bath. Hotel in a 13th-century building right in the heart of the historic area round the church of Gross St. Martin. The rooms are clean and comfortable with a '50s feel, which was when the hotel was last furnished. Also has a good restaurant with a notable wine list featuring over 300 wines.

Inexpensive

An der Tennishalle Schmitte, Köln-Rodenkirchen, Grossrotter Weg 1 (tel. 02233–22777). 26 beds, all rooms with bath. A must for tennis enthusiasts, with no fewer than five covered courts and eight open-air courts. Although located well outside the center of Köln, there are good connections into town by streetcar or S-Bahn. Head here for comfortable accommodations in pleasant surroundings, with a cellar wine bar and restaurant as well.

Brandenburger Hof, Brandenburger Str. 2–4 (tel. 0221–122889). 76 beds, some rooms with bath. Near to the main train station and the cathedral. Clean, modern rooms, and a friendly atmosphere.

Gartenhotel Ponick, Köln-Weiden, Königsberger Str. 5–9 (tel. 02234–76006). 53 beds, most rooms with bath. Pleasantly furnished hotel, situated in a quiet residential area outside the center of town, but within easy striking distance.

Geisler, Köln-Porz, Frankfurter Str. 172 (tel. 02203–61027). 89

beds, all rooms with bath. Modern hotel in the southern part of the city. Elegant lobby, and stylishly furnished and well-equipped rooms.

Pension Müller, Brandeburger Str. 20 (tel. 0221–124318/124692). 16 beds, some rooms with bath. Family-run pension, close to the center and all the major sights. "Thank-you" letters to the Müllers for their hospitality from all corners of the world decorate the lobby.

Youth Hostels

Jugdendgästehaus, Köln-Riehl, An der Schanz 14 (tel. 0221–767081).

Jugendherberge Köln-Deutz, Siegesstr. (tel. 0221–814711).

Camping

For general information, contact: ADAC, Alteburger Str. 375 (tel. 0221–379937).

Bootshaus Berger, Köln-Rodenkirchen, Uferstr. 53a (tel. 0221–392421). Open Mar. through Oct.

Campingplatz am Waldbad, Köln-Dünnwald, Peter-Baum-Weg 9 (tel. 0221–603315). Open year-round.

Städtischer Familienzeltplatz (Municipal Family Campsite), Köln-Poll, Weidenweg 46 (tel. 0221–836921). Open May through Sept.

Where to Eat

Köln has excellent facilities for eating and drinking. You can sample everything from top German and international cuisine to hearty regional specialties. For good, wholesome food at affordable prices, and an authentic German atmosphere, you can't beat the brewery restaurants. They all serve the local specialties, along with Kölsch, the light local beer; sometimes the brewery itself is on the same premises. However, low prices can also mean crowds, so arrive early to be sure of a table.

Moderate

Gasthaus zum Rheingarten, Frankenwerft 19 (tel. 0221–246054). Pleasant restaurant in the Altstadt (Old Town) with a good view of the river. Serves special dishes at lunchtime, but gets crowded in the evenings. Groups can order beer by the barrel. There's a beer garden as well.

"Gir" Keller, Lintgasse 14 (tel. 0221–240 1079). Open Mon. to Sun. from 6 P.M. In a 12th-century vaulted cellar, this restaurant specializes in Köln and Rhineland cuisine of the last 2,000 years. You can choose from a whole range of extraordinary dishes, including "a medieval feast in the tradition of our forefathers" and "bacon on figs," based on a recipe by the Roman gourmet Aplicius. Live music on different evenings.

Ratskeller, Altermarkt (tel. 0221–218301). Cellar-restaurant in Köln's historic city hall which, like its counterparts in other German towns, serves reliable international and German cuisine.

⊖**Zum Treppchen,** Köln-Rodenkirchen, Kirchstr. 15 (tel. 0221–392179). This is the place to go when you've had enough of the city. Surrounded by idyllic timbered houses and houseboats, the Treppchen with its beautiful beer garden is a favorite spot for excursions from Köln. It can be reached by boat or by taking the *U-Bahn* 16 to Rodenkirchen.

Inexpensive

Brauhaus Sion, Unter Taschenmacher 5–7 (tel. 0221–214203). Traditional family brewery and restaurant near the cathedral.

⊖**Früh am Dom,** Am Hof 12–14 (tel. 0221–212621). Substantial portions of filling fare are served in this ever-popular establishment. It's always crowded and not just because it's so close to the cathedral and the main train station.

Gertrudenhof am Neumarkt, Apostelnstr. 2a (tel. 0221–232474). Offers special lunchtime menus, including both soup and dessert, which are good value for money. Near the busy shopping areas of Mittelstr. and Schildergasse.

⊖**Obergärige Hausbrauerei Päffgen,** Friesenstr. 64–66 (tel. 0221–135461). The last of the real brewery restaurants and the most typical of the local taverns (köllsche Weetschaffte). The majority of its customers are regulars, and this has helped guarantee an unvarying quality in the standard of food and drink served here down the years. The Kölsch (local light beer) is brewed on the premises. Don't offend the waiter, or *Köbes* as they are nicknamed, by ordering Coca Cola, or, even worse, Altbier, which is unique to Düsseldorf. There's a small garden shaded by chestnut trees.

Beer Halls

Bierdorf Colon, Breite Str. 29 (tel. 0221–248989). Located opposite the opera house and under a shopping gallery, this is a complex of 18 different pubs, a disco, and the Colon theater which puts on free shows at 10 P.M.

Biermuseum, Buttermarkt 39 (tel. 0221–2401579). 18 different beers on draught. Also recommended are the steaks and the *Kassler* (pickled pork) roast. Beer garden, too.

➜ **Deutsches Bierhaus,** Roonstr. 33 (tel. 0221–240 1881). This is a real beerkeller, 418-square yards of it, and enormously popular. There are 17 different beers on draught and many bottled specialties, including Schäffbier, which must be stored for one year at a temperature of 25° before drinking. Good-value snacks are also available.

Klimperkasten, Alter Markt 39 (tel. 0221–216759). Piano music accompanies the Kölsch beer and snacks. There's a collection of mechanical musical instruments that are made to work every hour.

Wine Taverns

Kunibert der Fiese, Am Bollwerk 1–5 (tel. 0221–235808). Why someone chose to name this very pleasant place "Kunibert the Nasty" is a mystery. It has a great selection of wines.

Weinhaus Lenz, Ursulaplatz 9–11 (tel. 0221–133709). This is the city's oldest wine bar, with furnishings from castles, palaces, and churches, and is just the place for a good glass of wine. Try the house specialty, vegetables in aspic with fried potatoes *(Gemüsesülze)*.

Cafés

Reichard, Unter Fettenhennen 11 (tel. 0221–233892). Elegant café facing the cathedral. Serves an enormous selection of cakes and pastries, an excellent breakfast-buffet, and a small range of meals. There's a terrace and winter garden.

Riese, Schildergasse 103 (tel. 0221–211160). In the busy pedestrian mall. This is where you should try one of Köln's specialties, *Eissplitter-Torte,* a half-frozen cake made with ice-cream.

Zimmermann, Herzogstr. 11–13 (tel. 0221–231501). A paradise of cakes and pastries.

What to See and Do

MAJOR ATTRACTIONS. Altstadt (Old Town). Spread round the Romanesque church of Gross St. Martin, between Alter Markt and Rheingarten. Medieval houses, pointed gables, and winding alleys make this, the heart of old Köln, especially attractive. Traditional buildings have been meticulously restored and carefully combined with modern, residential architecture. It's a lively area at night, with many restaurants, cafés, and bars.

Beethovenpark, *Neuendörfer Allee. (From the cathedral take the*

U-Bahn 9, 11, 12, or 6 to Neumarkt, then change to streetcar 7 for Hermeskeiler Platz.) Within this beautiful city park is the **Decksteiner Weiher** lake, which remains ever popular. Row boats can be rented. There's also a café/restaurant.

Dom (Cathedral), *Domplatz. Guided tours in English Mon. to Fri. 10–11 and 2:30–3:30, Sat. 10–11, Sun. 2:30–3:30. No entrance fee. Treasury open Mon. to Sat. 9–4:30 (summer to 5:30), Sun. 12:30–4:30. Tower open Mon. to Sun. 9–5.* At the heart of the city stands this magnificent cathedral, a perfect example of High Gothic architecture and one of the largest cathedrals in Europe. Almost miraculously, it was largely untouched by the devastating bombing of the war and its soaring stone spires are an enduring symbol of the city's proud spirit. Building began in 1248, though the cathedral was only finally completed 632 years later, in 1880. From the outside, it is a majestic mass of buttresses and flying buttresses; inside the masses of stone rise up almost ethereally to the 43.5-meter-high (143 ft.) vaulting. The slender nave is flanked by four aisles.

Among the many art treasures are: the **Gero Cross,** one of Europe's oldest, largest, and most important sculptures, dating from 975; the **Shrine of the Three Kings,** an outstanding example of goldsmiths' work from the Rhine-Maas area and the cathedral's most valuable object; the famous *Dombild* **altar painting** by Stephen Lochner (circa 1450) which depicts the *Adoration of the Magi,* and is flanked by the patron saints of Köln, St. Gereon and St. Ursula; and the **High Altar,** dating from 1322, and covered by a single, 4.5-meter (15 feet) slab of black marble with snow-white figure decorations on all sides.

There are also **stained-glass windows** of breathtaking beauty from every epoch from the 13th- through to the 20th-century. Of particular significance are the two windows illustrating the Scriptures (dating from 1260 and 1275) in the ambulatory of the choir, the five magnificent Renaissance windows (1507–09) in the north side-aisles, and the famous Kings' Window in the choir clerestory which depicts the *Adoration of the Magi* and dates from 1310.

The finely carved oak **choir stalls** (1310) can seat over 100 people and are the largest of their kind in Germany. The **choir screens,** with their 42 paintings, also date from the early 14th century.

It is worth climbing the **spire,** nearly 100 meters (328 ft.) high, for the superb view of Köln and the distant mountains.

Gross St. Martin, *Martinspförtchen 8.* Romanesque church, built on the ruins of a Roman storehouse in the 12th century. The imposing central tower is a landmark in the city.

Museum Ludwig and Wallraf-Richartz-Museum, *Bischofs-gartenstr. 1. Open year-round Tues. to Thurs. 10–8, Fri. to Sun. 10–6; closed Mon.* Located between the cathedral and the Rhine, and one of Europe's most important art museums. It was opened in 1986 and contains a vast collection of paintings from the Middle Ages to the 20th century. The Dutch and Flemish schools are well-represented, with works by Rembrandt, Rubens, Van Dyck, and Hals. Here, too, are paintings by such grand masters as Tiepolo, Canaletto, Boucher, Renoir, Bonnard, Monet, Sisley, Pissarro, and Cezanne. The Ludwig Museum is entirely dedicated to 20th-century art and covers everything from sculpture to paintings to environmental works. It has a particularly outstanding collection of Picassos.

Rheinpark/Zoo, *Köln-Deutz, Kennedy-Ufer.* Köln's largest and newest park is connected by cable car across the Rhine with the Zoo. Buy a combined ticket in the Rheinpark which includes the cable car fare and zoo entrance fee. The zoo has 7,000 animals from 700 different species. *Open summer, Mon. to Sun., 9–6, winter, Mon. to Sun., 9–5. (Entrance in Riehler Str. 173).*

Römisch-Germanisches Museum (Roman-Germanic Museum), *Roncalliplatz 4. Open year-round Tues., Fri., Sat., and Sun. 10–5, Wed. and Thurs. 10–8.* Imaginatively-conceived museum, near the cathedral and the main train station, which focuses on Roman archeological finds from the Köln area. Standouts include the Diony-sian Mosaic, the tomb of Publicius, and prehistoric artifacts from the Rhineland.

OTHER ATTRACTIONS. Altes Rathaus (Old City Hall),

Rathausplatz, Alter Markt. Impressive ensemble of buildings from different periods dating back as far as 1130. Of particular note is the **Hansasaal** of 1349, the Renaissance **entrance hall** (1569–73), and the **tower** (1407–14) whose tuneful peal of bells can be heard daily at noon and at 5 P.M.

Botanischer Garten (Botanical Gardens), *Köln-Riehl, Am Botanischen Garten. (Reached by streetcars 15, 11, 16.)* About 12,000 different types of plants have been cultivated here. The southern part, called "Flora," was opened in 1864 and is laid out in the style of an English landscape garden. There are also several greenhouses with tropical and sub-tropical plants.

Brauerei-Museum (Brewery Museum), *Küppers Kölsch Brauerei, Köln-Bayenthal, Alteburger Str. 157. Open year-round Sat. 11–4.* A 100-year-old brewery, still in perfect working order.

Kölnisches Stadtmuseum (Köln City Museum), *Zeughasstr.*

*1–3. Open Tues., Wed., and Fri. to Sun. 10–5, Thurs. 10–8; closed
Mon.* This museum, dealing with the history of Köln, is housed in the
original city arsenal, built between 1594 and 1606 on the remains of
the Roman wall. The structure has a late Renaissance entrance gate by
Peter Cronenborch.

Mittelalterliche Stadtmauer (Medieval City Wall). The remains
of three medieval city gates have been preserved: the **Eigelsteintor** at
Ebertplatz, the **Hahnentor** at Rudolfplatz, and **Severinstor** at
Chlodwigplatz. There are also remains of the city wall on the
Hansaring and Sachsenring roads.

Museum für Angewandte Kunst (Museum of Applied Arts), *An
der Rechtsschule.* Scheduled to open in spring 1988. The whole
spectrum of the applied arts from early medieval times to the present
day is displayed in this new museum. There's a special Islamic section,
and a fascinating fashion collection covering 200 years of costume
history.

Tours

Sightseeing tours in English are organized by the tourist office,
Verkehrsamt der Stadt Köln, Unter Fettenhennen 19. The two-hour
bus tour starts at the tourist office and takes in monuments of Roman
architecture, the medieval city gates, Romanesque churches, the
cathedral, the city hall, Gürzenich, the modern city and main shopping
areas, the Rhine Park and Dance Fountain, and the trade fairgrounds.
May through Oct. tour departures are daily at 10, 11, 1, 2, and 3. Nov.
through Apr. tours are daily at 11 and 2 only. Cost is DM 17.

Between May and Sept., there are also guided walking tours of the
city. These tours last two hours and start daily at 4:30 from the tourist
office. Cost is DM 7.

During July and Aug., the tourist office offers a Kölner Abend
(Cologne Evening) on Fri. and Sat. at 8 P.M. This tour includes a bus
ride through the city, a boat trip on the Rhine, a cold dinner with
Kölsch beer, and a visit to a wine tavern and to the Colonius TV tower.
Cost is DM 35.

Most hotels in Köln also sell the **Kölner Knüller,** a special tourist
pack that includes a voucher for the sightseeing tour and a
Museumspass that will get you into most of the city's museums. Cost
is DM 22.

BOAT TOURS. The landing stages of the companies listed below are
located round the Hohenzollern Bridge next to the cathedral.

Dampfschiffahrt Colonia, Lintgasse 18 (tel. 0221–211325).

Departures from May through Sept. daily, every 45 minutes from 10–4. Cost is DM 6.

Köln-Düsseldorfer Deutsche Rheinschiffahrt AG, Frankenwerft 15 (tel. 0221–20881). Departures from end of Mar. through Sept. every hour from 10:30–2:15. Cost is DM 6.50.

Rhein-Mosel Schiffahrt, Konrad-Adenauer-Ufer (tel. 0221–121600). Departures from Mar. through Oct. daily, every 45 minutes starting at 10. Cost is DM 6.

Shopping

A shopping expedition round the center of Köln should start at the cathedral at the junction with **Hohe Str.** where the extensive pedestrian mall begins. Hohe Str. itself has many exclusive stores and small classy shops which attract thousands of window-shoppers. Those in search of less expensive items should go to **Schildergasse,** which runs between the lower end of Hohe Str. and Neumarkt. Here there are plenty of large shops and department stores with good-value merchandise. Other streets recommended for shopping (or window-shopping) are: **Mittelstr., Hohenzollernring, Ehrenstr.,** and **Breite Str.** Anyone interested in antiques should head for **St. Apern-Str.**

The most obvious souvenir to buy in Köln is the famous *Kölnisch Wasser* **(Eau de Cologne),** which is sold by the well-known manufacturer "4711," whose shop of the same name is in Glockengasse.

Entertainment and Nightlife

Most of Köln's nightclubs are concentrated in the following areas: Friesenstr. and Friesenwall, Hildeboldplatz and Maastrichterstr. (between Hohe Str. and city hall), near Hohenzollernring. For respectable evening entertainment, go to the Altstadt area around the Gross St. Martin church.

For detailed information about what's going on in the city, check the *Monatsvorschau,* a monthly program of events issued by the tourist office, or buy the monthly magazine, *Köln im . . . ,* which is available from newsstands and bookshops, price DM 2.

DISCOS. Alter Wartesaal, Hauptbahnhof (tel. 0221–431006). Open Fri. and Sat. only 10 P.M.–3 A.M. Entrance fee DM 15 (includes a DM 10 drinks voucher). Concert hall and disco in the old waiting room of the main train station. Things really get going here when other places start closing.

Filmdancing, Köln 80, Im Weidenbruch (tel. 0221–641010). Open Wed. to Sun. from 7:30 P.M. Entrance fee DM 3.50; drinks from

DM 4.50. A disco for movie buffs. Comedies and family movies are shown in three parts from 9 P.M. and there's dancing during the breaks.

Savoy Ballroom, Hohenstaufenring 25 (tel. 0221–247714). Open Wed. to Sat. 9–3. Disco in a converted cinema, with nostalgic '40s-style decor. Also has live jazz.

Subway, Aachener Str. 82–84 (tel. 0221–517969). Open Tues. to Sun. from 9 P.M. From Wed. to Sun. this is a disco for a mainly young crowd. On Tues., there's live jazz played by nationally- and internationally-known bands.

LIVE MUSIC. Luxor, Luxemburger Str. 40 (tel. 0221–219506). Open Sun. to Thurs. to 2 A.M., Fri. and Sat. to 3 A.M. Entrance fee on weekends DM 9 (includes a DM 7 drinks voucher). Up to 20 live performances monthly by jazz, rock, punk, and new-wave groups. (Tickets cost between DM 13–DM 17.)

Papa Joe's Jazzlokal "Em Streckstrump," Buttermarkt 37 (tel. 0221–217950). Open Mon. to Sun. 7:30–3 A.M., Sun. 11–3:30 P.M. Live music every evening, concentrating on traditional jazz, swing, and Dixieland.

Stadtgarten, Venloer Str. 40 (tel. 0221–516039). Concert hall with 200 seats for jazz concerts. Also a cinema which shows specialized productions.

Tanzbrunnen (Dance Fountain), Rheinparkweg (close to the fairground tower). Open May through Sept., Fri. 3:30–8 P.M., Sat. at 8 P.M., and Sun. 11–4 P.M. An open-air stage in the Rhine Park where folk, rock, and pop concerts are held. Also open-air dance parties. There's room for up to 10,000 people, with 2,500 seats——and it's very popular.

THEATERS AND CONCERTS. Kölner Philharmonie, Bischofs-gartenstr. 1 (Information: tel. 0221–240 2100; box office: tel. 0221–233854). Opened in 1986, this ultra-modern, circular concert hall under the new Wallraf-Richartz-Museum can seat up to 2,000 people. It puts on an extensive program of events, including concerts by the city's two main orchestras, the Gürzenich and the WDR (West German Broadcasting Company), as well as by international orchestras.

Oper der Stadt Köln, Offenbachplatz 1 (tel. 0221–212581). Rich repertory of high-class classical opera through to modern musicals.

TICKET OFFICES. For information about upcoming events and reservations, try:

KVB-Passage, Neumarkt (tel. 0221–214232).

Kaufhof, Schildergasse (tel. 0221–216692).

Rudolfplatz (tel. 0221–246945).
Saturn, Hansaring 98 (tel. 0221–121912).

◆

S P L U R G E S

Dinner at Weinhaus in Walfisch, Salzgasse 13 (tel. 0221–219575). Make the effort to find this wonderful 17th-century restaurant; it's located a block or so back from the Rhine in the Old Town between Hohenzollernbrücke and Deutzerbrücke. Behind its black-and-white timbered facade lurks the most atmospheric eating in Köln. Choose carefully, and prices won't be too high, either. Venison is a longtime favorite specialty, though you must order it for two.

◆

BONN

Bonn was catapulted onto the international scene in 1949 when it was chosen as the new capital of the German Federal Republic. Although the youngest capital in Europe, its history stretches back 2,000 years. Under the name of Castra Bonnensia, it was an important link in the Roman defense line along the Rhine and was first mentioned, by the historian Tacitus, in A.D. 69.

During the 13th century, the powerful prince electors of Köln moved to Bonn and established the city as a worthy capital of their domain. In 1244 Bonn was granted formal City Rights. Over the following centuries the city became the base of such notables as Ferdinand of Wittelsbach, bishop of Köln from 1601, and, in the 18th century, the Prince Electors Joseph Clemens and Clemens August, who transformed the city into a Baroque jewel. It was in Bonn, in 1770, that Beethoven was born.

Until 1949 Bonn was considered a somewhat sleepy university town, no more than the gateway to the romantic Rhine valley. Even today there are those who think that Bonn's most important asset is its surrounding countryside: the legendary Siebengebirge (Seven Hills) and the fertile valley of the Kölner Bucht (Cologne Bight). There's some truth to this; despite its status as the seat of government, Bonn has managed to retain the charm of a small town. In its streets, markets, shops, pedestrian mall, parks, and the beautiful residential area of Südstadt, the pace of life is unhurried—despite the presence of 38,000 students and countless diplomatic and government personnel.

Yet there can be no doubt that this is a world capital, and a vast administrative center. Proof is supplied in plenty by buildings such as the modern Federal Chancellery, the Bundeshaus (or the German Federal Parliament building), the building for the Members of Parliament, and a proliferation of other high-rise government buildings close to the banks of the Rhine.

Our ● symbol = Highly recommended.

GETTING IN FROM THE AIRPORT. Buses run from Köln-Bonn International Airport to the main train station in Bonn every half hour. Departures start at 6:50 A.M. and continue until 10:30 P.M. The trip takes half an hour and costs DM 6 one way, DM 9 round-trip. Bus departures from the main train station back to the airport start at 5:40 A.M. and 9:40 P.M.

USEFUL ADDRESSES. Tourist Offices. The main tourist office in Bonn is the Tourist Information Cassius-Bastei, Münsterstr. 20 (tel. 0228–773466), located close to the main train station. It provides information about the city, can handle all enquiries, and runs a free accommodations service; there's no charge for advance hotel reservations, either. The office is open Mon. to Sat. 8 A.M.–9 P.M., Sun. and public holidays 9:30–12:30.

Hotel reservations can also be made in advance by writing to Kongressabteilung des Presse-und Werbeamtes, Stadthaus, Berliner Platz 2, 5300 Bonn.

There's another tourist information booth in Bonn-Bad Godesberg, Kurfürstenallee 2–3 (tel. 0228–773927). Open Mon. to Thurs. 2–4, Fri. 8–12; closed Sat. and Sun.

Embassies. U.S.A., Bonn-Bad Godesberg, Deichmanns Aue (tel. 0228–3391); Canada, Friedrich-Wilhelm-Str. 18 (tel. 0228–231061); Great Britain, Bonn-Bad Godesberg, Friedrich-Ebert-Allee 77 (tel. 0228–234061).

Lost and Found. Fundbüro, Stadthaus, Berliner Platz (tel. 0228–772592); Bundesbahnfundstelle, main train station (tel. 0228–7151).

Emergencies. Medical, tel. 0228–671011; Pharmacy, tel. 0228–11500; Police, tel. 110.

Post Office. The Main Post Office at Münsterplatz 17 is open all day.

Car Hire. Autohansa, Römerstr. 4 (tel. 0228–631433); Avis, Adenauerallee 4–6 (tel. 0228–223047); Redcar, Bonner Str. 48 (tel. 0228–355075).

Taxis. (tel. 0228–555555).

Getting Around

Bonn has a complicated public transportation system comprising buses, subways, streetcars, and commuter trains. Fares vary according to distance and the time of day. Buy a **Tagesnetzkarte** (combined ticket which can be used on all forms of public transportation and is valid for 24 hours), price DM 6. Another useful combined ticket, which covers the environs of Bonn as far as Köln, costs DM 8. Also good value is the **Umweltschutzkarte** which is valid for three days' travel in Bonn, its environs, and Köln; price DM 15. The Bonn-only ticket costs DM 12.

Tourist tickets are available from the information office of the public transport company (SWB), and in the shopping mall under the main train station (tel. 0228–711820).

An alternative way of exploring Bonn is by bike. Bikes can be rented for around DM 10 per day or DM 32 per week; call 0228–631433. A biking map of Bonn *(Fahrrdakarte)* is available in all bookstores for DM 9.90.

Where to Stay

Moderate

Astoria, Hausdorffstr. 105 (tel. 0228–239507). 77 beds, all rooms with bath. Located close to the government quarter, this modern hotel has individually furnished rooms and provides a breakfast-buffet. Dinner served for residents only.

Drachenfels, Bonn-Bad Godesberg, Siegfriedstr. 28 (tel. 0228–343067). 34 beds, all rooms with bath. Built around 1900, but with modern comforts and pleasant rooms, this hotel is peacefully located right on the banks of the Rhine. It has views of both the Drachenfels mountain and the river.

Godesburg-Hotel, Bonn-Bad Godesberg, Auf dem Godesberg 5 (tel. 0228–316071). 22 beds, all rooms with bath. An ultra-modern hotel, built within the ruins of 13th-century Godesburg Castle, which has fine views over Bad Godesberg and the Rhine valley. Wood and glass are the dominant features of its interior, and there's a covered terrace, a wine tavern, and the Siebenbirge (Seven Mountains) Restaurant as well.

●**Schaumburger Hof,** Am Schaumburger Hof 10, Bonn-Plittersdorf (tel. 0228–364095/6). 63 beds, some rooms with bath. The nostalgic charm which pervades this timbered hotel on the Rhine enables you to overlook the fact that the rooms are rather old-fashioned and that few of them have bathrooms en suite. The building dates back to 1755 and it was here, on the terrace, shaded by lime trees, that Beethoven sipped his wine and, later, where Queen Victoria met Prince Albert. Simple, reliable cooking in the restaurant, though there's a notable wine list featuring over 180 different wines.

Inexpensive

Bergischer Hof, Münsterplatz 23 (tel. 0228–633441/2). 48 beds, some rooms with bath. On a pedestrian mall facing the cathedral, this is a clean and comfortable hotel with large bedrooms and a restaurant.

Youth Hostels

Jugendgästhaus, Bonn-Bad Godesberg, Horionstr. 60 (tel. 0228–317516).

Jugendherberge, Haagerweg 42 (tel. 0228–281200).

Camping

Campingplatz Genienaue, Bonn-Mehlem, Im Frankenkeller 49 (tel. 0228–344949). Located at the far end of Bonn-Bad Godesberg, and reached by buses 12, 13, 18, 19.

Where to Eat

Many restaurants in Bonn offer the "Bonn-Menu," a good-value fixed-price costing around DM 12. Listing of all Bonn's restaurants is available from the tourist information Cassius-Bastei, Münsterstr. 20 (tel. 0228–773466). It's called *Bonn bittet zu Tisch* (Bonn Asks You to Dinner) and costs DM 0.50.

Moderate

Daufenbach, Brüdergasse 6 (tel. 0228–637944/45). Small restaurant offering home-cooking; a great place for a quiet dinner and a glass of German wine.

Em Bahnhöffje, Bonn-Beuel, Rheinaustr. 116 (tel. 0228–463436). A one time train station now houses this small restaurant and its huge terrace overlooking the Rhine and the promenade running parallel to it.

●**Gasthaus im Stiefel,** Bonngasse 30 (tel. 0228–634806).

Bonn's most atmospheric restaurant; serving excellent local specialties. It's right next door to Beethoven's birthplace and is an absolute *must* on the younger traveler's tourist trail.

Im Bären, Acherstr. 1–3 (tel. 0228–633200). The oldest restaurant in town with a history stretching back to the Middle Ages. Serves German specialties; this is the place for frothing steins of beer and delicious homemade sausages.

Maternus, Bonn-Bad Godesberg, Löbestr. 3 (tel. 0228–362851). For years this place has been something of an institution in Bonn. Politicians, journalists, and artists all congregate to gossip and to eat. Excellent-value local specialties and fine Moselle wine.

Inexpensive

Hähnchen, Münsterplatz 21 (tel. 0228–652039). Located right in the heart of the city, this is a place without frills but it's always full. The good-value fixed-price menu *(Gedecke—soup, main course, dessert)* changes daily.

Cafés

Bonngut, Remigiusplatz 4 (tel. 0228–637212). Café/bistro for those who want to see and be seen. It's in a pedestrian mall, so the best view is from the tables outside.

Dahmen, Poststr. 2 (tel. 0228–634934). The modern surroundings obscure this traditional café's long existence. Great pastries to accompany your coffee; it's just a stone's throw from the main train station.

Müller-Langhardt, Markt 36 (tel. 0228–637446). The ideal place to stop for a cup of coffee and a slice of cake after a stroll round the fruit- and vegetable-market. Specialties include *Baumkuchen* and *Mokkamandelcremetorte* (coffee and almond cake).

What to See and Do

MAJOR ATTRACTIONS. Alter Friedhof (Old Cemetery), *Bornheimer Str. Open Mar. through Aug., Mon. to Sun. 7 A.M.–8 P.M., Sept. through Feb., Mon. to Sun. 8 A.M.–6 P.M. Guided tours on Tues. and Thurs. at 3 P.M.* The cemetery was established in 1715 and later became the burial place for many famous artists, composers and scientists.

Beethoven Haus, Bonngasse 20. *Open year-round, Mon. to Sat. 9–1 and 3–6, Sun. 9–1.* This is where Beethoven was born in 1770; today it houses one of the most important Beethoven collections in the world, including his last grand piano. There are letters, documents, scores, paintings, an extensive library, and an ear trumpet or two among his other personal possessions. The room in which he was actually born is furnished with just a marble bust of the master himself.

Botanischer Garten (Botanical Gardens), *Poppelsdorfer Schloss, Meckenheimer Allee 171. Open Apr. through Sept., Mon. to Fri. 8–7, Sun. 9–1, closed Sat.; Oct. through Mar., Mon. to Fri. 8–4:30, closed Sat. and Sun.* Well worth a visit, especially to see the 10 new greenhouses with exotic plants (open Mon. to Fri. 10:30–noon, 2–4).

Godesburg (Godesburg Castle), *Bonn-Bad Godesburg, Auf dem Godesburg. Open Apr. to Oct., Mon. to Sun. 10–6.* Built in 1210, the castle was destroyed in 1583, but, amazingly, the 32-meter-high (105 ft.) watch tower survived; it offers a wonderful view.

Münster Cathedral, *Münsterplatz. Open Mon. to Sun. 9:30–5:30.* This 900-year-old basilica was one of the most important churches along the Rhine in the Middle Ages; in 1314 and 1346 it was the coronation church of two Holy Roman Emperors. It is a fine example of late-Romanesque architecture with five towers, including a soaring central spire. The **cloisters** and the **crypt** are both noteworthy.

Rheinisches Landesmuseum, *Colmanstr. 14–16. Open year-round, Tues., Thurs., and Fri. 9–5, Wed. 9–8, Sat. and Sun. 10–5; closed Mon.* One of the largest museums in the Rhineland, focusing on the history, art, and culture of the Rhine Valley from the Roman occupation to the present day. There are numerous artifacts from Roman settlements in the area—paintings, glass, porcelains, sculpture, furniture, and a wealth of contemporary Rhineland art. Here also is the skull of **Neanderthal man,** who was discovered in 1856 just outside Düsseldorf.

St. Klemens Kirche, *Bonn-Beuel (Schwarzrheindorf), Dixstr. Open year-round, Mon. to Sat. 9–6:30, Sun. 12–6:30.* Two late-Romanesque churches (consecrated in 1151) built on top of each other and linked by an octagonal opening underneath the cupola. This double-chapel design enabled the Archbishop and the nobility to share the same service with the humbler congregation. There are some particularly fine frescoes.

OTHER ATTRACTIONS. Freizeitpark Rheinaue. An extensive park, close to the government quarter, with 48 km (30 miles) of footpaths running through it. There's a flea market on every third Saturday of the month, and many other open-air events as well. Visit the lake and follow the **archeological trail** which takes you through Rhenish history. Refreshments are available at the Parkrestaurant Rheinaue, open Mon. to Sun. 11–7.

Museum Alexander König, *Adenauerallee 150–164. Open year-round, Tues. to Fri. 9–5, Sat. and Sun. 9–12:30; closed Mon. and public holidays.* One of the three most important zoological collections in Germany.

Poppelsdorfer Schloss, *Meckenheimer Allee 171.* Small Baroque palace, once part of the Electoral Residence. It was built between 1715–40; today it is part of the university and is surrounded by the Botanical Gardens.

Rathaus (City Hall), *Marktplatz.* Baroque structure with an imposing outside staircase, built in 1738 to a design by the French architect Michael Leveilly. The pink, gold, and white Rococo facade was restored after the war.

Städtisches Kunstmuseum, Rathausgasse 7. *Open year-round Tues. and Thurs. 10–9, Wed. and Fri. to Sun. 10–5; closed Mon.* An important collection of 20th-century German paintings, including works by August Macke, the Rhenish Expressionists, and German post-1945 painters.

Universität (University of Bonn), *Am Hof.* Before becoming the capital of the Federal Republic, Bonn was essentially a university town, and it is not surprising that the university occupies one of the city's most impressive buildings, the **Küfurstliches Schloss.** This late-Baroque palace, with its fine Hofgarten and ornate gate, the **Koblenzer Tor,** was built in the 18th century by the powerful electors of Köln and completed in 1725. It is linked to Poppelsdorfer Schloss by a beautiful avenue of chestnut trees.

Tours

Guided tours are organized by the tourist information Cassius-Bastei. The tours last about two and a half hours and take in all the major sights of the city: the southern part of Bonn with its fine, late 19th-century architecture; Poppelsdorf Castle; Bad Godesberg with its residential and diplomatic quarters, and Redoute; the main government buildings; Beethoven's birthplace and the university; the pedestrian precinct with the old city hall; and Münster Cathedral.

Tours depart from the tourist office at Münsterstr. 20. Apr. 21 through June and the whole of Oct. tours are Mon. to Sun. at 10; July through Sept., Mon. to Sat. at 2; Nov. 7 through Dec. 19 and Jan. 10 through Apr. 11, Sat. only at 11. Cost is DM 14.

BOAT TRIPS. Among the most popular excursions from Bonn are boat trips on the Rhine. Two companies run day trips starting at the Alter Zoll landing stage, Brassert-Ufer, opposite Rheingasse. **Bonner Personenschiffahrt,** Brassert-Ufer Am alten Zoll (tel.

0228–636542); and **Köln-Düsseldorfer Deutsche Rheinschiffahrt AG,** Frankenwerft 15, 5000 Köln 1 (tel. 0221–2088–288).

Boat trips which start and end at the Schaumburger Hof landing stage in Bonn-Plittersdorf are operated by **Personenschiffahrt Siebenbirge,** Rheinallee 59 (tel. 0228–363737).

There are numerous boat trips going farther afield toward Koblenz or Mainz or down river to Köln. Prices vary according to the length of the trip. The destinations described below are all within easy reach of Bonn and make for a pleasant day out of town.

Königswinter. The picturesque, old town center has many wine taverns. Visit Drachenburg Castle and Drachenfels (Dragon's Crag) where you can simply stroll along, ride on a donkey, or take Germany's oldest cogwheel railroad (1883) for magnificent views over the Rhine valley and the Siebenbirge (Seven Mountains). The round-trip takes one hour and costs DM 9.30.

Linz. A scenic old town with fortifications dating back to the Middle Ages and a city hall built in 1392. The round-trip takes around four hours and costs DM 15.50.

Unkel. Well-known for its wine and beautiful timbered houses. Recommended wine taverns are: Im Lämmchen, Traube, and Rheinhotel Schulz. The round-trip takes around three hours and costs DM 12.50.

Shopping

Bonn is an agreeable place for shopping. Most shops are located on the pedestrian mall between the main train station, Münster Cathedral, the university, and the Rathaus (City Hall) on Marktplatz, where a market takes place every morning. There are numerous shops, and prices are often lower than in Köln, and distinctly lower than in Düsseldorf.

Entertainment and Nightlife

The tourist office sells a monthly brochure called *Bonn Information* (price DM 1) detailing all upcoming events.

DISCOS. Biskuithalle, Siemensstr. 12 (tel. 0228–622698). Open Wed., Fri. and Sat. 9–5 A.M.; closed on nights before public holidays. Rather anonymous, huge disco with an excellent sound and light show.

Madox, Münsterstr. 11 (tel. 0228–630090). Open Mon. to Sun. 8:30–1 A.M. Small and friendly disco.

LIVE MUSIC. Jazz Galerie, Oxfordstr. 34 (tel. 0228–639324). Open Mon. to Sun. 8–3 A.M. Live concerts and sessions featuring everything from Salsa to Free jazz.

FESTIVALS. Bonner Sommer. This open-air festival, which takes place all round the city, features folklore from different parts of the world, theater, puppet shows, lots of musical events, and art happenings. Lasts from May to Oct.

Pützchens Markt, Bonn-Beuel. A great fun-fair which attracts up to a million visitors every year. Takes place around the second week in Sept. on a Fri. and Sat.

THEATERS AND CONCERTS. For information contact Kulturamt der Stadt Bonn, Rathaus Bad Godesberg, Kurfürstenallee 2–3 (tel. 0228–774533 and 0228–774518/19). Tickets can be bought at the Konzert- und Theaterkasse, Mülheimer Platz 1 (tel. 0228–773666/773667). Open Mon. to Fri. 11–1 and 4–6, Sat. 11–1 only.

Beethovenhalle, Wachsbleiche (tel. 0228–631321). This is Bonn's main venue for concerts and congresses. It's a modern concert hall and home to the city's distinguished Orchester der Beethovenhalle. Every two years the Beethoven Festival takes place here, attracting visitors from all over the world.

Kulturzentrum in der Brotfabrik Beuel, Kreuzstr. 16 (tel. 0228–475424). Open Mon. to Sun. 2–5, one hour before events. Cultural center which houses a gallery, theater, and cinema. There's also the Fabrikkneipe pub, open Mon. to Sun. 7–1 A.M.

Oper, Am Boeselagerhof 1 (tel. 0228–773668). The Bonn opera house ranks as highly as those in Munich and Hamburg. The ambitious director engages first-class, international stars to sing here. Operas are always sung in their original language.

◆

S P L U R G E S

Dinner at Em Höttche, Markt 4 (tel. 0228–658596). Atmosphere is guaranteed in this 14th-century inn, as well as fine, if definitely Teutonic, dining—there are no nouvelle niceties here. Exposed brick walls, sturdy beams, and a huge fireplace set the mood. Try salmon if it's on the menu; it's always freshly caught. The wine list is extensive, but you can save by ordering one of the excellent-value house wines. Reservations are essential. The restaurant is located by the Baroque town hall.

◆

DÜSSELDORF

One of the greatest cities in the Ruhr, Germany's most industrialized region, Düsseldorf is also the capital of the state of Northern Rhineland Westphalia. In 1988 the city celebrates its 700th anniversary and there will be a variety of events and exhibitions to mark the occasion.

Although the Rhine flows through the city, it is said that Düsseldorf does lies not on the Rhine but on the "Ko," as its most famous and fashionable boulevard, the Königsallee, is nicknamed. Here, in addition to the elegant cafés, stores, and big banking houses, you will see little boys turning cartwheels in front of you; they are called *Radschläger*, and will expect you to give them a few pfennigs as a reward. It is an old tradition going back to the wedding of Elector Johann Wilhelm, the city's much-loved ruler in the 17th century. During the great procession a wheel of the wedding coach became loose and a ten-year-old boy saved the day by attaching himself to the wheel, gripping the hub, and cartwheeling with it to the end of the parade.

But there's much more to Düsseldorf besides the "Ko." The city is an internationally important commercial center, and hosts numerous trade fairs and congresses. It's also a major cultural center, one whose eminence in this field is not new. The poet Heinrich Heine was born here in 1797, while Johannes Brahms, Robert Schumann, and Goethe all lived in Düsseldorf. The city is said to put on some of the finest theatrical performances in Germany; it's a major film distribution center; and it's home to another industry that lies halfway between art and trade: graphic design. In addition, there are rich collections from the fields of art, literature, and science housed in the many museums and galleries.

Spacious parks and gardens are dotted around much of the city, while 1987 saw Düsseldorf hosting the Federal Garden Show. Stroll along the broad promenades lining the river, through the Rheinpark, and farther downstream, through Nordpark with its fountains and flower gardens, including the famous Japanese gardens, and sculptures.

For entertainment of a livelier kind, there is the Old Town (Altstadt). Though it's less than one square mile, there are some 200 beer-houses, bars, and restaurants teeming with life and activity. Added to all of which, there are historic monuments, castles, and churches to be visited, as well as river excursions and other places of interest nearby.

PRACTICAL INFORMATION

GETTING IN FROM THE AIRPORT. An S-Bahn commuter train will take you from Düsseldorf Airport to the city's main train station in 12 minutes. Bus 727 also runs from the airport to the main train station; the trip takes 22 minutes and one-way fare is DM. 3. There are up to 30 trains a day linking the airport to various other towns in the Rhine and Ruhr.

Facts and Figures

USEFUL ADDRESSES. Tourist Offices. Information on the city, sightseeing tours, theater tickets, hotel reservations, and any special requirements are handled by the Verkehrsverein der Stadt Düsseldorf, Immermannhof opposite the main rail station, Konrad-Adenauer-Platz, P.B. 8203, 4000 Düsseldorf (tel. 0211–350505). The office is open Mon. to Sat. 8–11, Sun. and holidays 4–10.

Another room reservations service *(Zimmernachweis)* is located in the main train station; open Mon. to Sat. 8–10, Sun. 4–10.

For advance information on Düsseldorf, write Werbe-und Wirtschaftsförderungsamt, Mühlenstr. 29, 4000 Düsseldorf (tel. 0211–8993827/3866).

Consulates. Consulate General of the U.S.A., Cecilienstr. 5 (tel. 0211–490081); Consulate General of Canada, Immermannstr. 3 (tel. 0211–353471); Consulate General of the United Kingdom, Georg-Glock-Str. 14 (tel. 0211–43740).

Lost and Found. Fündburo (city), Heinrich-Ehrhardt-Str. 61 (tel. 0211–899 3285), open Mon. to Fri. 8:30–12:30; VRR (public transport), Graf-Adolf-Platz 5 (tel. 0211–582 1469), open Mon. to Fri. 8–12 and 1–4; main train station (tel. 0211–3680454), open Mon. to Fri. 8–1.

Emergencies. Medical (tel. 0211–597070); Dental (tel. 0211–666291); Pharmacy (tel. 0211–1141); Police (tel. 110).

Post Office. Postamt 1, Immermannstr. (corner of Charlottenstr.). Open Mon. to Sat. 8–9 P.M., Sun. 10–6. There is also a post office at the airport.

Car Hire. Avis, Berliner Allee 32 (tel. 0211–329050), and at the airport (tel. 0211–421 6748); Hertz, Immermannstr. 48 (tel. 0211–357021/24), and at the airport (tel. 0211–421 6485).

Taxis. Tel. 0211–33333.

Getting Around

The city and suburbs are well-served by an inter-connecting transportation system comprising streetcars, S-Bahn (suburban trains), buses, and U-Bahn (subway), the whole scheduled to be in full operation in 1988. The whole network belongs to the VRR or Verkehrsverund Rhein-Ruhr. Fares are uniform for all forms of transport. But buy a 24-hour **visitors' ticket,** price DM 8.50, valid for the whole public transport system. It also allows you to take two children under 14 free of charge. It's available from all ticket booths and offices, from bus and tram drivers, and from VRR ticket machines. Make sure you cancel it in one of the automatic endorsing machines *before* starting your journey.

Where to Stay

In line with her position as the richest city in the Federal Republic, Düsseldorf has some outstandingly good hotels. Rates accordingly tend to be higher than just about anywhere else in Germany. Enquire about special weekend rates and the lower rates which apply during the quieter periods between trade fairs and the main vacation seasons. There are over 10,000 beds in the city, but within a radius of 30 km (19 miles) the figure rises to over 40,000, so consider staying in one of the many good-value private pensions and inns in the suburbs.

Moderate

Dase, Düsseldorf-Holthausen, Bonner Str. 7 (tel. 0211–799071). 56 beds, all rooms with bath. Located on the outskirts of Düsseldorf, this comfortable hotel is within easy reach of the downtown area on public transportation. A special "Nordic" breakfast-buffet is available.

Minerva, Cantadorstr. 13a (tel. 350961/62). 20 beds, all rooms with bath. Family-run hotel in a quiet side street near the main train station. The rooms are modern, well-furnished, and clean. A breakfast-buffet is provided; service is friendly.

⬤**Schloss Hotel,** Düsseldorf-Benrath, Erich-Müller-Str. 2 (tel.

0211–719570). 23 beds, all rooms with bath. Despite being part of the Düsseldorf conurbation, the village of Benrath has managed to retain its own individual character and is within easy reach of center city. The hotel, situated opposite the famous Rococo castle with its beautiful grounds, has modern rooms which have all been furnished to a uniform standard. There's also a restaurant.

Wilke, Düsseldorf-Oberkassel, Adalbertstr. 11 (tel. 0211–573189). 12 beds, all rooms with bath. The elderly lady who runs this small, homey hotel in a peaceful residential area, is a movie fan and has decorated the lobby with signed photographs of once-famous German actors. The rooms are immaculately clean and tidy, though somewhat heavily furnished. Pretty garden as well.

Inexpensive

Amsterdam, Stresemann-Str. 20 (tel. 0211–84058/59). 24 beds, some rooms with bath. Bed-and-breakfast pension, located conveniently close to the Königsallee. The rooms are clean, though furnished in a rather old-fashioned style; the ones at the back are quieter. A good breakfast is provided.

Gästhaus Benkwitz, Kölner Str. 26 (tel. 350031/32). 23 beds, some rooms with bath. 3 apartments. On the top floor of a five-story building. The rooms are large, modern, and clean, but rather simply furnished. Bed-and-breakfast only.

Modern, Düsseldorf-Oberkassel, Leostr. 15 (tel. 0211–589013/51108). 8 beds, some rooms with bath. Small pension, run by a young couple, which provides an average standard of accommodation. It's situated on the other side of the Rhine, just 10-minutes' walk from the Old Town.

Tal, Talstr. 36 (tel. 0211–370051/2). 40 beds, some rooms with bath. Although this small hotel, built on an extension of the Königsallee, is surrounded by several high-rise office blocks it has retained a certain dated charm. Inside, very little has been altered since the hotel was first opened in the '50s. The rooms are clean and the atmosphere is convivial.

Youth Hostel

Düsseldorf Youth Hostel, Düsseldorfer Str. 1 (tel. 0211–574041). 80 beds. Easy to reach from center city.

Camping

Camp Unterbacher See, Düsseldorf-Unterbach (tel. 0211–899 2038). Recreation area on the north bank of lake Unterbach.

Swimming, boating, surfing, and sailing school. Open Easter through Sept. 15.

Düsseldorf-Lörick, Oberlörick (tel. 0221–591401). On the Rhine. Swimming and boating facilities. Open Apr. through Oct.

Where to Eat

There are 2,400 restaurants in Düsseldorf, but eating in them is likely to prove an expensive experience. For plain food at affordable prices, go to the Old Town, or try one of the brewery restaurants all of which serve local specialties and Düsseldorf's famous Altbier, a dark and mature beer. Among the top local dishes, look for: *haxe* (shin of pork); *sauerbraten* (stewed marinated beef); *reibekuchen* (potato fritters); *halwe hahn* (cheese on a rye roll); or grilled *bratwürst* (sausage).

Moderate

Dampfnudel, Hohe Str. 2 (tel. 0211–131594). Small bistro which serves both regional and international cuisine, as well as an interesting range of cocktails. Try the yeast dumpling which gave its name to the place.

●**Mövenpick-Café des Artistes,** Königsallee 60 (tel. 0211–320314/17). A place you can always rely on for a good meal, delicious cakes, and a fine selection of wines. It's located in one of Düsseldorf's newest and most stylish shopping malls, the "Ko" Passage, which is, needless to say, otherwise very expensive.

●**Zur Auster,** Berger Str. 9 (tel. 0211–324404). This landmark fish restaurant has been going strong for 165 years. All manner of top-quality fish dishes and oysters prepared anyway you like them.

Inexpensive

En de Canon, Zollstr. 7 (tel. 0211–329798). Small restaurant with a garden, which serves special dishes at lunchtime. A bit quieter than some places as it's not right in the center of the Old Town.

Meuser, Düsseldorf-Niederkassel, Alt-Niederkassel 75–79 (tel. 0211–51272). Located on the left bank of the Rhine, this traditional and atmospheric inn dates back to 1641. It's popular with Düsseldorfers who come here for the two famous local specialties: *Altbier* and *Speckpfannekuchen* (pancakes filled with bacon).

Schumacher Bräu, Oststr. 123 (tel. 0211–326004). A brewery restaurant which offers a good choice of regional dishes. There is a pleasant courtyard as well.

Cafés

CaféHofkonditorei Bierhoff, Oststr. 128 (tel. 0211–360 3366). Glittering café in the Savoy Hotel, renowned for over 100 years for its excellent pastries.

Konditorei-Café Otto Bittner, Königsallee 44 (tel. 0211–80421). Café with pleasant sidewalk terrace situated on Düsseldorf's most elegant boulevard.

What to See and Do

MAJOR ATTRACTIONS. Altstadt (Old Town). Düsseldorf's historic area is worth visiting not only for its restaurants, taverns, and bustling nightlife, but for the important monuments and old buildings dotted around it. Standouts include the Gothic Stiftskirche **St. Lambertus,** with its twisted spire; the 16th-century **Rathaus** (City Hall), rebuilt after World War II; the round **Castle Tower,** the only surviving part of the 13th-century city castle; and the equestrian statue of **Elector Johann Wilhelm II,** who ruled Düsseldorf in the 17th century and greatly contributed to the city's cultural development.

Goethe-Museum, *Jägerhofstr. 1. Open year-round Tues. to Fri. 10–5, Sat. 1–5, Sun. 10–5; closed Mon.* More than 37,000 exhibits— manuscripts, first editions, paintings, sculptures, and medals—all relating to Germany's foremost man of letters. The collection was started by Anton Kippenberg, once the owner of the Insel-Verlag publishing house. It is now the third largest Goethe museum in Germany after those in Frankfurt and Weimar.

Hetjens-Museum/Deutsches Keramikmuseum (German Ceramics Museum), *Palais Nesselrode, Schulstr. 4. Open year-round Tues. to Sun. 10–7; closed Mon.* An outstanding collection of ceramics from the Stone Age to the present, housed in an impeccably restored Rococo palace. There are exhibits from all over the world— ancient Egypt, the Americas, Europe, and the Orient.

Kunstmuseum Düsseldorf (Municipal Art Gallery), *Ehrenhof 5. Open year-round, Tues. to Sun. 10–5; closed Mon.* The museum is particularly famed for its glass collection, one of the largest in the world and crowned by a unique collection of Art Nouveau exhibits, including pieces by Tiffany. Also well-represented are Medieval, Baroque, and contemporary sculpture, arts, and crafts. There are some fine paintings, too, among them Rubens' *Venus and Adonis,* plus works by Van Dyck, Goya, Tintoretto, Boucher, and the German moderns.

Kunstsammlung Nordrhein-Westfalen (North Rhine Westphalian Art Collection), *Grabbeplatz 5. Open year-round, Tues. to Sun. 10–5; closed Mon.* A glittering collection of 20th-century paintings by the luminaries of modern art—Picasso, Braque, Chagall, Dali, Magritte, Matisse, and Warhol among others. There is a substantial collection of works by Paul Klee.

Rheinturm (Telecommunications Tower). *Open year-round, daily 10–11. Elevator costs DM 4.* The highest building in Düsseldorf, and the best overall vantage point; it's located next to the new State Parliament building. It has a revolving restaurant on the top floor, and there are superb views of the city and into Holland.

St. Andreas, *Andreasstr.* Built between 1622–29 as a court church, the choir contains the **mausoleum** of the Electors of the Palatinate, including the tomb of Johann Wilhelm II.

Schloss Benrath. The most beautiful Rococo castle in Northern Rhineland, surrounded by formal gardens, lakes, and parkland. It was built between 1755–73 by the Elector Karl Theodor as a summer residence, and many of its splendid rooms are open to the public. The west wing houses the local **history museum.**

Stiftskirche St. Lambertus (Collegiate Church of St. Lambertus), *Altstadt.* The twisted spire of this Gothic basilica has made it one of Düsseldorf's main landmarks. Built between 1288 and 1394 on the remains of a Romanesque church, it contains Gothic wall paintings, a remarkable late-Gothic tabernacle, the Renaissance tomb of the 16th-century Duke Wilhelm the Rich, and a bronze door by the German sculptor Edward Matare. The church **treasury** has some fine pieces of silver.

OTHER ATTRACTIONS. Parks and Gardens.
Düsseldorf is a city of parks, the oldest of which was laid out as long ago as 1767. From Graf-Adolf-Platz to the "Kö" (Königsallee), through the Hofgarten as far as the old trade-fair hall, then on through the Nordpark (pausing at the Japanese gardens) you can walk through a continuous green belt the entire way to the new trade-fair complex.

Another pleasant walk will take you along the river bank through the **Rheinpark,** which stretches for nearly a mile from Ehrenhof, north of the Altstadt, to Theodor Heuss bridge.

Also of interest is the **Botanical Garden,** in the grounds of the university, and the **Aqua-Zoo,** a futuristic construction in the Nordpark housing aquariums, terrariums, and displays on natural history.

Stadtmuseum (City Museum), Bäckerstr. 7–9. *Open year-round,*

Tues., Thurs., Fri., and Sun. 10–5, Wed. 10–8, Sat. 1–7; closed Mon.
Interesting museum devoted to local history and culture, and featuring
paintings of local dignitaries, furniture, etchings, maps, and coins.

Tours

Sightseeing bus tours are organized by the tourist office and run
daily from Apr. through mid-Oct.; the rest of the year on Sat. only.
Departures at 2:30 from Bussteig 10 (bus stop 10) Friedrich-Ebert-
Str., opposite the main train station. The tour lasts two and a half
hours and includes a boat trip on the Rhine and a visit to the Rhine
Tower. Cost is DM 18.

The tourist office can also arrange special tours and bilingual
guides, as well as conducted tours for groups; call 0211–350505 for
details.

EXCURSIONS. During the summer boats ply up and down the Rhine
several times a day. There are KD landing stages all along the Rhine
promenade, as well as those of local passenger ship companies. Boats
belonging to city public transport association, Rheinische
Bahngesellschaft, sail regularly between Kaiserwerth to the north of
Düsseldorf and Benrath to the south. There is also a hydrofoil service
between Mainz and Düsseldorf. For information phone KD (tel.
0221–20881).

Kaiserwerth. North of the city on the Rhine, reached by streetcars
11 and D, and in summer by river boat. Visit to see the ruins of the
palace built by Emperor Barbarossa and the Suitbertus Cathedral
dating from the year 1000, with 13th-century works of the Köln
Goldsmiths' School, and the shrine containing the mortal remains of
Suitbertus, the Anglo-Saxon missionary who was active in this area
around 700. Additionally, there are Baroque gabled houses.

Neandertal. About 16 km (ten miles) from Düsseldorf and reached
by bus 43 from the main train station. This is where, in 1856, the
remains of an Ice-Age man, known ever since as Neanderthal Man
were found. The museum illustrates life in the Ice Age; a model of
Neanderthal Man has been reconstructed in the place where he was
first discovered. There is also a reserve stocked with animals of the Ice
Age—bison, wild horses, and wild cattle.

Shopping

Düsseldorf has the reputation of being West Germany's most elegant
shopping mecca—and is, in fact, the country's center for high fashion.
It goes without saying that there's not much in the way of bargains to

be found here, so unless you've saved up specially for a buying splurge, window-shopping is probably the likeliest bet for the budget traveler. But don't miss the opportunity to wander along Königsallee, known locally as the "Kö," with its numerous and exclusive shops, and arcades and malls selling furs, leather, jewelry, antiques, and books.

Entertainment and Nightlife

The Altstadt (Old Town) is the heart of Düsseldorf's nightlife. This is where you'll find a wide choice of pubs, taverns, and bars—some with restaurants, some with dancing as well. There are also organized nightclub tours available, which include drinks, dinner, and a visit to one or two nightspots. For details, contact the tourist office (tel. 0211–350505).

THEATERS AND CONCERTS. There are more than 20 theaters in Düsseldorf offering everything from opera to puppets. Advance reservations are recommended. Most tickets can be bought from the tourist office in Konrad-Adenauer-Platz; opera tickets must be purchased direct from the opera house.

Deutsche Oper am Rhein, Heinrich-Heine-Allee 16a (tel. 0211–89081); box office (tel. 369911). First-class opera, and resident ballet company, too.

Düsseldorfer Schauspielhaus, Gustav-Gründgens-Platz 1 (tel. 0211–363011).

Robert-Schumann-Saal, Ehrenhof 4a (tel. 0211–899 3829/6129). Düsseldorf's music conservatory, and an important venue for classical music concerts.

Tonhalle, Ehrenhof 1 (tel. 0211–899 5540); box office (tel. 0211–899 6123). Home of the highly-regarded Düsseldorf Symphony Orchestra; opened in 1978 in the former Planetarium building on the edge of the Hofgarten, and one of Germany's most beautiful concert halls.

S P L U R G E S

Dinner at Im Schiffchen, Kaiserwerther Markt 9 (tel. 0211–401050). Düsseldorf is an expensive city—it's the richest in Germany—and its inhabitants have developed a distinctly Dallas-style way of life. Conspicuous consumption, allied to a certain *hauteur*, is the only passport to success here. If this is your style, too, and your bank balance can stand it, make for Im Schiffern out in the suburb of

Kaiserwerth. The restaurant—it's set in an 18th-century building—is nouvelle with a vengeance. It's also quite superb. This may be one of the best restaurants in Europe, let alone in Germany. It's hard to say just what it will cost, but you should figure on paying at least DM 100 per person without wine. Reservations are essential.

◆

HAMBURG

Standing at the mouth of the river Elbe, one of Europe's greatest rivers, Hamburg was for centuries the busiest port in Europe, and is still the biggest in Germany. Every year some 15,000 ships sail up the lower Elbe carrying cargoes from all over the world. Many tourists also arrive here by sea.

Hamburg, or the "Hammaburg," was founded originally in 810 by Charlemagne. From its earliest days, the city's prosperity has depended on commerce. The first port was built in 1189, and in the mid-13th century the city entered into a mercantile partnership with neighboring Lübeck that developed into the Hanseatic League, a powerful commercial union of North Sea and Baltic cities of immense wealth and influence during the later Middle Ages. Even today, Hamburg calls itself a "Free Hanseatic City." But Hamburg is important not just as a great commercial center. It is also the hub of Germany's media.

Nearly all the country's principal newspapers and magazines are based here, as are numerous press agencies and public relations firms. Likewise, Germany's largest film and television studios are located in the city, and it is the center for both the record and tape industries.

Water dominates Hamburg. This is partly because of the harbor, but equally central to the scene is the Alster. Once little more than an insignificant waterway, it was dammed during the 18th century to form a lake. Divided into two at its southern end, this lake is known as the Binnenalster (Inner Alster) and the Aussenalster (Outer Alster), the two separated by a pair of bridges. It is surrounded by stately hotels, gardens, and private mansions, and altogether makes a fine sight. The center of the city is here.

Although the war took its toll on Hamburg, there are many elegant new buildings, perhaps more functional and less ornate than the old. Apart from the museums and sights, there is much to offer in the way of entertainment: numerous restaurants, cafés, bars, discos, live-music venues, theaters, and concert halls, and no fewer than nine glass-roofed shopping malls. And there is the district of St. Pauli, near the harbor, dedicated to nightlife. Here you will find club after club, catering to all tastes and all of them using sex—in one form or another—as a selling point. The whole area has a unique vitality, and is one of the main features of contemporary Hamburg—a thoroughly cosmopolitan city.

Our ● symbol = Highly Recommended.

PRACTICAL INFORMATION

GETTING IN FROM THE AIRPORT. Fuhlsbüttel, Hamburg's international airport, lies 11 km (seven miles) northwest of the city center. Regular bus services connect the airport to the city. Airport buses leave the Central Bus Station in Hamburg every 20 minutes from 5:17 A.M.–9:31 P.M., and the airport from 6:30 A.M. The journey takes about 25 minutes and the fare, including luggage, is DM 7.

There is also the Airport Express bus (no. 110) which runs every ten minutes between Ohlsdorf S-Bahn and U-Bahn Station and the airport. A ticket costs DM 2.80.

Facts and Figures

USEFUL ADDRESSES. Tourist Offices. The main branch of the Hamburg Tourist Office is in Bieberhaus, near the main train station at Hachmannplatz, (tel. 040–248700). Opening times are Mon. to Fri. 7:30 A.M.–6 P.M., Sat. 7:30 A.M.–3 P.M. In addition to their comprehensive hotel guide, they also publish an official monthly program, *Hamburger Vorschau* (price DM 2), which is available from any of their offices, and lists museums, and upcoming shows, theater performances, and special events. Also useful is the illustrated journal *Hamburg Tips* (price DM .50) which details seasonal events.

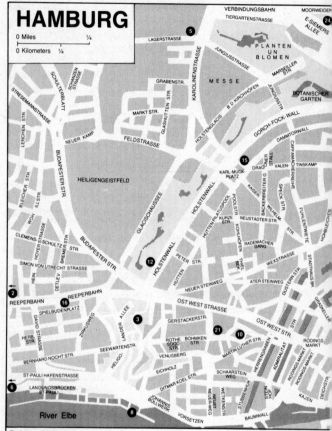

HAMBURG

0 Miles ¼
0 Kilometers ¼

Points of Interest

1 Alster Cruise Tour
2 Altonaer Museum
3 Bismarck Memorial
4 Deutsches Schauspielhaus
5 Fernsehturm
6 Fisch Markt
7 Hamburgische Staatsoper
8 Harbor Tour
9 Hauptbahnhof
10 Krameramtswohnungen
11 Kunsthalle
12 Museum für Hamburgische Geschichte

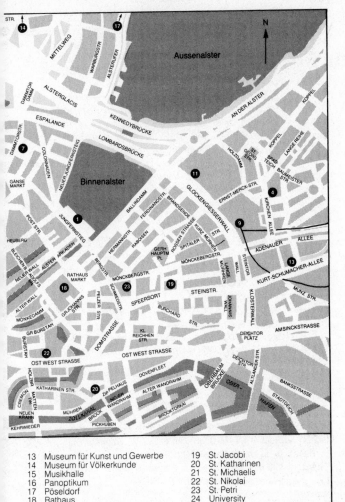

13	Museum für Kunst und Gewerbe	19	St. Jacobi
14	Museum für Völkerkunde	20	St. Katharinen
15	Musikhalle	21	St. Michaelis
16	Panoptikum	22	St. Nikolai
17	Pöseldorf	23	St. Petri
18	Rathaus	24	University

For practical assistance in booking accommodations, the Hotelnachweis (Hotel Accommodation Service) in the main train station at Kirchenallee/Hachmannplatz exit (tel. 040–248 70230) is open daily 7 A.M.–11 P.M. Alternatively, try the Tourist Office in the Arrivals Hall at Fuhlsbüttel Airport (tel. 040–248 70240), which is open daily 8 A.M.–11 P.M.

Hamburg Tip, at Gerhart-Hauptmann-Platz, also provides a full information service, with a central theater-ticket agency and a travel bureau for booking excursions and other trips. Another information pavilion is Hafen Tip (tel. 040–313977), which is part of the Harbor Information Center and is conveniently located between entrances 4 and 5 of the St. Pauli Landing Stages. Both Hamburg Tip and Hafen Tip are open Mon. to Fri. 9 A.M.–6 P.M.

Consulates. Consulate General of the U.S.A., Alsterufer 28 (tel. 040–441061); Consulate General of the U.K., Harvestehuder Weg 8a (tel. 446071); Consulate General of Canada, Esplanade 41–47 (tel. 040–230045).

Lost and Found. Städtisches Fundbüro mit Fundbüro der Hamburger Hochbahn (city and public transport), Bäckerbreitergang 73 (tel. 040–351851). Open Mon. to Fri. 8 A.M.–3:30 P.M. Nearest subway station: Gänsemarkt.

Medical Emergency. Tel. 040–228022.

Post Office. The post office in the main train station at Hachmannplatz is open 24 hours.

Car Hire. Auto Sixt, Ellmenreichstr. 26 (tel. 040–241466); Avis, Drehbahn 15–25 (tel. 040–341651); Hertz, Amsinckstr. 45 (tel. 040–230045).

Taxis. Tel. 040–441011; Tel. 040–656211; Tel. 040–682001.

Getting Around

Hamburg has an excellent public transportation system which incorporates subways (U-Bahn), an extensive suburban train network (S-Bahn), rapid transit trains (Schnellbahnen), and a fine bus service. There are 192 bus routes, and night buses (numbers 600–640) run all night, departing hourly from the Rathausmarkt and the main train station.

The entire system is inter-linked and tickets and fares are uniform, as well as being valid for the whole system, including the harbor passenger ferries. A day ticket valid for travel anywhere in the large central zone costs DM 7. There are also two good tourist tickets, valid for one or more days, that can be used on all public transport in the city

HAMBURG U-BAHN, S-BAHN, AND SUBURBAN RAIL SYSTEM

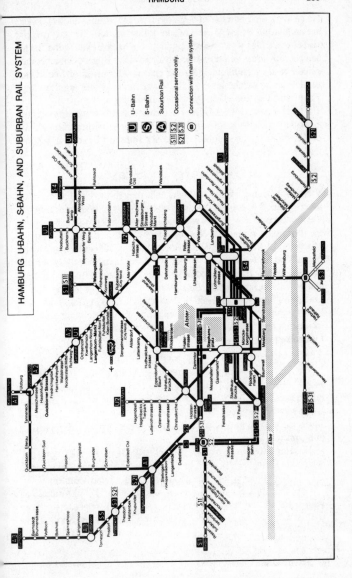

for an unlimited number of journeys. On any given day, both tickets are valid from 9 A.M.–4:30 A.M. the following day. The **city tourist ticket** costs DM 8 per person per day; the **area ticket** (good for the surrounding areas as well as the city) costs DM 13 per person per day. Accompanying children up to the age of 12 can travel free. Other tickets can be purchased from the automatic machines at all stations. The S-Bahn is free of charge for the disabled.

The Hamburg Tourist Office can provide details about all the tickets available and maps of the system. Further information is also obtainable from the Hamburg Passenger Transport Board (HHV), (tel. 040–322911).

Where to Stay

Rates in Hamburg can be high, and, though the city has over 300 hotels, there is a real shortage of good-value accommodations. Stick to the less expensive pensions and guest houses, most of which are near the Dammtor station, at Stephansplatz in Harvesthude, and on the other side of the river Alster. Also, as the city is host to many major events and conventions, it is best to book in advance through the Hotelnachweis (Hotel Accommodation Service) at the main train station in Hachmannplatz (tel. 040–2487 0230), or at the Tourist Office in the Arrivals Hall of Fuhlsbüttel Airport (tel. 040–2487 0240). Finally, it is always worth enquiring about special weekend and off-season rates that are offered by most hotels in Hamburg, as in other German towns.

Moderate

❤**Am Nonnensteig,** Nonnensteig 11 (tel. 040–473869). 32 rooms, all with bath. Situated in one of Hamburg's most popular residential areas, but still close to the center, this pension in an Art Deco villa attracts many artists, actors, and journalists. The rooms are furnished with an individual touch, and overall there is a very pleasant atmosphere.

Baseler Hospiz, Esplanade 11 (tel. 040–341921). 160 rooms, all with bath. Conveniently close to the city center, this family-run hotel is clean and well-cared for. The rooms have all modern comforts.

Graf Moltke, Steindamm 1 (tel. 040–280 1154). 100 rooms, all with bath. This modern, functional hotel is right opposite the main train station. The breakfast buffet is served in the Coffee Shop, where it is also possible to order light snacks in the evening.

Inexpensive

Amsterdam Garni, Moorweidenstr. 34 (tel. 441419). 34 rooms, most with shower. One of six pensions in the Dammtorpalais, just a couple of minutes' walk from the center. The large, welcoming rooms are all spotless. A good breakfast is provided.

● **Pension Meyer,** Rohrweihenweg 9 (tel. 7966359). 12 rooms and an apartment with balcony, all with bath. Although this small pension lies 12 km (seven miles) north of the center (good links to the city by public transport), it makes a terrific low-cost option for tourists on a budget. The house specialty is *Katenschinken*.

Pension Schmidt, Holzdamm 14 (tel. 2802119). 17 rooms, all with bath. In one of Hamburg's best locations, with a fine view of the Aussenalster. Breakfast is served in the large, comfortable rooms.

Youth Hostels

There are four main Youth Hostels in Hamburg for which a YH identification card is needed; there's no age limit.

Auf dem Stintfang, Alfred Wegener Weg 5 (tel. 040–313488). In a good location near the St. Pauli Landing Stages.

Hamburger Jugendpark Langenhorn, Jugendparkweg 60 (tel. 040–597350). For groups only.

Horner Rennbahn, Rennbahnstr. 100 (tel. 040–651 1671). Outside the center near the Horn Race Course and U-Bahn station.

Horner Rennbahn Gästehaus, Rennbahnstr. 100 (tel. 040–651 1671). Attached to the Horner Rennbahn listed above.

Camping

Camping Anders, Kielerstr. 650 (tel. 040–570 4498).
Camping Brünning, Kronsaalweg 86 (tel. 040–540 4994).
Campingplatz Bucholz, Kielerstr. 374 (tel. 040–540 4532).
Campingplatz Ramcke, Kielerstr. 620 (tel. 040–570 5121).

Where to Eat

Food in Hamburg is for the most part good quality and good value. One can also find some of Germany's top restaurants, but these are too expensive for most tourists on a budget. Aside from the hamburger, the city is known for its seafood and probably the most famous fish dish is *Aalsuppe* (eel soup), which is comparable to the Marseille *bouillabaisse*. Other Hamburg specialties include *Stubenküken* (chicken), *Vierländer Mastente* (duck), *Birnen, Bohnen und Speck* (pears, beans, and bacon), and the sailor's favorite, *Labskaus*.

Moderate

Block-House, Gänsemarkt-Passage (tel. 040–346005). Open daily

11 to midnight. One in a reliable chain of steakhouses found all over town. The service is quick and friendly, the steaks are excellent and accompanied by crisp, fresh salads. Other branches at Kirchenallee 50; Wandsbek Schlossstr. 48; Rotherbaum Grindelhof 73; Pöseldorf Mittelweg 122.

Schmitz, Maria-Louisen-Str. 3 (tel. 040–484132). Open Sun. to Fri. 12–3 and 6–10; closed Sat. and four weeks during July and Aug. This small, cozy restaurant, with its beautifully scoured wooden tables, serves both local specialties and international dishes. Only the freshest produce is used.

Inexpensive

☻Alsterhaus, Jungfernstieg 16 (tel. 040–359011). This famous department store is a must for every visitor and the food department offers something to suit all tastes. Here, too, you'll find the best-value glass of champagne in town to cheer you up should the Hamburg weather live up to its (bad) reputation!

Fischkajüte, St. Pauli Landungsbrücken, Brücke 5 (tel. 040–314162). Open Mon. and Tues., Thurs. to Sun. 11–8; closed Wed. The oldest fried-fish restaurant in Germany, located at the St. Pauli Landing Stages, with a splendid view of the bustle and activity of the harbor.

Kanzelmeyer, ABC-Strasse 8 (tel. 040–344296). Open Mon. to Sat. 12–midnight; closed Sun. Right in the center of the city, this popular restaurant has been serving Hamburg specialties for 80 years. Quick, clean, and inexpensive.

Pasta & Pizza Ricci, Gerhofstr. 18 (tel. 040–342261). Open daily 11–midnight; Sat. and Sun. to 2 A.M. An Italian restaurant, rather functionally furnished, but the many inexpensive specialties are appetizing and authentic.

Schlachterei Beisser, Eppendorfer Baum 4 (tel. 040–337365). An Imbiss (snack bar) in one of the best butcher's shops in town. Here you can sample spicy sausages, tasty meatballs, and nourishing *Erbsensuppe* (pea soup).

Silberkugel/Hamburgs Grosse Pizza, Hanseviertel (tel. 040–351635). Open 7:30 A.M.–11 A.M. and 7:30 P.M.–11 P.M. A choice of pizzas in three different sizes to suit your appetite. Also various potato dishes. The service is quick and the food tasty.

☻Zum Ochsenwirt am Schlacthof, Sternstr. 96 (tel. 040–433545). Open from 3 A.M. Enormous portions of good quality meat are served in this establishment in the vicinity of Hamburg's slaughterhouse. Definitely worth a visit for a hearty meal.

Wine Taverns

Bistrot à Vin, Grosse Bleichen 36 (tel. 040–351635). Located in the Hanseviertel Shopping Gallery. This has become *the* meeting place for the wine connoisseurs of Hamburg. There are over 400 wines to sample and light snacks are served to accompany the wine-tasting. Promotional offers on special wines are always available.

Weinstuben am Grossneumarkt, Grossneumarkt 10 (tel. 040–346689). Cellar tavern adorned with wood paneling. Serves mainly Alsatian, Pfälzer, and Badische wines. Soups and wholesome dishes of *matjes* (herring) and *schwarzbrot* (black bread) can be ordered with the wine.

Zur Traube, Karl Theodor Str. 4 (tel. 3909347). In a side street behind the Ottenser Market Square. Rustic decor that has been the same since 1936. Over two-dozen different kinds of "open" wine, and 50 different bottled vintages. Snacks, too.

Cafés

Alsterpavillon, Jungfernstieg 54 (tel. 040–345052). Overlooking the Inner Alster lake, this is a Hamburg institution where everybody meets and is *the* place to be seen. First-class confectionary and cakes.

Andersen, Wandsbeker Marktstr. 153 (tel. 040–684042). Here, Hans Christian Andersen's fairy tales are transformed into cakes. No additives, only a little sugar, and a lot of tasty ingredients are used to create the finest, fanciest cakes in town.

Vernimb, Spitalerstr. 9 (tel. 040–324455). The ideal place for a cup of coffee after shopping in the area around Mönckebergstr. Situated on a "bridge" over the pedestrian precinct, it has a fine view onto Spitalerstr. Pyramid cake is a specialty.

➡ Witthüs Teestuben, Elbchaussee 499A (tel. 040–860173). Open Mon. to Sat. 3–11, Sun. 11–11. Very good home-made bread and cakes (wholemeal only), and delicious snacks are served in this delightful, old thatched-roof house. Candlelight and background classical music help create a gentle ambiance. During the summer, there are also tables outside in the beautiful Hirschpark in Blankenese.

What to See and Do

MAJOR ATTRACTIONS. Kunsthalle (City Art Museum), *Glockengiesserwall. Open year-round, Mon. to Sun. 10–5.* This is Hamburg's—indeed North Germany's—major art museum, located right by the main train station. You'll find works by practically all the great northern European masters from the 14th to the 20th century, as well as by painters such as Goya, Tiepolo, and Canaletto. There's a vast collection of 19th-century German painting, which many people, frankly, find rather dreary, but the Impressionists—Monet, Renoir, and Sisley—help lighten the mood. An almost equally sizeable collection of 20th-century works, with Picasso, Klee, Matisse, Moore, Calder, and Caro well to the fore, trace the development of modern painting and sculpture. For many visitors, however, the highlight of the museum is the *Grabow Altarpiece,* painted in 1379 by a painter known only as Master Bertram. The central scene is of the Crucifixion, but the numerous side panels show the story of man from Genesis to the Nativity.

Rathaus, *Marktplatz. Guided tours in English from Mon. to Fri. every hour between 10:15 and 3:15, Sat. and Sun. between 10:15 and 1:15.* This is Hamburg's city hall, an immense heap of a building— there are 647 rooms—built at the end of the 19th century and resting on 4,000 oak piles. No one is likely to claim that this gigantic building, complete with towering central clock-tower, is the most graceful structure in the city, but for the sheer opulence of its interior, it's hard to beat. Although you only get to see the state rooms, the tapestries, huge staircases, glittering chandeliers, coffered ceilings, and mighty portraits convey forcefully the wealth of the city in the last century, and give a rich insight into bombastic municipal taste.

St. Michaelis, *Krayenkamp 4.* Not only is this just about the only Protestant Baroque church in northern Germany, it's also very much the symbol of Hamburg, or, at least, its 132-meter-high (433 ft.) tower is anyway. The tower—called, simply, "Michael" by the Hamburgers—is a weighty and cumbersome structure, topped by a tapering green spire on an oriental-looking dome. You get a great view from the summit. Masochists can climb the 449 steps; everyone else will take the elevator (DM 2.5). However, it only operates mid-Mar. through Oct., Mon. to Sat. 9–5:30. The building has had a checkered past. It was built originally between 1750 and 1762, but largely destroyed by fire in 1906. Rebuilt, it was then almost entirely destroyed by Allied bombing in 1943—bombing which claimed the lives of 50,000 Hamburgers. The present building, a faithful copy of the original, went up in the '50s.

OTHER ATTRACTIONS. Alsterpark, Harvestehuderweg. A beautiful park on the Alster, with a wonderful view of the city skyline. Tends to get very crowded on weekends.

Altes Land (Old Land). *Reached by ferry from St. Pauli Landungsbrücken (Brücke 3) to Lühe. Ferry runs May through Sept.,*

Mon. to Sun. every hour between 9–5, price DM 11. This traditional fruit-growing region, with its vast timbered farmhouses and many canals, is particularly worth a visit in May when the fruit trees are in blossom or during August when the cherry harvest is taking place.

Blankenese. *Reached easily by S-Bahn and bus 48.* A picturesque village where once only fishermen and sailors lived, but now considered one of the most desirable addresses in Hamburg. Wander through the maze of narrow streets and terraces, past quaint cottages with little gardens, and up a total of 4,864 winding steps which lead to the 87-meter-high (285 ft.) **Süllberg,** from which there is a magnificent view over the river Elbe. Blankenese also has a very lively **market** on Bahnhofsstrasse (open Tues., Fri., and Sat.).

Grossneumarkt. Located between the city center and St. Pauli, this area has blossomed into a delightfully atmospheric quarter full of pubs and clubs. Take a stroll along **Peterstr.** to see the restored brick and half-timbered houses and the monument to **Brahms,** Hamburg's most illustrious son.

Hagenbecks Tierpark (Zoo), *Stellingen Hagenbeckallee, (U-Bahn: Hagenbecks Tierpark). Open summer Mon. to Sun. 8–7, winter Mon. to Sun. 8–4:30.* Originally founded in 1907, this extensive zoo in the northwest suburb of Stellingen has long enjoyed a reputation for modernity and innovation. It was the first zoo anywhere to keep animals in open-air pens, and now has about 2,500 different species.

Hirschpark. *(Main entrance: Mühlenberg; S-Bahn station: Blankenese.)* Beautiful landscaped park on the river Elbe, with ancient trees and a game enclosure. There's a classical residence called **Hirschparkhaus** and a charming **café** in a thatched-roof house.

Krameramtswohnungen, *Krayenkamp 10–11 (U-Bahn: Rödingsmarkt.) Open year-round, Mon. to Sun. to 7 P.M.; apartment open Tues. to Sun. 10–5. No entrance fee.* One of the few relics of old Hamburg, these timbered houses were built in 1676 by the Merchants' Guild for the widows of its members. One apartment, furnished in the original period style, can be visited. There's also an art gallery, café, and a restaurant.

Museum für Hamburgische Geschichte (Hamburg Historical Museum), *Holstenwall 24. Open year-round, Tues. to Sat. 10–2 and 2–5; closed Sun. and Mon.* Here's where you can find out all about Hamburg's history, especially its maritime heritage. The **Historic Emigration Office** is also housed here. Opened in 1984, it is Germany's first historical documentation center for the history of emigration. Between 1850 and 1914 almost five million people passed through Hamburg's harbor on their way to the U.S., Canada, and Australia. The collection has a data store with the names of all those who left Germany between those years. Visitors interested in researching their immigrant forefathers need only provide the name and year of emigration from Germany. A search through the archives costs $30–$60 and provides a certificate stating all personal data, family members, and town of origin.

Museum für Kunst und Gewerbe (Arts and Crafts Museum), *Steintorplatz 1. Open year-round, Tues. to Sun. 10–5; closed Mon.* You'll find the Arts and Crafts Museum just south of the main train station. This is one of the most fascinating and comprehensive collections of its kind, both in terms of the historical periods covered by the museum and their geographical range. There are medieval tapestries and Picasso posters; Japanese objects and Italian Renaissance religious artifacts. The highlight is probably the collection of German Art-Nouveau objects, the largest of its kind in the world.

Övelgönner Museumshafen (Harbor Museum). *Reached by bus to Anleger Neumühlen. Open Sat. and Sun. 11–8; closed Jan. and Feb. and when the river Elbe is frozen.* With Hamburg's long and proud history as a major port and trading city, it is perhaps not surprising that she can boast a maritime museum which actually floats! Inside, you'll see sailboats, freighters, fire-ships, and all manner of sea-related exhibits.

Planten un Blomen. *(Main entrance: Stephansplatz; U-Bahn: Stephansplatz.) Open year-round, Mar. through Sept. daily 7–10; Oct. through Feb. daily 7–8.* Right in the city center, a large park with many rare trees and shrubs, beautiful flower-beds and several greenhouses with exotic plants. There's a miniature railway for trips round the park, and during the summer there are concerts and an illuminated water organ.

Schloss Ahrensburg *(S-Bahn: Ahrensburg.) Open year-round Tues. to Sun. 10–12:30, 1:30–5; closed Mon.* A Renaissance moated castle surrounded by magnificent parkland. The interior dates back to the 18th century. See also the castle church, a simple, post-Gothic structure with a delicate Baroque interior, and the 12 **Gottesbuden** (paupers' dwellings) in a low, semi-detached building which was constructed at the same time as the castle.

Vierlande/Marschlande. *Reached by boat from the Jungfernstieg landing stage.* Only 12 km (seven miles) from the city center is Germany's main fruit- and flower-growing region. It is a picturesque area dotted with villages, including **Curslack, Neuengamme, Altengamme,** and **Kirchwerder.** In Curslack, you can visit the oldest house in the Vierlande (Four Lands), the **Rieck-Haus,** which dates back to 1533. Also interesting is the **Bergedorfer Schloss,** a 13th-century moated castle. The roundtrip takes about six hours and costs DM 32.

Tours

The Hamburg tourist office organizes various sightseeing tours which start from Kirchenallee at the main train station. There are two city tours, one lasts two hours and costs DM 18; the other takes two and a half hours and costs DM 22. For further information about all available trips and tours, stop in at any of the Tourist Information Offices or call 040–220 1201.

HARBOR TOURS. Hamburg is the largest and busiest port in the Federal Republic of Germany. Particularly interesting for the first-time visitor is the **Stadt- und Hafenrundfahrt** (the combined City and Harbor tour) which takes two and a half hours, price DM 23, and includes a boat trip round the harbor.

Another way of exploring the life and activity of the port area is to take a normal harbor ferry, either number 77 to Kaiser-Wilhelm-Höft or number 66 to Stoltenkai, get off and walk along the quays taking in the many fascinating sights at your own leisure. To reach the harbor, take the S-Bahn and U-Bahn to St. Pauli Landungsbrücken.

BOAT TOURS. Three rivers pass through Hamburg: the Elbe, the Alster, and the Bille. Boat tours on all three rivers and on the city's many canals and waterways are a relaxing way of seeing the sights.

Alsterrundfahrten (round trips on the Alster). Duration about 50 minutes; price around DM 10; landing stage: Jungfernstieg.

Fleet-Fahrten organize tours which take in the canals, the duty-free harbor, and the warehouse town. Duration about two and a half hours; price around DM 20; landing stage: Jungfernstieg.

Kanalfahrten run boat trips that include the Inner and Outer Alster, romantic canals, and the more outlying areas such as Barmbek. Duration about two hours; price DM 13; landing stage: Jungfernstieg.

Shopping

Shopping facilities in Hamburg are excellent, with a wide range of shops to suit all tastes and pockets. But be warned, however, that like so many places in Germany budget shopping can often mean window-shopping.

As an international port and city, Hamburg's specialties are varied and the wares offered come from all over the world. There is a particularly large choice of English clothing, furniture, antiques and, of course, tea, as well as lobster, smoked salmon, and caviar. It is also well worth looking for some maritime souvenirs: ships in bottles, maps, charts, coins, and uniforms.

The city has nine shopping malls which make shopping a real treat, even when it's raining. The way through this dense network of arcades leads you through the cool, industrial-like architecture of the **Gänsemarkt-Passage;** the two adjacent passages of **Neuer Gänsemarkt** and **Gerhof;** the glass-roofed **Hanse-Viertel Galerie Passage,** which is over 200 meters (656 ft.) long; the **Galleria,** with its marble pilasters; the classical building of the **Alte Post;** the passage in the 100-year-old **Hamburger Hof** office building; and finally, through the **Landesbankgalerie.**

Department stores and shops in the lower price ranges line the **Mönckebergstr.** and **Spitalerstr.,** while more expensive shops are located in the streets around the **Jungfernsteig.** Bars and cafés proliferate.

Antique shops are concentrated in the city center in the **ABC-Str., Neue ABC Str., Poststr.,** and in the **Antique Center** in the **Markthalle.** Outside the city center, both **Blakenese** and **Pöseldorf** also have good antique shops. **Pöseldorf** is a small, modern shopping area on the Outer Alster, with trendy boutiques, pubs, and restaurants.

One of the city's most colorful and busy attractions is the **Fischmarkt** (Fish Market), held every Sun. from 6 A.M. It is by no means confined to fish, and everything from birds to bicycles is on offer. This is the kind of place where you can wander happily for hours.

The streets around the port—**Rödingsmarkt, Johannisbollwerk,** and the area directly behind them—all have interesting maritime and nautically-related shops.

Kaufrausch, Isestr. 74 (tel. 040–477154). In this reputable, if unconventional mini department store, you are likely to find just the right gifts and souvenirs for the folks back home.

Steinmetz und Hehl, Rödingsmarkt 20 (tel.040–364652). The all-in-one outfitters for seafaring men and women—everything from hats to an admiral's uniform!

Entertainment and Nightlife

The hottest spots in town are concentrated in the St. Pauli harbor area, on the Reeperbahn and in a little side street known as the Grosse Freiheit (or Great Freedom, and that's putting it mildly!). The shows themselves are expensive (and yes, you will see live sex acts on stage), but to walk through this area is an experience in itself and you can soak up the atmosphere without spending anything. It's *not* advisable, however, to travel through this part of the city alone, especially if you're a woman.

Indeed, if you have any doubts about the St. Pauli district, but want a peep anyway, the best bet is to join one of the organized tours arranged by the tourist office. The "Hamburg By Night" tour starts at 8 P.M. on Fri. and Sat., departing from Kirchenallee at the main train station. It will show you the nightlife for which the St. Pauli quarter is famous (or notorious, depending on your point of view), and will take you to a typical dive. For DM 80 per person, it's an expensive but safe way of seeing most—if not all—of what's on offer.

It's no understatement to say that while some of the sex clubs may be quite good fun and relatively harmless, a good many others are pornographic in the extreme. None gets going until about 10; all will happily accommodate you till the early hours. Order your own drinks rather than letting the hostess do it for you and pay for them as soon as they arrive, though check the price list again before handing the money over. If you order whisky, for example, you can be sure you will not get an inexpensive brand.

Sexual entertainment aside, Hamburg has a good selection of clubs, live music venues, discos, theaters, and concert halls where you can enjoy both contemporary and classical culture of a more conventional, but no less varied kind. The *Hamburger Vorschau,* published by the tourist office (price DM 2), gives information on events in town and provides details of theater programs, concerts, and exhibits. Another monthly magazine which concentrates on cultural activities is *Szene Hamburg,* available from all book stores and newsstands (price DM 3.50).

SEX-SHOWS. The following is a small selection of the many places to go, and includes only those which offer the less bizarre and/or sordid shows.

Colibri, Grosse Freiheit 34 (tel. 040–313233). Famous and expensive sex-show theater, considered by some to be the best, and certainly a magnetic attraction for many.

Safari, Grosse Freiheit 21 (tel. 040–315400). One of the top spots; quite classy, and with prices to match.

Salambo, Grosse Freiheit 11 (tel. 040–315622). Sex theater with an amazing show.

LIVE MUSIC. Hamburg is Germany's jazz capital. There are countless clubs, pubs, and cellars where every evening well-known artists of the scene pluck strings or pound keys. There are over 100 live-music venues to choose from; a choice few are listed below.

Birdland, Gärtnerstr. 122 (tel. 040–405270). Hamburg's newest jazz club with live jazz every day except Mon. and Tues. Swing, bebop, and modern.

Cotton Club, Alter Steinweg 27–31 (tel. 040–343878). The legendary, traditional jazz club. Smoky and intimate.

Fabrik, Barnerstr. 36 (tel. 040–391565). (S-Bahn: Altona.) This 19th-century former munitions factory is now a major venue for live concerts, theater events, and readings of contemporary literature. Regularly attracts a big audience; particularly recommended is the *Frühschoppen* jazz sessions which take place on Sun. mornings around 11.

Grosse Freiheit 36, Grosse Freiheit 36 (tel. 040–319 3649). Here's where the Beatles first appeared. Still holds many live concerts ranging from rock and funk to reggae and jazz. Also has discos.

DISCOS. Alsterufer 35, Alsterufer 35 (tel. 040–418155). Open Tues. to Sun; closed Mon. Bar, disco, restaurant, and gallery–not only for the very young. You must be properly dressed and in tune.

Offline, Eimsbütteler Chaussee 5 (tel. 040–439 8094). Attractive surroundings in which to bop to good music. There's an amazing laser show at midnight.

THEATERS AND CONCERTS. High-class drama, ballet, classical music, and opera is rampant in Hamburg. There are some 30 theaters, though tickets are often difficult to obtain and expensive. Consult the *Hamburger Vorschau* for monthly listings of theater and concert programs, complete with details of box-office opening times and performances.

Deutsches Schauspielhaus (German Theater), Kirchenallee 39 (tel. 040–248713). (S-Bahn and U-Bahn: Hauptbahnhof.) One of Germany's most prestigious theaters, staging modern productions of classic and avant-garde plays. Re-opened in 1984, the theater has been extensively restored to its turn-of-the-century splendour. A real treat to visit.

The English Theater, Lerchenfeld 14 (tel. 040–225543). (U-Bahn: Mundsburg.) Ideal for visitors; productions are in English only.

Hamburgische Staatsoper (Hamburg State Opera), Dammtorstr. 28 (tel. 040–351555). (U-Bahn: Gänsemarkt/Stephansplatz; S-Bahn: Dammtor.) Internationally renowned for the excellence of its productions and outstanding ballet ensemble, this 300-year-old opera house is still rated as one of the very best in Germany.

Musikhalle (Concert Hall), Karl Muck Platz. (U-Bahn: Messehallen.) Hamburg's most important concert hall, where its two major orchestras, the Philharmonisches Staatsorchester (Philharmonic Orchestra) and the Sinfonieorchester des Norddeutschen Rundfunks (North German Radio Symphony Orchestra), as well as other internationally-known orchestras and artists appear regularly. The hall, built in Baroque style, was opened in 1908 and seats 1,900 people.

NDR—Norddeutscher Rundfunk (North German Radio) Studio 10, Oberstr. 10 (tel. 040–413 2504). (U-Bahn: Klosterstern.) Concerts by the Radio Symphony Orchestra, as well as guest appearances by international artists.

Operettenhaus (Operetta House), Spielbudenplatz 1 (tel. 040–311171). (U-Bahn: St. Pauli.) The place for light opera and musicals.

TICKET OFFICES. Theaterkasse im Alsterhaus, Jungfernsteig 16 (tel. 040–3590 1323). Located in the famous Alsterhaus department store.

Theaterkasse Central, Gerhart-Hauptmann-Platz (tel. 040–324312). In the Hamburg Tip information pavilion.

Theaterkasse Garlic (tel. 040–342742). In the Hanse-Viertel shopping mall.

Theaterkasse O. Wickers, Tourist Office in Bieberhaus, Hachmannplatz (tel. 040–280 2848). At the main train station Tourist Office.

Excursion to Lübeck

If you're spending a few days in Hamburg, consider visiting Lübeck, just 65 km (40 miles) away to the north. It's a major attraction in its own right and deserves at least a day or two of your time. Lübeck, "Queen of the Hansa," was Hamburg's chief confederate in the Hanseatic League, and almost the equal of Hamburg as a powerful port, though it was the Baltic rather than the North Sea through which the city's trade passed. The old harbor buildings and docks along the river Trave provide visible evidence of the ancient prosperity of the port. Indeed it was already an important and privileged city in the 12th century, while in 1266, under the Hohenstaufen emperors, it became an Imperial Free City.

Even when the Hanseatic League fell into decline, Lübeck was able to maintain its role as a major commercial and trading center. By the 15th century, it was well-known not only for its chief export—salt—but as an artistic powerhouse.

Despite the severe damage inflicted on the city during World War II, many of its notable buildings have been carefully restored, and the historical wealth of the old town is obvious from the fine old brick buildings in the center. Lübeck is famous for its brick-work and the most spectacular example is city hall (Rathaus), which retains in part the black glazed tiles characteristic of the region.

GETTING THERE. Just 65 km (40 miles) northeast of Hamburg, Lübeck is linked to the national network of InterCity trains and can easily be reached from any major German city. The main train station is just a few minutes' walk from the city center. If you're traveling by car from Hamburg, take the E4 autobahn.

USEFUL ADDRESSES. Tourist Offices. The main tourist information office, Touristbüro des Lübecker Verkehrsvereins, Am Markt, (tel. 0451–72300/72339), can handle all enquiries and provides an accommodations service as well. A hotel reservation costs DM 5—which the hotel will then refund. Open Mon. to Fri. 9–6, Sat. 9–2, Sun. 10–12.

There is another tourist office in the main train station; open Apr. to mid-Oct., Mon. to Sat. 9–1 and 3–8, Sun. 11–3.

The tourist office sells several useful publications about what's going on in Lübeck. The monthly journal *Lübeck Aktuell* (price DM 1) gives up-to-date information on attractions and events in both Lübeck and Travemünde, with details of opening times. The guidebook *Lübecker Altstadtbummel am Abend* (price DM 4.80) provides suggestions for evening walks around the old town.

If you want information in advance of your visit, write Amt für Lübeck-Werbung und Tourismus, Beckergrube 95, 2400 Lübeck (tel. 0451–122 8109.) This office, however, cannot help with hotel reservations.

Lost and Found. City: Dr.-Julius-Leber-Str. 46–48 (tel. 0451–122 3256); public transport: Roeckstr. 49a (tel. 0451–888707).

Medical Emergency. Tel. 0451–71081.

Post Office. Main Post Office, Markt 1. Open Mon. to Fri. 8–6, Sat. 8–12.

Car Hire. InterRent, through the tourist office, Am Markt (tel. 0451–72300).

Taxis. Tel. 0451–81122; Tel. 0451–81112.

GETTING AROUND. All parts of Lübeck are accessible by bus and there are many bus routes which cover the surrounding areas as well. Buses in the center of town run till midnight. For further information call the Stadtwerke Lübeck (tel. 0451–8881).

WHERE TO STAY. **Altstadt-Hotel** (M), Fischergrube 52 (tel. 0451–72083). 30 rooms, most with bath, some with kitchen facilities. A well-furnished, modern hotel behind an historic facade. Conveniently located close to the town center. Noted for its friendly service.

Wakenitzblick (M), Augustenstr. 30 (tel. 0451–791792). 17 rooms, all with bath. Built on a terrace overlooking the lovely river Wakenitz, this hotel has attractively furnished, comfortable rooms. It also provides good and substantial breakfasts.

Oymanns Hotel (I), Hamberge-Hansfelde, Stormannstr. 12 (tel. 0451–891351). 20 rooms, all with bath. New hotel on the outskirts of Lübeck, peacefully located by the banks of the river Trave. Comfortable rooms and attentive service.

WHERE TO EAT. Whether you want to eat in a modern or historical setting, Lübeck has plenty of good restaurants where the cooking is reliable and the prices are reasonable. It's worthwhile contacting the Tourist Office about the *7-Türme-Gerichte* (''7-Tower-Dishes''), named after the seven towering steeples that characterize Lübeck's skyline. These are specialty dishes, served in different restaurants, for which you need to buy vouchers in advance from the tourist office. The cost per voucher is DM 15.

Also useful is the restaurant guide published by the tourist office, the *Lübecker Gaststätten-Führer,* price DM 4.80.

Bürgerkeller and Historische Weinstuben (M), Koberg 6–8, (tel. 0451–76234). Atmospheric restaurant and wine tavern in the vaulted cellars of the 13th-century Heiligen-Geist-Hospital, a former hospice for the poor. Local specialties are served, as well as international cuisine.

●**Schiffergesellschaft** (M), Breite Str. 2 (tel. 0451–76776). Open Sun. to Sat.; closed Mon. This former assembly-hall of the Shipping Guild is now probably the most famous restaurant in town. The building dates back to 1535, and the high paneled dining room, with its darkened paintings, models of ships, long tables, and benches, is a major tourist attraction. Be warned that it can get crowded. The fish dishes, in particular, are recommended. During the evening, sit in the ''heavenly'' Gotteskeller (God's Cellar) where drinks and light snacks are served.

CAFÉ. **Niederegger,** Breite Str. 89 (tel. 71036). Open Mon. to Fri.

9–6:30, Sat. 9–6, Sun. 10–6. A Lübeck institution, nationally- and internationally-renowned for its marzipan specialties which are exported worldwide. An amazing variety of marzipan-based products can be bought in the shop attached to the café. The cakes, too, are especially recommended.

MAJOR ATTRACTIONS. Dom (Cathedral), *Dominsel. Open summer, Mon. to Sun. 10–4; winter Mon. to Sun. 10–3.* Founded in 1173, this is Lübeck's oldest church and one of the most important brick buildings in northern Germany. The impressive interior has three naves and many art treasures, of which the most famous is the enormous, wood-carved **triumphal cross** made in 1477.

Holstentor (City Gate). The city's landmark, built in 1447, that's known to every German—it is on all DM 50 bills. Also houses an interesting **museum** on the history of Lübeck.

Marienkirche (St. Mary's Church), *Marienkirchhof. Open year-round, Mon. to Sun. 10–3.* Located next to the city hall, St. Mary's was planned and founded in the 13th century by wealthy townspeople as a counterpart to the cathedral. It is a perfect example of Gothic brick-building, majestic in scale, with a vast interior soaring to nearly 40 meters (131 ft.) and extending 80 meters (262 ft.) in length. Although the church has been carefully restored, most of the original interior features and art treasures were destroyed during an air raid in 1942.

Rathaus (City Hall), *Breite Str./Markt. Guided tours Mon. to Fri. at 11, 12, and 3.* One of the oldest and most beautiful city halls in Germany, dating back to 1230. It is a mix of Gothic, Renaissance, and Baroque architecture, united by street-level galleries fringing the Marktplatz. The characteristic facade has dark-green glazed tiles, and 15th-century turrets. Inside, you'll see portraits of early city luminaries, the Baroque **council chamber,** and the splendid covered **staircase.**

OTHER ATTRACTIONS. Benhaus Museum, *Königstr. 10/11.* The former home of a wealthy citizen, this authentically furnished house was built in 1777. Today, it also contains the **municipal art gallery** and exhibits 19th- and 20th-century paintings by German artists.

Drägerhaus Museum, *Königstr. 9.* Displays the art and cultural life of Lübeck between 1750 and 1914. Here, too, you can see items depicting the life and works of the famous German novelists, Thomas and Heinrich Mann.

Puppenmuseum, Kleine Petersgrube 4–6. *Open year-round Tues.*

to Sun. 9:30–6; closed Mon. An outstanding collection of German and European puppet- and marionette-shows spanning three centuries.

St.-Annen-Museum, *St.-Annen-Str. Open Tues. to Sun. 10–5 (to 4 in winter); closed Mon.* This early 16th-century convent, which has also served as a workhouse and a prison, now houses many of old Lübeck's art treasures including religious works and statues that had to be removed from the city's bombed churches. There are Gothic church altars, medieval sculptures, paintings, even toys. An exceptional series of period Lübeck rooms, with furniture and accessories, represent the domestic life of the city from the Middle Ages to the 19th century.

Stiftshöfe/Wohngänge. Characteristic of Lübeck, though not immediately obvious to casual visitors, are the unusually small houses, built in rows in the backyards of existing houses. They were put up by rich citizens as charity dwellings for widows and orphans. Today many of these little houses are beautifully restored and modernized. Go and see: **Dorneshof** behind Schumacherstr. 15; **Flüchtlingshof** (1639), behind Glockengiesserstr. 23–27; **Glandorpshof** (1612), behind Glockengiesserstr. 41–51; and **Glandorpsgang Haasen-Hof** (1727), behind Dr.-Julius-Leber-Str. 37–39.

TOURS. Sightseeing tours are organized by the tourist office; tickets should be bought in advance. On Sat. at 2 and Sun. at 11, you can take a guided walk round the town which includes a visit to the Rathaus (city hall). Cost is DM 6. Alternatively, there are guided bus tours starting daily at 10:30 (in May, Sept., and Oct. on Wed. and Sat. only) from Holstentor city gate. The tours last two hours and include a stop at the Rathaus and Marienkirche, as well as a visit to the heavily-guarded East German border.

THEATERS AND CONCERTS. Lübeck is limited so far as the performing arts and entertainment go. Even though classical music concerts are held in the city's historic churches, for a real cultural treat you have to go to Hamburg. It's best to contact the tourist office for information about what's currently going on in Lübeck and any forthcoming events.

SHOPPING. Although an historic town, Lübeck has all the shopping facilities of a modern city. The center is a pedestrian mall with many shops and department stores. If you want to buy souvenirs, go to the **tourist office** which has a good range of locally-made items, such as ceramic reliefs of Lübeck's beautiful, old buildings. And don't forget the **Niederegger** shop which sells the world-famous marzipan specialties.

◆

S P L U R G E S

Day Trip to Helgoland. If you have a yen for some real North-Sea air, take a day trip to the little island of Helgoland, 55 km (35 miles) northeast of Cuxhaven. Take the train from Hamburg to Cuxhaven (round-trip fare is DM 48) and then the ferry for the two-and-a-half-hour sailing to the island (round-trip fare is DM 53). The island may be tiny, but it's also a duty-free area, meaning that there are some real bargains to be picked up. If you aren't fond of sailing and the sea, however, think carefully about making the voyage; when the ferry gets to Helgoland you transfer to a smaller launch, and in rough weather this last leg can be unpleasant. Full details are available from **HADAG Seetouristik und Fährdienst AG,** Johannisbollwek 86–88, 2000 Hamburg (tel. 040–31961).

Dinner at Landhaus Scherrer, Elbchaussee 130 (tel. 040–880 1325). Elegance and style are the trademarks of this fine restaurant set in what was once a brewery. Fish predominates, as you might expect in this great seaport, especially shellfish. There's an immense selection of desserts—this is not a place to worry about your diet—and over 400 wines from which to choose. Reservations are essential. The restaurant is located in Altona, just outside the downtown area.

◆

BERLIN

Berlin is like no other city in the world. It's not just that it is a western city stranded in the heart of communist East Germany. It's not even because the city is divided in two, the western half administered jointly by France, Great Britain, and the U.S. (West Berlin is not technically part of the Federal Republic of Germany—West Germany, that is), and the eastern half administered by the Soviet Union. Of course, these extraordinary factors color, indeed dominate, life here; it could hardly be otherwise. But the heart of the oddity, the peculiarity, that is Berlin is that it has always been a city where the march of history and the tide of events have been faster and more unpredictable than anywhere else. The city is almost a microcosm—a sort of scale model—of the 20th century. All the violence, tragedy, humor, and vitality of mankind seem to be here. There's a sort of poetic justice about the fact that it was Berlin that was carved up between the victorious Allies at the end of the war in 1945. The intense, speeded-up quality of life in the city is not simply a reaction to its post-war circumstances. The point about Berlin is that it's always been like this.

The city contains many paradoxes and surprises. One that strikes almost every visitor is the enormous size of the place. It's much more than just a city. There are whole towns and villages here, and lakes, forests, and rivers, as well as the downtown area. Second, West Berlin contains only a small portion of historic Berlin. In fact, nearly all the really interesting parts of the old city are in the Soviet sector. No visitor should pass up the chance to spend at least half a day in East Berlin. And then there's the wall. Seen from the west, it seems rather a modest affair, no more than a simple concrete barrier daubed with graffiti. But climb one of the wooden viewing posts and you can look down into the empty corridor that runs parallel to it; entire streets and buildings were ruthlessly demolished to create it. On the far side are observation posts—you can easily see the guards in them—and miles of barbed wire. Between you and them are thousands upon thousands of anti-personnel mines. It's a chilling sight.

Getting to Berlin is easy; the city figures prominently on most tour operators' schedules. It is not an inexpensive city—food in particular can be expensive—but it certainly has accommodations and places to eat that fall within the budget range provided you take just a little bit more care. Though it can be cold and gloomy in winter, the range of activities makes Berlin very much a year-round destination. Exhibits, conventions, and festivals: every season has something to recommend it. Make sure, however, that you have made hotel reservations well in advance.

Points of Interest

1. Ägyptisches Museum
2. Altes Museum
3. Amerika Gedenkbibliothek
4. Antikenmuseum
5. Berlin Museum
6. Bode Museum
7. Brandenburger Tor
8. Checkpoint Charlie
9. Dahlem Museums;Botanischer Garten
10. Deutsche Oper
11. Deutsche Staatsoper
12. Englischer Garten
13. Europa-Center
14. Funkturm; I.C.C.
15. Grunewald
16. Kaiser Wilhelm Gedächtniskirche
17. Kreuzberg

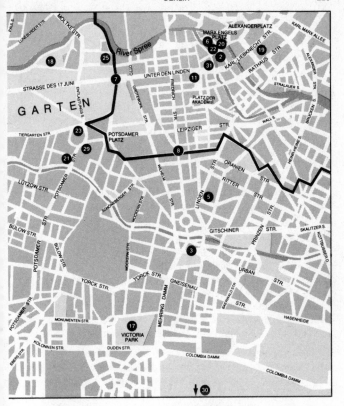

18 Kongresshalle
19 Marienkirche
20 Nationalgalerie
21 Neue Nationalgalerie
22 Pergamon Museum
23 Philharmonie
24 Rathaus Schöneberg
25 Reichstag
26 Schloss Bellevue

27 Schloss Charlottenburg
28 Siegessäule
29 Staatsbibliothek
30 Tempelhof Airport
31 Zeughaus
32 Zoologischer Garten

PRACTICAL INFORMATION
Getting There

BY PLANE. In addition to regular flights to West Berlin from the US (see *Planning Your Trip* for details), there are frequent services from all major West German cities. Despite substantial subsidies from the West German government, fares are high. Check out the savings offered by Air France, British Airways, and Pan Am on weekend, early-morning, and late-night flights. Note that Lufthansa is not permitted to fly to West Berlin.

GETTING IN FROM THE AIRPORT. There's a bus service from Berlin's Tegel airport to the main train station (Bahnhof Zoologischer Garten) in the center of town. The trip takes about 30 minutes. Buses leave every ten minutes; fare is DM 2.20 one way. A taxi will cost about DM 25.

BY TRAIN. Getting to Berlin by train from West Germany is easy. Services are operated jointly by West Germany's Deutsche Bundesbahn railroads and East Germany's Deutsche Reichsbahn. There are five major crossing points into East Germany for the ride to Berlin. Make sure you have your passport with you as you need to get a transit visa at the border. Holders of the DB rail card qualify for a great-value one-way fare of only DM 48. Other discounted fares may also be available through 1988, so be sure to check.

BY CAR. Car travel to East Germany is similarly simple. There are eight major crossing points, and the longest ride across East Germany is 208 miles (the shortest is 105). Buy your visa at the border. You will also need insurance and registration documents. Once in East Germany, observe all highway rules to the letter or you risk sudden and extravagant fines. Tolls are charged for using East-German highways and must be paid in western currency. The speed limit is 100 km an hour (62 mph); all front-seat passengers must wear seat belts.

Facts and Figures

USEFUL ADDRESSES. Tourist Offices. The main tourist office (Verkehrsampt Berlin) is located at Europa Center, 1000 Berlin 30 (tel. 030–262 6031), open year-round, daily 7:30 A.M.–10 P.M. The entrance is on Budapester Str. Write it in advance for free promotional materials, and lists of hotels and exhibits, etc. Pick up a copy of the free, English-language magazine *Berlin Turns On*.

There's a branch of the tourist office at Tegel Airport in the main Arrivals Hall (tel. 030–410 13145), open daily 8 A.M.–11 P.M. There's also a branch at the Dreilinden border crossing point for visitors arriving by car (tel. 030–803 9057), open daily 8 A.M.–11 P.M.

Consulates. American, Clayallee 170 (tel. 030–832 4087); British, Uhlandstr. 7–8 (tel. 030–309 5292/3/4).

Lost and Found. Fundbüro der Polizei, Platz der Luftbrücke 6 (tel. 030–6991); Fundbüro der BVG (for property lost on public transport), Potsdamer Str. 184 (tel. 030–216 1413).

Emergencies. Medical (tel. 030–310031); Pharmacies (also dental) (tel. 1141).

Post Offices. There is a post office in the Bahnhof Zoo train station, open 24 hours a day, and a post office at Tegel Airport, open daily from 6:30 A.M.–9 P.M.

Car Hire. Avis, Budapester Str. 43 (tel. 030–261 1881), and at Tegel Airport (tel. 030–41013147); Hertz, Budapester Str. 39 (tel. 030–261 1053), and at Tegel Airport (tel. 030–41013315); InterRent, Kurfürstendamm 178 (tel. 030–8818093), and at Tegel Airport (tel. 030–41013368).

Taxis: Tel. 6902/216060/261026/240202.

Getting Around

Berlin is a vast city and, except for the center, cannot be comfortably explored on foot. But there's an excellent integrated public transportation network, a blessing to the budget-conscious tourist.

The Berlin Transit Corporation (BVG), or Berliner Verkehrs-Betriebe, has 83 city bus routes and eight subway lines. Maps of the entire system and a timetable outlining all lines, fares, and first and last buses and subway trains are available from subway ticket offices.

The combined U-Bahn **(subway)** and S-Bahn **(suburban trains)** system is the best way to get around. There are 116 U-Bahn stations covering the whole city; the S-Bahn extends into outlying areas. Two U-Bahn lines also go through to East Berlin, as does one S-Bahn; the only stop is Friedrichstr. The extensive **bus** system, running to the most remote areas of West Berlin, provides an effective supplement to the train services (special night buses carry an ''N'' next to the number).

Fares are uniform on all forms of public transport (including the ferries from Wannsee to Kladow). One-way tickets cost DM 2.30 (children between 6 and 14 years, DM 1.50); multiple-ride tickets, good for up to five trips, cost DM 10.50 (children DM 6.50). Tickets are available from vending machines at many U- and S-Bahn stations and at U-Bahn ticket offices. You must cancel your ticket yourself in one of the red machines.

There is also a good-value tourist ticket (**Touristenkarte**) available, valid on all public transportation. These are good for either two days, at a cost of DM 16 (children DM 9.50), or four days, at a cost of DM 32 (children DM 19). Buy them from the main BVG ticket office at Kleistpark U-Bahn station or at the Bahnhof Zoo train station. Generally speaking, the multiple-ride ticket (**Sammelkarte**) costing DM 50 or the 24-hour ticket costing DM 8 (children DM 5) represent the best value. Alternatively buy the combined day ticket, which is valid on the whole network of public transport, including boats operated by the Stern und Kreisschiffart line; cost is DM 14.50 (children DM 7.50).

For **information** either call the BVG (tel. 030–216 5088), or go to their information office on Hardenbergplatz, directly in front of Bahnhof Zoo train station.

Should you fancy just a trip along Kurfürstendamm, take bus 19 or 29—the fare between Rathenhausplatz and Wittenbergplatz is only DM 1.

In the summer, special excursion buses (marked with a small triangle), operate from the Bahnhof Zoo U-Bahn station almost non-stop to Wannsee and the neighboring lakeside resorts.

Where to Stay

Though there are in excess of 340 hotels and pensions in the city, advance reservations are essential. The tourist office can supply free lists of all hotels and will make reservations for you. Most business hotels have discounted rates at weekends and out of season. Check into staying out of the downtown area, too. Rates can be lower and the efficient public transportation system makes getting in to the center easy.

If you fly into Tegel Airport and don't have a reservation, there's a board showing which hotels have rooms. The tourist office at the airport can also help with reservations.

Moderate

Berlin Mark Hotel, Meinekestr. 18 (tel. 030–88002/0). 217 rooms, all with bath. Located right in the center of town, this modern hotel largely caters to group travel, but the top two floors are reserved for individual travelers and families. All rooms are identically and functionally furnished. Facilities include a cafeteria and separate public rooms for groups. Located close to Kurfürstendamm U-Bahn station.

● Casino, Königin-Elisabeth-Str. 47a (tel. 030–30309/0). 24 rooms, all with shower. A former barracks for Prussian officers is the extraordinary setting for this clean and pleasant hotel quietly situated off Königin-Elisabeth-Strasse (a few minutes' walk from Theodor-Heuss-Platz U-Bahn station). All rooms are large and elegantly furnished. Besides the excellent breakfast you can enjoy snacks prepared by the friendly Bavarian owner, who also attends to the bar. There's a beer garden, where barbeques take place in summer. Special out-of-season rates are offered.

Comet, Kurfürstendamm 175 (tel. 030–882 7021). 33 rooms, all with shower. Located on the third and fourth floors of a typical turn-of-the-century Berlin apartment house, right on Kurfürstendamm, this immaculately clean hotel provides large and comfortable rooms and a quiet atmosphere. Facilities include a breakfast buffet and solarium; special out-of-season rates are offered. Located close to Konrad-Adenauer-Platz U-Bahn Station.

Franke, Albrecht-Achilles-Str. 57 (tel. 030–892 1097). 65 rooms, all with bath. This is a clean, modern, and comfortable hotel set in a quiet side street off Kurfürstendamm, close to Konrad-Adenauer-Platz U-Bahn station. There is a restaurant, and guests can use a nearby private swimming pool.

Motel Grunewald, Kronprinzessinenweg 120 (tel. 030–803 1011). 43 rooms, most with shower. A modern motel with rather small rooms, catering to those who prefer to stay outside the city close to the woods and the lakes (a few minutes' walk from the Wannsee and the Havel), yet only 15 minutes away from the center of town by S-Bahn. There is a restaurant.

Ravenna, Grunewaldstr. 8–9 (tel. 030–792 8031). 45 rooms, all with bath. This is a modern hotel located in the Steglitz district, close to Rathaus Steglitz U-Bahn station and the Botanical Gardens. All rooms are similarly and elegantly furnished. Facilities include breakfast buffet, restaurant, café, and bar. Special low rates are offered over Christmas and the New Year.

● Riehmers Hofgarten, Yorckstr. 83 (tel. 030–781 011). 21 rooms, all with shower. Part of a group of late 19th-century buildings of the same name, this hotel, which opened in 1985, is spacious and elegantly furnished; rooms overlooking the garden-like courtyards are quieter but more expensive. An excellent breakfast is served in the bistro-type room on the ground floor. Located close to Mehringdam U-Bahn station.

Inexpensive

Alpenland Hotel, Carmerstr. 8 (tel. 030–312 4898/316236). This is a simple but adequate hotel, with its own restaurant, set in the lively area around Savignyplatz close to Ku-Damm (Kurfürstendamm).

Econtel, Sommeringstr. 24 (tel. 030–344001). 205 beds, all rooms with shower. Low rates, especially for families, are the main attraction of this modern hotel, with identically-furnished rooms. For those who really want to be independent, have breakfast outside the hotel in a café, though there is a self-service restaurant as well as a small bar in the hotel itself. Located a few minutes' walk from Richard-Wagner-Platz U-Bahn station.

Hospiz Friedenau, Fregestr. 68 (tel. 030–851 9017/18). 16 rooms, 12 with bath or shower. This is a clean and comfortable hotel, quietly situated outside the center in the Friedenau district, with its own small garden. It is within walking distance of Innsbrucker Platz and Friedrich-Wilhelm-Platz U-Bahn station.

⬧ **Rialto,** Kurfürstendamm 96 (tel. 030–323 2937). 10 rooms, 8 with shower. Situated on the top floor of a typical Berlin apartment house, this small boarding house combines individually-furnished rooms with a personal atmosphere. Breakfast is provided. The exceptional roof garden and the splendid view over Kurfürstendamm add to the Rialto's attraction.

Youth Hostels

CVJM (YMCA), Einemstr. 10 (tel. 030–261 3791).
Jugendgästehaus Berlin, Kluckstr. 3 (tel. 030–261 1097).
Jugendgästehaus am Wannsee, Badeweg/corner of Kronprinzessinenweg (tel. 030–803 2034).
Studenthotel Berlin, Meiningerstr. 10 (tel. 030–784 6720).

Camping

For full details and reservations, write Deutscher Camping Club, Geisbergstr. 11, D-1000 Berlin 30 (tel. 030–246071).

Zeltplatz, am Krampnitzer Weg 111–117 (tel. 030–356 2797). Located in remote Kladow district. Open year-round.

Zeltplatz in Kohlhasenbruck am Griebnitzee, Neue Kreisstr. (tel. 030–805 1737). Located in Wannsee district. Open Apr. through Sept.

Where to Eat

Berlin boasts a staggering range of eating places, from plush temples of haute cuisine to street-corner snack bars. A good-value option for low-cost eating is the **Imbiss-Stände,** booths scattered all over town selling sausages and other quick bites to eat.

The three favorite specialties of Berlin are *Brockwurst* (a chubby frankfurter); yellow pea soup with *Brockwurst* and/or a slice of bacon; and *Eisbein,* a hunk of pork that would satisfy a caveman. **Berliner Kindl** restaurants, with outlets all over town, are a sure bet for *Eisbein.* A traditional summer specialty is *Aal grün mit Gurkensalat,* tiny pieces of eel cooked in a rich sauce and served with boiled potatoes and cucumber salad.

Moderate

Alter Dorfkrug, Alt-Lübars 8 (tel. 030–402 7174). (S-Bahn stop Waidmannslust, or bus no. 20). To the north of Berlin you will find this original inn in the last remaining village within the city. It's particularly enjoyable during the summer when you can sit in the beer garden after a walk through the nearby fields.

Berliner Stube, in the Hotel Steigenberger, Los-Angeles-Platz 1 (tel. 030–21080/210 8850). Open daily from 11 A.M. Don't let the rather exclusive surroundings of this top hotel scare you off: The Berlin specialties served here, always in large portions, are excellent and very good value.

➨**Hardtke,** Meinekestr. 27 (tel. 030–881 9827). Popular with many Berliners and about the best-value restaurant for affordable eating in the city. Enjoy a hearty meal, selected from a variety of Berlin specialties, in a traditional setting.

Leibniz-Klause, Leibnizstr. 46 (tel. 030–323 7068). Open daily from 11:30 A.M.–7 A.M. This restaurant tends to be packed around midnight, and an early breakfast is served from 2 A.M. onwards. The good-value lunches also attract many regular customers.

Mövenpick, Europa Center (tel. 030–262 7077). Four different restaurants in one offer everything from breakfast, lunches made from seasonal specialties, excellent cakes and ice creams, to wines from many different wine-growing regions.

Restaurant im Jüdischen Gemeindehaus, Fasanenstr. 79–80 (tel. 030–881 3031). Set in the parish house of the Berlin Jewish community, this restaurant serves Kosher food of a high quality; it's nearly always full so reserve in advance. The changing art exhibits in the same building are also of interest.

Inexpensive

➨**Alt-Berliner Weissbierstube,** in the Berlin Museum, Lindenstr. 14 (tel. 030–251 4015). (Nearest U-Bahn station Hallesches Tor). There is an admission fee. A buffet with Berlin specialties in atmospheric surroundings makes this a favorite with Berliners and tourists alike. Visit the interesting museum dealing with the history of the city first and have lunch here afterwards. But be sure to reserve a table!

Ashoka, Grolmannstr. 51 (tel. 030–313 2066). Open daily 12 noon–midnight. This Imbiss-type spot serving Indian-vegetarian dishes is ideal for a quick and inexpensive meal. Located right in the lively and interesting area around Savignyplatz close to Kurfürstendamm.

Club Culinaria, in the Wertheim department store, Kurfürstendamm 231. Open during shop-opening hours. Set in the basement of this well-known department store, and serving everything from a glass of champagne and fresh pasta to excellent roasts—and all at reasonable prices.

Maharani, Fuggerstr. 18 (tel. 030–213 4022). This is a friendly and clean restaurant offering a large variety of vegetarian and traditional Indian lamb dishes. It's located close by the KaDeWe department store.

Pizzeria Roma, Belzigerstr. 60 (tel. 030–781 1580). Opened many years ago and with a reputation for the biggest and cheapest pizzas in town, this is an obvious choice for a low-cost meal. Located within walking distance of Rathaus Schöneberg.

Rogacki, Wilmersdorfer Str. 145, close to Bismarckstr. (tel. 030–341 4091). This traditional fish shop, with attached Imbiss, is attracting a growing number of customers, not only for fish but for lobster and oysters, all of the same top quality.

Zille-Stuben, in the KaDeWe department store, Wittenbergplatz. This self-service restaurant in the city's most famous department store can be crowded, but it's tops for quality and value.

Cafés

●**Café Kranzler,** Kurfürstendamm 18 (tel. 030–882 6911). The most well-known of Berlin's older style cafés, with a long tradition echoing Berlin's pre-war café life. Located right in the heart of the city, and serving delicious cakes and ice creams. Sit outside in the summer and watch the world go by.

Einstein, Kurfürstenstr. 58. This café specializes in many different sorts of coffee, with or without cream or alcohol, as well as Austrian cakes and pastries. Live concerts and poetry readings are a feature. Located close to Kurfürstenstr. U-Bahn station.

Krone, Uhlandstr. 51. Specialties of the house include strudels and special breakfasts. Located close to Kurfürstendamm.

⬤ **Leysieffer,** Kurfürstendamm 218. Situated on the second floor of the former Chinese Embassy. In spite of the self-service counter it's an elegant spot, with a wide-range of cakes and light meals. The shop on the first floor displays many, rather expensive, specialties. You probably won't be able to resist the *Truffel* (truffels) or Leysieffer's own creation, *Die Himmlischen* ("heavenlies").

Melange, Knesebeckstr. 49. Quiet café set in a sidestreet off Ku-Damm, close to Technical University. Some tables are provided outside.

Möhring, Kurfürstendamm 213. Traditional café, well known for its exquisite cakes; also has a branch near the Schloss Charlottenburg, on Otto-Suhr-Allee 145.

Kneipen

Berlin has around 7,000 pubs, bars, dives, and such which all answer to the general description of "Kneipen"—somewhere where you can go for a beer, a snack, a chat with friends, or perhaps even a dance. Those around Olivaerplatz, Savignyplatz, Ludwigkirchplatz, and in the Greenwich Village-like Kreuzberg area (around Chamissoplatz) are all popular and lively, and sometimes quite noisy. Below, we list a few of the many on offer in the above areas, with or without music, where a beer and a little Berlin atmosphere won't cost you the earth.

Bogen 597, Savignyplatz, S-Bahn Passage. Located literally under the S-Bahn—you'll hear and feel the trains rumbling over your head—this is a snug little place with a pleasant atmosphere, good beer, and a fine selection of wines.

Wilhelm Hoeck, Wilmersdorfer Str. 149 (tel. 030–341 9194). Come to Berlin's oldest Kneipe to meet Berliners as they are; you won't be disappointed!

Joe am Ku-Damm, Kurfürstendamm 225–226, corner of Joachimstaler Str. (tel. 030–883 6273). The central location and authentically bustling atmosphere of this Kneipe ensure that it's nearly always packed. Live music on Wed., Thurs. and Sun.

Ku-Dorf, Joachimstaler Str. 15 (tel. 030 883 6666). For those who dislike walking too far, you'll find 18 different Kneipen under one roof here; it's just a few meters away from Kurfürstendamm.

⬤ **Leydicke,** Mansteinstr. 4 (tel. 030 216–62973). A historic spot, where the proprietors distill their own wines and liqueurs—a must for every tourist to Berlin.

Nolle, Nollendorfplatz (tel. 030–2167546). Located in a former subway station (above the ground); sit in an old U-Bahn carriage or dance to the live dixie-jazz music. Berlin specialties from the buffet and good beer are on offer. Come Sunday morning and stroll around the flea market here.

What to See and Do

MAJOR ATTRACTIONS. Dahlemer Museem (Dahlem's Museums). *Open year-round, daily 9–5; closed Mon. No entrance fee. The restaurant is open during museum-opening hours.* One of Berlin's three most important museum complexes. It houses the following: **Gemälde Galerie** (Painting Gallery), *entrance on Arnim Allee 23.* This is undoubtedly one of Germany's finest collections of paintings— no fewer than 26 Rembrandts (including the famous *Man in a Gold Helmet,* as well as the *Vision of Daniel,* and *Samson and Delilah*) and 14 Rubens are on view, as well as a host of works by other great masters, such as Dürer, Brueghel, Titian, and Raphael. **Kupferstichkabinett** (Etchings Gallery), *Studiensaal.* This is an important collection of drawings, prints, and illustrated books from the 15th to 20th centuries. Of particular note are the Rembrandt drawings and the etchings by Dürer, Holbein, and Cranach. **Museum für Islamische, Indische and Ostasiastische** (Islamic, Indian and Far Eastern Museum), *Lansstr. 8.* Contains a fine collection of Oriental art, including sculptures and miniatures from India and porcelain and lacquer-ware from China and Japan. **Museum für Völkerkunde** (Ethnological Museum), *Lansstr. 8.* Houses a marvelous collection of ethnic works from all over the world. Sections are devoted to ancient America, Africa, the South Seas and South and Southeast Asia. Includes Mayan carvings, masks from the South Seas, Benin bronzes and a whole host of other treasures. **Skulturengalerie** (Sculpture Gallery), *Lansstr.* Contains European sculpture from antiquity to the 18th century. Particularly noteworthy are the German medieval works and those from the Italian Renaissance.

Europa Center, *Tauentzienstr. The platform is open year-round, daily 10 A.M.–12 midnight.* A symbol of post-war West Berlin, this is the largest multi-purpose shopping and entertainment mall in Europe, with over 100 shops, cafés and restaurants, as well as movie theaters and sports facilities. The trip up to the 22nd floor is well worth it, especially at night, for spectacular views of West and East Berlin.

Funkturm (Radio Tower). *Open year-round, daily 10 A.M.–11:30 P.M.* (Nearest U-Bahn station Messedamm). Another of the city's landmarks offers an equally dazzling view of the city from its

126-meter (413-ft.) high observation platform, reached by stairs (for the super fit only) or elevator. The tower was constructed in 1926 for the Berlin Trade Fair. There is a restaurant about half-way up, open from 11 A.M.–9 P.M.

Grünewald. The Grünewald, which extends over 32 sq. km (20 sq. miles), is the largest of Berlin's woods, belonging to the districts of Wilmersdorf and Zehlendorf. It makes for a great day trip. In the eastern part are the lakes of **Hundekehlesee, Grünewaldsee, Krumme Lanke,** and **Schlachtensee,** are all linked by canals. We recommend excursions to any of these lakes for delightful walks or swimming in the summer (also rowing on the Schlachtensee). It is also worth visiting the **Teufelsberg** "rubble" mountain (constructed from the city's debris after the war), which in the winter is the scene of skiing and tobagganing, and the **Grünewaldturm** tower (with restaurant), from where there is a stunning view. Close to Lake Grünewaldsee is **Jagdschloss Grünewald,** a hunting lodge dating back to 1542, which contains a representative collection of Dutch and German paintings and some interesting hunting trophies and guns. During the summer concerts are held in the courtyard. (The Grünewald can be reached as follows: *Grünewaldturm,* excursion buses from Bahnhof Zoo Station; *Grünewaldsee and Jagdschloss Grünewald* (near the Forsthaus Paulsborn restaurant), U-Bahn station Oskar-Helene-Heim, access by Clayallee and Huttenweg; *Hundekehlesee,* S-Bahn Grünewald; *Krumme Lanke,* U-Bahn station Krumme Lanke, access by Fischerhuttenstr.; *Schlachtensee,* S-Bahn station Schlachtensee; *Teufelsberg and Teufelsee lake,* S-Bahn station Heerstr.).

Kaiser Wilhelm Gedächtniskirche (Kaiser Wilhelm Memorial Church), *Breitscheidplatz.* Built in honor of Wilhelm I between 1891 and 1895 in neo-Romanesque style, the church's bombed ruins, now containing a modern octagonal church with impressive stained-glass windows, stand as a perpetual symbol of the destruction of Berlin in World War II.

Kulturzentrum Tiergarten (Cultural Center). *Open year-round, daily 9–5; closed Mon.* Several museums, some still under construction, are located on the edge of Tiergarten Park, and form the second of Berlin's major museum complexes. The following two are open to the public: **Kunstgewerbemuseum** (Museum of Applied Arts), *Tiergartenstr. 6.* Opened in 1985, it houses a wonderful collection of arts and crafts from the Middle Ages to the late 19th century. The highlight is the **Guelph Treasure,** stunning examples of medieval church treasures in gold and silver. **Musikinstrumentenmuseum** (Museum of Musical Instruments), *Tiergartenstr. 1*. Added to the Philharmonie in 1984, this is fascinating for anyone with a taste for musical history. Among the instruments of the famous on display is Frederick the Great's flute and Grieg's piano.

Neue Nationalgalerie (National Gallery), *Potsdamer Str. 50*. Set in a modern construction of glass and steel; here you'll find a wide-ranging collection of 19th- and 20th-century painting, including works by Manet, Renoir, Klee, and Ernst, with changing exhibits of contemporary art.

Rathaus Schöneberg (Town Hall), *John F. Kennedy Platz* (nearest U-Bahn station Rathaus Schöneberg). *Open Wed. and Sun. only 10–4*. Built in 1911, this is the seat of the **Berlin Senate** and **House of Deputies,** and the hub of Berlin political life since 1948. It was also the scene of President Kennedy's famous speech to the Berliners in 1963. You can climb the belfry (374 steps) and take a closer look at a replica of America's **Liberty Bell,** donated to Berliners in 1950 by the United States.

Schloss Charlottenburg (Charlottenburg Palace). *Open year-round daily 9–5; closed Mon*. The third of Berlin's museum complexes, this is the former summer residence of the kings of Prussia; the building dates from 1695, when the central part was built for Sophie Charlotte, wife of Frederick I. The rest of the building was added over the years. A guided tour will take you through the **state apartments** with their memories of the great kings and queens of Prussia. The palace was badly bombed during the war, but has subsequently been restored lavishly. It houses the following museums: **Ägyptisches Museum** (Egyptian Museum), *located opposite the palace. Open year-round, daily 9–5; closed Fri*. Contains a wealth of treasures from ancient Egypt, including the most famous portrait bust in the world, that of **Nefertiti,** Queen of Aken-Aton the Heretic, and finds from the excavations at Tell-El-Amarna. **Antikenmuseum und Schatzkammer** (Museum of Antiquities and Treasury), *located next to the Egyptian Museum. Open year-round, daily 9–5; closed Fri*. Greek and Roman treasures are displayed upstairs, glittering silver and gold—some dating back over 3,000 years—downstairs in the treasury; a visit to this museum is a must for anyone interested in jewelry from the classical world. **Museum für Vor- und Frügeschichte** (Prehistoric and Proto History Museum), *located in the west wing of the palace. Open daily 9–5, closed Fri*. Contains archeological finds, mainly European, from prehistoric times to the early Middle Ages.

The park surrounding Charlottenburg is also worth visiting. Part of it is laid out as a French Baroque garden and another is designed in the English landscape tradition. Tucked away in these extensive grounds are the **mausoleum,** where some of the Prussian royal family are buried, and the **Belvedere,** a pretty retreat housing a porcelain collection, built with a view of the lake.

Siegessäule (Victory Column), *am Grosser Stern*. Erected in 1872–3 in front of the Reichstag, this 67-meter- (210-ft.-) high column with a figure of winged **Victory** crowning it commemorates the Prussian campaigns of 1864, 1866, and 1870–71. The view takes in the Brandenburger Tor and Unter den Linden in East Berlin; climb the 285 steps—there is no elevator.

Zitadelle Spandau (Spandau Citadel), *Strasse der Juliusturm, (nearest U-Bahn station Zitadelle)*. Not to be confused with the nearby Spandau Prison where Hitler's former deputy, Rudolf Hess, was imprisoned until his death in 1987, this moated castle, standing at the confluence of the Spree and Havel rivers, dates back to 1160. The **Juliuturm** (Julius Tower) is the only remaining part of the 12th-century fortress and from 1874–1919 housed the Imperial War Treasury. Visit the **museum** which catalogs the history of Spandau in the impressive belfry. There is also an atmospheric and reasonably-priced restaurant.

OTHER ATTRACTIONS. Bauhaus-Archiv/Museum für Gestaltung (Bauhaus Archives and Museum), *Klingelhoferstr. 13–14. Open year-round daily 11–6; closed Tues*. Collections charting the history of the *Bauhaus* (1919–33), architect Walter Gropius' innovative school of arts and design in Weimar and Dessau.

Berlin Museum, *Lindenstr. 14. Open year-round, daily 11–6; closed Mon*. Once the Court of Justice, today the law courts have been converted into a museum showing 300 years of Berlin arts and culture. There is also a good restaurant.

Botanischer Garten (Botanical Gardens), *entrance either on Unter den Eichen 5–16 (S-Bahn station Botanischer Garten), or Königin Luise Str. 6–8 (U-Bahn station Dahlem Dorf, or bus 1 or 68). Open year-round, daily 8–8; Sun. and public holidays 10–8*. These are the largest botanical gardens in Germany and among the most important in the world, with over 18,000 different plants. A special attraction are the 16 greenhouses from the turn-of-the-century—the one housing the tropical plants is the highest in the world. There is also a **Botanical Museum** *(open Tues. to Sun. 10–5)*.

Brücke Museum (Bridge Museum), *Bussardsteig 9. Open year-*

round, daily 11–5; closed Tues. The museum houses works by the Berlin Expressionist school The Bridge, which was active in the city before World War I. Set in a delightful park-like residential area.

Glienicker Park, *located close to Königstr. in the Zehlendorf district. (Nearest S-Bahn station Wannsee, or bus 6).* This is a beautiful landscape park dating back to the mid-19th century. Within the park you will find the **summer residence** of Prince Carl of Prussia, who decorated the palace with classical treasures from Carthage and other Roman towns. Parts of the palace are now used as a restaurant. From here you can take beautiful walks either through the park and the woods or along the Havel river to the Moorlake restaurant; **Blockhaus Nikolskoe** (a well-known excursion restaurant with a beautiful view over the Havel river); a log house built in 1819 by Frederick Wilhelm III for his daughter, wife of the Crown Prince Nicholas of Russia; or as far as **Pfaueninsel** (Peacock Island), which is reached by ferry. On the island you'll find many historic buildings, of which the picturesque **chateau,** resembling a partly-ruined castle, is especially interesting. It was built by Frederick Wilhelm II for his mistress, the Countess Lichtenau *(open Apr. through Sept., Tues. to Sun. 10–5).*

Museum für Verkehr und Technik (Transport Museum), *Trebbiner Str. 9. Open Tues. to Fri. 9–6, Sat., Sun. 10–6. Nearest U-Bahn stations Gleisdreieck and Mockernbrucke, or bus 29.* The development of industrialization and means of transport is imaginatively charted. There is a special railway exhibition.

Olympiastadion (Olympic Stadium). *Nearest U-Bahn station Olympia.* Constructed by Hitler for the infamous 1936 Olympics (but also used for numerous Nazi rallies after the games), this remains the largest sports arena in the country, accommodating 95,000 spectators. It was here that the legendary Jesse Owens won his four gold medals in 1936.

Reichstagsgebäude (Parliament Building), *Platz der Republik.* Built in 1884–94, the interior was destroyed in 1933 through arson; the reconstructed building was then almost completely destroyed at the end of the war. Constructed in a bombastic high-Renaissance style, the building was restored in 1970 and is today used for receptions and political conferences. Walk along the Berlin wall—it's a matter of yards away—to the observation platform directly opposite the Brandenburger Tor for the impressive view into East Berlin.

Tiergarten, *entrance on Hardenbergplatz, or on either side of the Strasse des 17. Juni.* Berlin's equivalent of Central Park covers an area of 630 acres. Originally intended for royalty only, it is now a favorite place for Berliners for picnics, soccer, extensive walks over the 25-km (16 miles) of paths, or simply lazing around. Close to Lake Neuer See there is a café. Hire a row boat on the lake. Scattered throughout the park you will find monuments of important historical personalities.

Zoologischer Garten (Zoo), *Hardenbergplatz 1 (tel. 030–261101). Entrance also on Budapester Str. through the magnificent Elephant Gate. Open Nov. through Mar., daily 9–5; Apr. through Oct., daily 9–7.* This is the oldest zoo in Germany, founded in 1841. It always was, and still is, popular with Berliners, and is a delightful place to visit. Over 11,000 animals are excellently housed and imaginatively displayed. In the center of the zoo you will find a large restaurant. The **aquarium,** destroyed during the war, was reopened in 1983 and today is one of the biggest and most modern in the world. (Note that it is cheaper to buy a combined ticket to both the zoo and aquarium.)

Tours

There are a number of excellent orientation tours in English around the city that take in all the main sights and places of interest. A two-hour trip around West Berlin will cost you around DM 20, and a combined tour of West and East Berlin around DM 50, plus an extra DM 15 for an official East German guide.

You can also take an organized tour to Potsdam and Sanssoucis in East Germany, Frederick the Great's favorite residence, built in 1744. This half-day tour costs around DM 99, including lunch. Remember that passports are essential for visits and tours to East Berlin or Potsdam.

For further information contact the following companies: *Berliner Baren Stadtrundfahrt* (BBS), Rankstr. 35, corner of Kurfürstendamm (tel. 030–213 4077); *Berolina Stadtrundfahrtne,* Kurfürstendamm 220, corner of Meinekestr. (tel. 030–883 3131); *Bus Verkehr Berlin* (BVB), Kurfürstendamm 225 (tel. 030–882 2063/882 6847); *Severin & Kühn,* Kurfürstendamm 216, corner of Fasanenstr. (tel. 030–883 1015).

An especially interesting way to tour the city is by boat on the Spree and Havel rivers and on Berlin's many canals. For further information call the tourist office.

Shopping

The principal shopping area in Berlin is **Kurfürstendamm** itself and its sidestreets as far as Olivaer Platz. Another good area is

Tauenzienstrasse, between Gedachtniskirche and Wittenbergplatz. At the latter square you'll find **KaDeWe,** the largest department store in Europe and a must for any shopping enthusiast—the food department has to be seen to be believed. Even if you have to stick to window-shopping, this place can be lots of fun.

Antiques abound in Berlin. The best areas are in the **Eisenacherstr./Motzstrasse** district and the area around **Keithstrasse,** as well as along **Ku'Damm.** Prices are high, however, and many shops are rather specialized. For lower prices and more variety, head for the famous **Trödelgeschäfte** (second-hand and junk shops). The best Trödel areas are in **Kreuzberg,** around the Bergmannstr., and in Neukoln near the **Flughafenstr.** You might also stumble across something unique at the fleamarket **(Berliner Flohmarkt)** on Strasse des 17. Juni (near Technical University), held every Saturday and Sunday morning from 8, nearest U-Bahn Tiergarten.

Other good shopping areas are **Schlossstrasse** in the **Steglitz** district, where you'll find many department stores and shops as well as the shopping malls **Forum Steglitz** (nearest U-Bahn station Walter-Shreiber-Platz) and **Wilmersdorferstrasse** (nearest U-Bahn station Wilmersdorfer Strasse, or S-Bahn station Charlottenburg).

If you're after an unusual souvenir, visit **Berliner Zinnfigurenkabinett,** Knesebeckstr. 88 (tel. 030–310812), where you will find everything from tin Prussian soldiers to Bavarian Christmas crib figurines. Or try **KPM,** the Royal Porcelain Factory (Staatlich Preussische Porzellanmanufactur), Wegelystr. 1 (tel. 030–39009215); nearest S-Bahn station is Tiergarten. They've been turning out high-quality porcelain here since 1763. Many of the pieces a budget tourist can only admire in the shop at Kurfürstendamm 26 are sold here at knock-down prices.

Entertainment and Nightlife

Information about what's going on in town is available through the tourist office. Alternatively, get the monthly magazine *Berlin Programm* (DM 2.50), or the fortnightly *Tip* (DM 3.20) and *Zitty*. They cover all events (cinemas, theaters, exhibits, special events, etc.) and are available from newsstands and bookstores.

Berlin's nightlife has always been famous, not to say infamous. The world at large has visions of smoky cellars and decadence in many manifestations, largely fostered by movies such as *Cabaret*. Most tour companies have nightclub tours which will take you round the city and include dinner, entrance fee to two nightclubs (with shows), and three drinks. These tours are on offer during weekends only and cost around DM 100.

LIVE MUSIC. Eierschale, Podbielskiallee 50 (tel. 030–832 7097). Open daily from 8, no entrance fee. (Nearest U-Bahn station Podbielskiallee). The traditional place for live music (old-time jazz or country music), with disco and restaurant. There is also a garden. You will find a branch of the Eierschale at the Memorial Church on Rankestr. 1 (tel. 030–882 5305).

Go In, Bliebtreustr. 17 (tel. 030–881 7218). Open daily from 8:30. Established many years ago, this is the best place for folk music.

Metropol, Nollendorfplatz 5 (tel. 030–216 4122). Open daily from 10. (Nearest U-Bahn station Nollendorfplatz). Huge and inexpensive disco; live concerts, too. Upstairs you will find the **Loft**—for punk, rock, and funk.

DISCOS. Blue Note, Courbierestr. 13 (tel. 030–247248). Open daily from 11. This is an attractive place without the usual disco music—jazz, bebop, and Latin-American rhythms really get people going.

Dschungel, Nurnberger Str. 53 (tel. 030–246698). Open from 10, closed Tues. For years this has been *the* place to go in Berlin; it's still one of the funkiest discos in town.

THEATERS AND CONCERTS. Berlin has always been, and remains, a leading center for theatrical events. There are many ticket offices around town, of which only those centrally located are listed here: **Theaterkasse Sasse,** Kurfürstendamm 24 (tel. 030–882 7360), close to Café Kranzler; **Theaterkasse im Europa Center** (tel. 030–261 7051/52); **Theaterkasse Centrum,** Meinekestr. 25 (tel. 030–882 7611). All ticket offices are open during normal shopping hours. There are also ticket offices in the two big downtown department stores: **KaDeWe,** Tauenzienstr. 21–24 (tel. 030–248036), and **Wertheim,** Kurfürstendamm 231 (tel. 030–882 2400).

Deutsche Oper Berlin (Opera House), Bismarckstr. 35 (tel. 030–341 4449). Box office open Mon. to Fri. 2–8, Sat. and Sun. 10–2, and one hour before start of performances. (Nearest U-Bahn station Deutsche Oper, or bus no. 1). Even though a good seat at the opera is expensive, opera-lovers may be tempted to splurge on tickets for one of the productions which have made the Berlin Opera House so famous.

Schaubühne am Lehniner Platz, Kurfürstendamm 153 (tel. 030–890023). Box office open Mon. to Sat. 10–7, Sun. and public holidays 10–2 and from 5. (Bus nos. 19, 29, 69). This is Germany's most modern theater: Its high-quality modern and classical productions have given it an international reputation.

Philharmonie, Matthäikirchstr. 1 (tel. 030–254 880). Box office open Mon. to Fri. 3:30–6, Sun. and public holidays 11–2. This impressively modern, asymmetrical building is the home of the Berlin Philharmonic Orchestra. If you are keen to take in a concert, reserve seats in advance by writing either to the above address, or, for performances during August, September, and October, when the Berlin music festivals (Berliner Festspiele) take place, write **Festspiele GmbH,** Kartenbüro, Budapester Str. 50, D-1000 Berlin 30 (tel. 030–25489/100), open Mon. to Fri. 10–4; this will almost certainly guarantee you tickets which are otherwise next to impossible to obtain.

ICC (International Congress Center), Messedamm (tel. 030–30381). (Nearest U-Bahn station Kaiserdamm). Ultra-modern building containing a series of halls which are used for congresses as well as concerts.

Konzertsaal der Hochschule der Künste (Concert Hall of the Academy of Fine Arts), Hardenbergstr., on the corner of Fasanenstr. (tel. 030–3185/2374). (Nearest U-Bahn stations Zoologischer Garten or Ernst-Reuter-Platz. Box office open Mon. to Fri. 3–6:30, Sat. 11–2. With 1,360 seats, this "garage of symphonies," as it is mockingly called, is the second largest concert hall in Berlin.

SFB–Grosser Sendesaal, Haus des Rundfunks, Masurenallee 8–14. Home of the Radio Symphonic Orchestra and the first purpose-built radio concert-hall in Germany. Constructed before the war, it was reopened after extensive renovations in 1987. Tickets from the SFB Pavilion, Mon. to Fri. 9–1, Wed. 2–8.

Visiting East Berlin

HOW TO GO. Formalities for Western visitors to East Berlin (or "Berlin, Capital of the GDR," to give the place its official name) are surprisingly few. Anyone planning just a day trip need take only their passport; you buy your visa—it costs DM 5—as you cross the border. You can take either the U-Bahn or the S-Bahn to Friedrichstr in East Berlin or, more atmospherically, cross over at Checkpoint Charlie at Kochstr. You will have to change DM 25 per person as you enter the country.

You can take in as much Western currency as you like, but must declare it. Keep the currency declaration form you'll be given or you won't be allowed to take the money back out with you. East Germany marks—officially pegged to the West German mark—may neither be imported or exported. You can take out any goods you buy in East Germany provided their total value does not exceed 100 marks. Keep all receipts to show the East German customs.

A number of sightseeing tours to East Germany are available; see "Tours" above. All formalities will be organized for you if you take one of these trips, but, again, don't forget your passport.

Finally, if you are approached in East Germany by anyone offering to sell you East German marks at rates in excess of the official exchange rate, you should under no circumstances agree. Changing money anywhere other than at an official exchange office in East Germany is a criminal offence. The consequences if you are caught far outweigh any temporary advantages, however tempting they appear, as anyone who has had the opportunity to see an East German prison from the inside will confirm.

USEFUL ADDRESSES. Tourist Office. Informationzentrum der Berlin Information, Panoramastr. 1 (tel. 212 4675). Open Mon. 1–6, Tues. to Fri. 8–6, Sat. and Sun. 10–6.

Embassies. American, Neustadtische Kirchstr. 4–5 (tel. 220 2741); British, Unter den Linden 32–34 (tel. 220 2431).

Emergencies. Police (tel. 110); Medical (tel. 1259); Pharmacies (tel. 160).

Post Office. The main post office is located at the corner of Ostbahnhof and Strasse der Pariser Kommune. It is open round the clock.

WHAT TO SEE AND DO. Despite some long-overdue sprucing up as part of the 750th-birthday celebrations of Berlin in 1987, East Berlin remains a distinctly shabby place, not least in comparison to its bustling and vibrant neighbor to the west. However, it is by no means lacking in places of major cultural and historical interest. Despite having torn down most of the older pre-war buildings and replaced them with high rises of mind-numbing ugliness—in fact these monuments to socialist know-how and city planning exercise a weird and rather awful fascination, especially those around Alexanderplatz— the East Germans have done much to restore the few that remain. Highlight of a visit is probably the Museumsinsel, or museum island, in the river Spree, site of the Boden Museum and Pergamonmuseum.

MAJOR ATTRACTIONS. Altes Museum (Old Museum), *Museumsinsel. Open year-round, Wed. to Sun. 9–6; closed Mon. and Tues.* Among the large collections of etchings and drawings by

EAST BERLIN
(NOT ALL STREETS SHOWN)

0 miles ½ ½
0 kilometers ½ ½

Points of interest

1 Altes Museum
2 Berlin Cathedral
3 Bodemuseum
4 Brandenburg Gate
5 Brecht House; Dorotheer Cemetery
6 Checkpoint Charlie
7 Humboldt University
8 Klosterkirche (ruin)
9 Komische Oper
10 Marienkirche
11 Märkisches Museum
12 Museum für Deutsche Geschichte
13 Museum für Naturkunde
14 Nationalgalerie
15 Nikolaikirche
16 Palast der Republik
17 Pergamon Museum; Neues Museum
18 Platz der Akademie: Schauspielhaus; French and German Cathedrals; Huguenottenmuseum
19 Postal Museum
20 Rathaus
21 St. Hedwig's Cathedral
22 State Opera
23 Synagogue ruins
24 TV Tower

— East/West border

contemporary East-German artists are a number of fine Bottiicellis and other Old Masters.

Bodemuseum, *Museumsinsel. Open year-round, Wed. to Sun. 9–6; closed Mon. and Tues.* The museum houses an important Egyptian collection, including the **"Burial Cult Room"** and the **"Papyrus Collection,"** as well as displays of early-Christian and Byzantine art. You will also find Italian masters of the 14th to 18th centuries and Dutch masters of the 17th century.

Brandenburger Tor (Brandenburg Gate). This massive triumphal arch was built by Carl Langhans in the late 18th century and is the only survivor of the original 14 city gates. Intended originally as the architectural conclusion to Unter den Linden, today it is a poignant symbol of the divided city. It is crowned with a giant quadriga—a horse-drawn chariot—driven by the Goddess of Peace.

Museum für Deutsche Geschichte (Museum of German History), *Unter den Linden. Open year-round, Mon. to Thurs. 10–7, Sat. to Sun. 10–4; closed Fri.* This former city arsenal, set in a magnificent Baroque building, was later used as a hall of fame glorifying Prusso-German militarism. Today, it impressively charts German history from 1789 to the present, though with a Marxist bias which may surprise Western visitors.

Nationalgalerie (National Gallery), *Museumsinsel. Open year-round, Wed. to Sun. 9–6; closed Mon. and Tues.* The gallery is mostly devoted to 19th- and 20th-century paintings and sculptures, including works by Cezanne, Rodin, and Degas, and one of Germany's most famous portrait artists, Max Liebermann.

Neue Wache (New Guard House), *Unter den Linden.* Formerly the Royal Guard House, today it houses the **Memorial to the Victims of Fascism and Militarism.** An eternal flame burns in a glass cube in the center of the hall, while in the tomb beneath stand urns containing the ashes of an unknown resistance fighter and an unknown soldier. There is an impressive changing-of-the-guard every half hour, with a more lavish parade on Wed. afternoons at 2:30. Opposite this neo-Classical building is the **German State Opera,** built between 1740 and 1743.

Palast der Republik (Palace of the Republic), *Marx-Engels-Platz.* This immense modern building, filled with heroic communist murals and vast chandeliers, dominates the huge open space of Marx-Engels-Platz. The general effect is crushing and soulless, though the sheer scale alone makes it impressive.

Pergamon Museum, *Museumsinsel. Open year-round, Wed. to Sun. 9–6; closed Mon. and Tues.* This is one of Europe's great museums, filled with treasures collected by indefatigable 19th- and early 20th-century German archeologists. The highlight, beyond question, is the **Pergamon Altar,** an enormous Greek temple dating from 180 B.C. As to illustrate legendary Prussian efficiency, it was transferred piece by piece to Berlin and reassembled here.

OTHER ATTRACTIONS. Alexanderplatz. What was once a sort of Piccadilly Circus and Times Square combined is now a large plaza surrounded by monumental high rises, among them the **Centrum Warenhaus,** the city's largest department store (it's filled with an array of depressing goods; prices may be low but quality is appalling). Rising high above it all is the **TV Tower,** a huge symbol of modern East German virility and technological progress.

Berliner Rathaus (Red Town Hall), *Rathausstr., on Alexanderplatz.* Berlin's town hall, an interesting Italianate building dating from 1869, is called the "Red Town Hall" not because of the political bias of its inhabitants but simply because it's built of red bricks. The giant 74-meter (240 ft.) tower and massive frieze running round the entire building are the dominant features.

Friedrich Werdersche Kirche (Friedrich Werdesche Church), *Werderscher Markt.* Berlin's most famous architect of the 19th century, Friedrich Schinkel, designed this church in neo-Gothic style; it was destroyed in 1945 and after painstaking restoration work was reopened in 1987 as an exhibition hall. (In the Berlin Museum in West Berlin you'll find a panoramic view of downtown Berlin in the 19th century; it was actually painted on the roof of this church by an artist called Gartner).

Humboldt Universität (Humboldt University), *Unter den Linden.* Built for the brother of Friedrich II of Prussia, it became a university in 1810 and is now the largest in East Germany; Marx and Engels were its two most famous students.

Kunstgewerbemuseum (Arts and Crafts Museum), *Kopenick Palace. Open Wed. to Sat. 9–5, Sun. 10–6; closed Mon. and Tues.* Situated in the suburb of Kopenick, this is a lovely setting for a collection of European arts and crafts of four centuries; there are also special exhibits.

Märkisches Museum, *Am Köllnischen Park 5. Open Wed. and Sun. 9–6, Thurs. and Sat. 9–5, Fri. 9–4; closed Mon. and Tues.* East Berlin's museum of cultural history contains a special section devoted to *Automaphones,* or "self-playing" musical instruments; they are on show Wed. 11–12 and Sun. 4–5.

Platz der Akademie (formerly Gendarmenmarkt). Located between the French and German cathedrals, with the **German Theater** in the center, this square was once the most beautiful in Berlin. Painstaking restoration is gradually bringing it back to life.

St. Hedwigskathedrale (St. Hedwig's Cathedral), *Bebelplatz*. This is the main Catholic church in Berlin. Built in 1747, it was bombed during the war, and, though the exterior has been carefully restored, the interior is predominantly modern.

◆

S P L U R G E S

Dinner at the Berlin Grill, Hotel Berlin, Kurfürstenstr. 62 (tel. 030–26050). Despite some individual touches, like flowers on the table, the mood here is more international than specifically German. Perhaps that's no surprise in so internationally-minded a city. At all events, those with a taste for plush, elegant, and rather sophisticated dining will feel very much at home. The service is attentive, and the food, occasionally superb, is always first class. Reservations are essential.

A Night at the Hotel Kempinksi, Kurfürstendamm 27 (tel. 030–881091). This is one of Europe's grand hotels, one that traces its origins back to two separate establishments: the Hotel Bristol and the Kempinski Restaurant. The comfortable rooms are all stylishly decorated, and most have marble bathrooms. There are three elegant restaurants, plus a sauna, a pool, a solarium, and a massage and fitness center. Anyone who's just come back from East Berlin need only spend a night here to appreciate just how real are the differences between East and West. Rates are tops, but ask about special weekend deals.

◆

INDEX

Index

Map page numbers appear in **boldface**

FODOR'S TRAVEL GUIDES

Here is a complete list of Fodor's Travel Guides, available in current editions; most are also available in a British edition published by Hodder & Stoughton.

U.S. GUIDES

Alaska
American Cities (Great Travel Values)
Arizona including the Grand Canyon
Atlantic City & the New Jersey Shore
Boston
California
Cape Cod & the Islands of Martha's Vineyard & Nantucket
Carolinas & the Georgia Coast
Chesapeake
Chicago
Colorado
Dallas/Fort Worth
Disney World & the Orlando Area (Fun in)
Far West
Florida
Fort Worth (see Dallas)
Galveston (see Houston)
Georgia (see Carolinas)
Grand Canyon (see Arizona)
Greater Miami & the Gold Coast
Hawaii
Hawaii (Great Travel Values)
Houston & Galveston
I-10: California to Florida
I-55: Chicago to New Orleans
I-75: Michigan to Florida
I-80: San Francisco to New York
I-95: Maine to Miami
Jamestown (see Williamsburg)
Las Vegas including Reno & Lake Tahoe (Fun in)
Los Angeles & Nearby Attractions
Martha's Vineyard (see Cape Cod)
Maui (Fun in)
Nantucket (see Cape Cod)
New England
New Jersey (see Atlantic City)
New Mexico
New Orleans
New Orleans (Fun in)
New York City
New York City (Fun in)
New York State
Orlando (see Disney World)
Pacific North Coast
Philadelphia
Reno (see Las Vegas)
Rockies
San Diego & Nearby Attractions
San Francisco (Fun in)
San Francisco plus Marin County & the Wine Country
The South
Texas
U.S.A.

Virgin Islands (U.S. & British)
Virginia
Waikiki (Fun in)
Washington, D.C.
Williamsburg, Jamestown & Yorktown

FOREIGN GUIDES

Acapulco (see Mexico City)
Acapulco (Fun in)
Amsterdam
Australia, New Zealand & the South Pacific
Austria
The Bahamas
The Bahamas (Fun in)
Barbados (Fun in)
Beijing, Guangzhou & Shanghai
Belgium & Luxembourg
Bermuda
Brazil
Britain (Great Travel Values)
Canada
Canada (Great Travel Values)
Canada's Maritime Provinces plus Newfoundland & Labrador
Cancún, Cozumel, Mérida & the Yucatán
Caribbean
Caribbean (Great Travel Values)
Central America
Copenhagen (see Stockholm)
Cozumel (see Cancún)
Eastern Europe
Egypt
Europe
Europe (Budget)
France
France (Great Travel Values)
Germany: East & West
Germany (Great Travel Values)
Great Britain
Greece
Guangzhou (see Beijing)
Helsinki (see Stockholm)
Holland
Hong Kong & Macau
Hungary
India, Nepal & Sri Lanka
Ireland
Israel
Italy
Italy (Great Travel Values)
Jamaica (Fun in)
Japan
Japan (Great Travel Values)
Jordan & the Holy Land
Kenya
Korea
Labrador (see Canada's Maritime Provinces)
Lisbon
Loire Valley

London
London (Fun in)
London (Great Travel Values)
Luxembourg (see Belgium)
Macau (see Hong Kong)
Madrid
Mazatlan (see Mexico's Baja)
Mexico
Mexico (Great Travel Values)
Mexico City & Acapulco
Mexico's Baja & Puerto Vallarta, Mazatlan, Manzanillo, Copper Canyon
Montreal (Fun in)
Munich
Nepal (see India)
New Zealand
Newfoundland (see Canada's Maritime Provinces)
1936 . . . on the Continent
North Africa
Oslo (see Stockholm)
Paris
Paris (Fun in)
People's Republic of China
Portugal
Province of Quebec
Puerto Vallarta (see Mexico's Baja)
Reykjavik (see Stockholm)
Rio (Fun in)
The Riviera (Fun on)
Rome
St. Martin/St. Maarten (Fun in)
Scandinavia
Scotland
Shanghai (see Beijing)
Singapore
South America
South Pacific
Southeast Asia
Soviet Union
Spain
Spain (Great Travel Values)
Sri Lanka (see India)
Stockholm, Copenhagen, Oslo, Helsinki & Reykjavik
Sweden
Switzerland
Sydney
Tokyo
Toronto
Turkey
Vienna
Yucatán (see Cancún)
Yugoslavia

SPECIAL-INTEREST GUIDES

Bed & Breakfast Guide: North America
Royalty Watching
Selected Hotels of Europe
Selected Resorts and Hotels of the U.S.
Ski Resorts of North America
Views to Dine by around the World

AVAILABLE AT YOUR LOCAL BOOKSTORE OR WRITE TO
FODOR'S TRAVEL PUBLICATIONS, INC., 201 EAST 50th STREET, NEW YORK, NY 10022.